Advance praise for *Staging Fairyland*

"Is there more to say about the folktale? Yes! And Schacker says it astutely and beautifully; examining the history of the folktale through the lens of pantomime and theatricality in the nineteenth century, Schacker reveals the meaning of materiality in performances on stage and in costume. From conceptions of childhood to cross-dressing, Schacker redeems the folktale from its current cinematic commodifications and gives it back to us in rich historical and performative detail, rereading and creatively revising the history of folktale scholarship in the process. Essential and engaging work!"

—Deborah Kapchan, New York University

"Jennifer Schacker's *Staging Fairyland* is a historical landmark book that expands our understanding of the intertextuality and interconnections of folklore and fairy tale. Brilliantly conceived and written, Schacker's study of the fairy-tale pantomime in the nineteenth century is a major contribution to interdisciplinary studies and the study of folklore and fairy tales. Her book fills major gaps in the history of the fairy tale as a pervasive and memetic genre. Indeed, it will contribute to our contemporary reconfiguration of the fairy tale by demonstrating how performance genres like the pantomime are part and parcel of this messy, magical genre. In this respect, Schacker is a scholarly wizard who has transformed the invisible into clear visibility."

—Jack Zipes, University of Minnesota

"*Staging Fairyland* is discipline-crossing, horizon-expanding scholarship at its imaginative best. Schacker's wide-ranging exploration of the experience of fairy tales across media and modalities of performance, from print to pantomime, scholarly imagining to popular entertainment, offers a powerful critical corrective to conventional disciplinary divisions of intellectual labor. This book has the potential to revolutionize the historiography of folklore."

—Richard Bauman, Distinguished Professor Emeritus of
Folklore and Ethnomusicology, Indiana University

"*Staging Fairyland* tells the engrossing story of two disciplines, folklore studies and theater studies, that ought to have partnered long ago but haven't even been properly introduced to one another until now. Had they found each other earlier, they certainly would have discovered what Jennifer Schacker has so convincingly proved: long before Victorians coined the word *folklore* and ushered in the 'golden age' of children's literature, fairy tales abounded onstage in the fantastic plots and magical characters of English pantomime, and they continued to thrive there even as folklorists sought for greater authenticity in the field, eschewing the limelight and tinsel but hearing essentially the same tales. This is interdisciplinary research of the highest order and a dream come true for scholarly specialists and general readers alike."

—Joseph Roach, Sterling Professor of Theater, Yale University

"Essential, overdue, and brilliantly conceived, *Staging Fairyland* explores the British pantomime tradition of enacting fairy tales. Jennifer Schacker demonstrates that the verbal Cinderella possesses her own, long-closeted stepchild: the children's holiday dramas that have exerted an unacknowledged impact on the ways in which the world now visualizes and understands fairy-tale classics. Schacker presents the panto as a 'spirit . . . that continues to haunt the history of the fairy tale' and, thanks to her, readers will now see the tales in an added, dramatic dimension."

—Carl Lindahl, editor of *Perspectives on the Jack Tales* and
American Folktales from the Collections of the Library of Congress

"Pantomime, that long-lived but lesser-known folk theater genre, gets its full due in Jennifer Schacker's wonderful *Staging Fairyland*. But more important, she uses specific details of the art—its history, narratives, fairy-tale characters, costuming, cross-dressing, satire, and subversion—to awaken the dormant discourse between folklore, theater, and performance studies. All this and more, written in Schacker's elegant, discerning style, *Staging Fairyland* gives its own bravura performance ready to be enjoyed by a diverse audience of scholars, performers, educators, theater-makers, and theater-goers."

—Kay Turner, adjunct professor of performance studies at
New York University and co-editor of *Transgressive Tales:
Queering the Grimms* (Wayne State University Press, 2012)

STAGING FAIRYLAND

SERIES IN FAIRY-TALE STUDIES

GENERAL EDITOR
Donald Haase, Wayne State University

ADVISORY EDITORS
Cristina Bacchilega, University of Hawai'i, Mānoa

Stephen Benson, University of East Anglia

Nancy L. Canepa, Dartmouth College

Anne E. Duggan, Wayne State University

Pauline Greenhill, University of Winnipeg

Christine A. Jones, University of Utah

Janet Langlois, Wayne State University

Ulrich Marzolph, University of Göttingen

Carolina Fernández Rodríguez, University of Oviedo

Maria Tatar, Harvard University

Jack Zipes, University of Minnesota

*A complete listing of the books in this series can be found online at
wsupress.wayne.edu*

Staging Fairyland

Folklore, Children's Entertainment, and Nineteenth-Century Pantomime

JENNIFER SCHACKER

WAYNE STATE UNIVERSITY PRESS
DETROIT

ISBN 978-0-8143-4590-0 (paperback)
ISBN 978-0-8143-4591-7 (hardcover)
ISBN 978-0-8143-4592-4 (e-book)

Library of Congress Control Number: 2018943985

Published with the assistance of a fund established by Thelma Gray James of Wayne State University for the publication of folklore and English studies.

Wayne State University Press
Leonard N. Simons Building
4809 Woodward Avenue
Detroit, Michigan 48201-1309

Visit us online at wsupress.wayne.edu

CONTENTS

Acknowledgments

The process of writing a book of this kind often feels like a fairy-tale quest: long and arduous, sometimes discouraging and lonely, profoundly (even comically) absurd—but also transformative. True to Vladimir Propp's folk-tale model, this journey required that I leave the security of home (or at least my disciplinary home of folklore studies), and at times it felt like I was battling my share of demons (mostly internal). As I exit the forest, I have to thank the numerous magical helpers who supported and guided my adventures in fairy-tale history.

This project was launched with the generous support from the College of Arts at the University of Guelph and a three-year grant from the Social Sciences and Humanities Research Council of Canada. That funding base allowed me to benefit from collaboration with two talented and conscientious research assistants: Ingrid Mündel, who worked brilliantly and enthusiastically on the project from the beginning, and Amanda McCoy, who brought her bilingualism and technical savvy to the project. The expertise and generosity of Leslie McGrath and Martha C. Scott at the Osborne Collection of Early Children's Books—an absolute gem for the city of Toronto—made my use of the Osborne's materials particularly rewarding and productive. I am also grateful to Moira Marsh of the Herman B. Wells Library at Indiana University and Mrs. S. A. Crabtree, director of Special

Collections at University of Kent, Canterbury, who provided me with access to the rich store of Victorian panto materials held in the Pettingell Collection at the Templeman Library. The enthusiastic responses of scholars I respect deeply—most notably Dick Bauman, Henry Glassie, and Donald Haase—as well as those of students I have taught at the University of Guelph, have helped me to maintain my own passionate commitment to this fundamentally multimedial and unruly history. When confidence wavered, Henry Glassie's declaration that "we need that book on pantomime" propelled me forward.

In the fourteen years that I have been thinking, talking, reading, and writing about fairy-tale theater, other book projects were conceived and brought to fruition; these were the result of deeply rewarding collaboration with my friend Christine A. Jones. Our conversations and debates about fairy-tale history expanded my perspective on tales, oral and written. The impact of those cross-disciplinary ventures is evident throughout *Staging Fairyland*. I have likewise benefited from feedback on numerous conference papers, organized panels, book chapters, and journal articles in which I rehearsed the arguments that form the foundation of the present study. Earlier versions of material in *Staging Fairyland* appeared in *Journal of American Folklore* (see Schacker 2007), *The Individual in Tradition: Folkloristic Perspectives* (see Schacker 2011), and *Marvels & Tales: Journal of Fairy-Tale Studies* (see Schacker 2012 and 2013). I am deeply grateful to Harry Berger, Giovanna Del Negro, Donald Haase, Ray Cashman, Tom Mould, and Pravina Shukla for their meticulous editing of that earlier work. The feedback and suggestions of the anonymous readers of *Staging Fairyland* helped me to make this book stronger, in tandem with Annie Martin, Carrie Teefey, Jude Grant, and the rest of the editorial team at Wayne State University Press. My dear friends Melinda Sutton Downie and Freda Love Smith have been unwavering sources of wisdom, encouragement, and good cheer, as have my parents, Maxine and David Schacker. My Guelph colleagues Daniel O'Quinn and Susan Brown each provided invaluable insight and advice at important moments in the writing process. I am particularly grateful to Danny for serving as sounding board and reader as my manuscript neared the finish line. No quantity of lunches out or mittens knitted could repay my debt to him.

From start to finish, I have been blessed to have Greg Kelley as my best friend and best editor, my companion and partner in all. This project grew along with our life together—even as Jax Mill and Chloe Mill transformed from quirky children to brilliant (and still quirky) adults, and Frida Kelley grew from magical baby to folklore-loving, tale-telling, riddle-solving kid. My love for and friendship with Greg underpins it all, is the foundation of anything that I have managed to achieve or accomplish in the past decade. It is to Gregory that I dedicate this book.

Introduction

The Fairies' Repertoire

IN 1878, THE year the Folk-Lore Society was founded in London, the Birmingham newspaper editor and writer John Thackray Bunce published a children's "introduction to the study of Folk-Lore" (v) focusing specifically on the genre of the fairy tale: *Fairy Tales, Their Origin and Meaning; with Some Account of Dwellers in Fairyland*. Released in October, this book was sold during the same season that traditionally saw the publication of a variety of fairy-tale-related products. At this time of year, one could purchase new anthologies of tales, both field based and literary; Christmas annuals for children, which frequently featured literary fairy tales; and toy theaters, toy books, and souvenir scripts from the fairy-tale pantomimes that had emerged as staples of nineteenth-century family entertainment.

In an introductory note addressed to adults, Bunce explains his goal: to stimulate in young people sufficient interest that their reading of his book would be followed by that of some important recent works of scholarship, namely the "writings of Mr. Max-Müller; the 'Mythology of the Aryan Nations,' by Mr. [George William] Cox; Mr. [William] Ralston's 'Russian Folk Tales'; Mr. [Walter K.] Kelly's 'Curiosities of Indo-European Folk Lore'; the Introduction to Mr. [John Francis] Campbell's 'Popular Tales of the West Highlands,' and other publications, both English and German" (1878, v–vi). The class of adult book buyers Bunce addresses in his introductory statement presumably would have both the resources and desire to provide their children with a reading knowledge of German and a working knowledge of an emergent line of philological inquiry. These may appear to be no ordinary fairy-tale consumers, but the vision of possible childhood reading imagined by Bunce also does not seem to have been inconceivable circa 1878, as strange as it may seem to a reader in 2018. Bunce's ambitions set his fairy-tale book apart from others that were targeted at children, but there is one way in which *Fairy Tales, Their Origin and Meaning* is typical of nineteenth-century writings on folklore and the fairy tale: it assumes that readers, young, and old, will possess a multimedial repertoire of narrative that includes popular theater.

During the formative decades of folklore's disciplinary history, the musical, slapstick, spectacular and highly profitable performance form known as pantomime was a significant medium for the transmission of stories, especially fairy tales that had permeated English popular culture before the advent of British folklore study and the development of field research methods. The narrative and performative possibilities of fairy tales were played out onstage yearly, situated in dynamic relationship to print culture and informing the production and reception of folklore research and related discourses in ways that are frequently overlooked. *Staging Fairylands* addresses that gap.

A musical and comedic form of theater that has drawn heavily on fairy-tale plotlines, characters, and motifs for over two centuries, pantomime has been curiously absent from histories of the fairy-tale genre and would seem to be outside the central concerns of folklore study, as a discipline. For the most part, British pantomime has made use of a repertoire of tale and nursery-rhyme characters distinct from those introduced to audiences through international, field-based folklore scholarship: nineteenth-century pantomime drew most of its narrative material from literary tales popular in translations from French as well as select British lore immortalized in chapbook form. Importantly, the conventions of contemporary pantomime performance emerged concurrently with the development of folklore as both a field of study and popular interest. These domains are frequently brought into dialogue in Victorian writings, including Bunce's writing for children.

When Bunce addresses young readers directly, he presents his introduction to the discipline of folklore as a kind of magical journey. It is one undertaken in a spirit of festive adventure, suitable to the season, and it is made in the company of a benevolent adult: himself. "We are going into Fairy Land for a little while," he writes, "to see what we can find there to amuse and instruct us this Christmas time. Does anybody know the way? There are no maps or guidebooks, and the places we meet with in our workaday world do not seem like the homes of the Fairies. Yet we have only to put on our Wishing Caps, and we can get into Fairy Land in a moment" (1878, 1). Bunce presents the world of Victorian folklore research as a kind of magical fairyland in and of itself, aligning it with other domains and practices figured as "fairylands" by Victorian writers. These include the worlds of theater, commerce, scientific discovery, and the domains of fiction and the imagination.[1] "Fairyland" was thus anything but *terra incognita*: despite references to its mysteries, Bunce is clearly able to assume adult and child familiarity with its varied and changeable landscape, as he is their familiarity with the genre of the fairy tale, including its established association with Christmastime publications and entertainments. He suggests that this is terrain that children cannot navigate alone: natural dwellers in fairyland they may be, but he implies that they require adult guidance—provided here by himself and, it would seem, the unseen team of folklorists whose

---

1   On "fairyland" as a powerful conceptual trope in Victorian theater, see Tracy C. Davis's "'Do You Believe in Fairies?' The Hiss of Dramatic License" (2005). Fairy imagery, as it was used to imagine both the space of the modern theater and the marketplace, are objects of analysis in Molly Clark Hillard's *Spellbound: Fairy Tales and the Victorians* (2014), and the use of fairyland and fairy-tale tropes in Victorian science writing for children is the focus of Melanie Keene's *Science in Wonderland: The Scientific Fairy Tales of Victorian Britain* (2015).

work he surveys and whose theories underpin the curated, controlled view of this popular (and always potentially unruly) genre that Bunce wishes to promote.

As Bunce continues, he calls on children's established repertoire of story and "dear old friends whom we have known and loved ever since we knew anything" to serve as companions in their seasonal adventure. He references some specific characters associated with English tales, like the Jacks of beanstalk and giant-killing fame, but the majority of those invoked by name are drawn from English renderings of French-derived tales, including characters from the *Arabian Nights' Entertainments,* by way of Antoine Galland's French translation (he lists Aladdin and Sindbad); Charles Perrault's tales (Sleeping Beauty, Puss in Boots, Cinderella); and those of Marie-Catherine d'Aulnoy (the Yellow Dwarf) (1878, 2). All these fairy-tale characters were standard stage roles by this point in time. Bunce then asks his implied child reader to recall other "dwellers in fairyland": alongside named figures from well-known stories are descriptions of stock types with whom the reader is assumed to be quite familiar, identifiable by speech, action, and appearance. He writes of "evil-mouthed fairies, who always want to be doing mischief" as well as good fairies, "beautifully dressed, and with shining golden hair and bright blue eyes and jewelled coronets, and with magic wands in their hands, who go about watching the bad fairies, and always come just in time to drive them away, and so prevent them from doing harm" (3). Bunce follows here in a long tradition of associating blondeness with beauty, virtue, and magic (see Warner 1994a, 362–69), but he is also invoking theatrical models in which stock character types are signaled by costume, props, and makeup. Indeed, he suggests that these fairies will be familiar to his child readers precisely because they are akin to "the sort of Fairies you see once a year at the pantomime" (1878, 3).[2]

---

2   In modern pantomime, the evil characters (the baddies) make ample and outrageous use of costume and makeup, embodying the "artifice and excess" about which Millie Taylor writes (2007, 147–60). They can also be among the most

In this folklore-research fairyland, Bunce indicates that there are fairy guides available who are "more beautiful, and more handsomely dressed, and more graceful in shape" than those who populated the stage productions of fairy tales, whether good or evil; and, he writes, they are "not so fat, and do not paint their faces, which is a bad thing for any woman to do, whether fairy or mortal" (1878, 3). One can detect in Bunce's moralizing coda the strains of anti-theatricality, grounded in a valorization of bodily and characterological authenticity, as well as an anxious response to female sexuality, coded in his comments on fat.[3] But the discursive turns through which Bunce steers his reader—from folklore as a discipline, to fairy tale as childhood reading material, to pantomime as family entertainment—also suggest the highly dialogic relationship between these cultural spheres. Bunce's claims about best-possible fairies, ones found in books and not onstage, ones that may even personify folklore research, call out to what Deborah Vlock refers to as "an imaginary text"; in this case, it is a repertoire of fairy-tale material that is not strictly textual but also richly and repeatedly experienced in/as performance. That repertoire is wide and diverse but also subject to reconfiguration based on hierarchies of cultural forms and their ideological underpinnings. The available models of the genre, emblematized by Bunce as a procession of possible fairy bodies, are subject to critical evaluation; some are celebrated, others relegated to the shadows. Importantly, this repertoire was the province of both children and adults, folklorists included, for whom the Christmas pantomime informed a "theatrical mode of reading" (Vlock 1998, 18–19) and a theatrically inflected mode of discourse, even by those who seem to have valued pantomime the least.

charismatic of players, and sometimes they are headliners; this trend had begun by Bunce's day, but this fact may be one with which he was uneasy.

3   Bunce's critique is complicated by the fact that the part of a female villain as well as that of the good fairy (the "benevolent agent" whose magic initiates a pantomime's transformation scene) were occasionally played by men, especially in early nineteenth-century productions; see David Pickering, ed., *Encyclopedia of Pantomime* (1993, 22).

As I write these words, the narrative genre popularly known as fairy tale remains both ubiquitous and elusive: fairy tales seem to be everywhere in contemporary popular culture—adapted or referenced in film, television, video games, advertising, graphic novels, popular music, fashion, and fiction. For decades, a set of fairy-tale plotlines, characters, motifs, and narrative devices has figured as part of Americans' and Canadians' shared narrative vocabulary, deemed by E. D. Hirsch to be an essential part of "cultural literacy."[4] No matter one's stance on Hirsch's philosophy and its implications for the politics of culture, a select canon of fairy tales has certainly surfaced with renewed vigor in past decades: Hirsch's claim would seem to have as much validity in 2018 as it did in 1988.

Yet anyone who has scratched the surface of fairy-tale history quickly comes to the realization that the range of tales well known today represents only a small fraction of a centuries-long, complex heritage, one that crisscrosses the lines of oral, written, visual, and performed traditions. Our understanding of the fairy tale's diverse and multimedial history relies largely on print and material artifacts, including the riches of nineteenth-century popular culture targeted at both children and adults, when a broader range of fairy tales than those that constitute the current canon enjoyed tremendous popularity. The archive of documents and artifacts that have made up fairy-tale history can pose particular challenges for those of us who focus on the processes of collection, recording, entextualization, publication, and theorizing of oral traditions—those practices that began in the early to mid-nineteenth century and remain central to folklore scholarship today.

4   In a 1990 essay titled "Literature, Education, and Cultural Literacy," Walter H. Clark Jr. itemized the 125 works of literature included in Hirsch's *Cultural Literacy: What Every American Needs to Know* (1988). Among these were "Beauty and the Beast," "Hansel and Gretel," "Jack and the Beanstalk," "The Princess and the Pea," "Puss in Boots," "Rumpelstiltskin," "Sleeping Beauty," "Snow White," and "The Three Bears" (see Clark 1990, 50–51).

One such challenge concerns questions of genre and terminology: much folkloristic study of these materials tends to avoid the term *fairy tale* (popular as it may be in current mainstream parlance) because it can encompass both a set of literary traditions and a range of oral narratives. The distinctive histories, contexts of meaning, and social uses of specific iterations of tales are often elided or left obscure when lumped together in this way. For over two centuries, "fairy tale" as a category also has been associated with young readers and listeners, whether one takes that association literally and focuses on actual audiences, or acknowledges the strategic mobilization of the association as it has been used to invoke a discourse of innocence and narrative transparency. "Fairy tales" are thus situated in a politics of culture that trivializes and marginalizes forms considered to be *of* the folk as it does those deemed to be *for* children. Such radical (but somehow seductive) oversimplification is as evident in scholarly writings that make oblique references to the genre as it is in common parlance and popular culture. In current folklore scholarship, the preferred term is one used two hundred years ago by Jacob and Wilhelm Grimm, *Märchen*, while many of the English terms used loosely and interchangeably in past centuries—including "popular tale" and "nursery tale"—have become obsolete. Nevertheless, in this book I have chosen to embrace and interrogate the term *fairy tale*, slippery and changeable a framework as it is, with an interest in how the term crosses and challenges borders—especially in the specific historical and cultural contexts considered here: those of nineteenth-century English popular culture and early folklore scholarship.

Another challenge when studying fairy-tale history concerns available "texts." Our understanding of the fairy-tale genre has been shaped by material histories of tales as well as ideological agendas that have become so naturalized that they can be taken for granted. When it comes to folk narratives, tellings in the past have come down to us through a tradition of field-based collection rendered in print, often in formats that were targeted at a broad audience. Those artifacts can never be taken to represent a full and accurate portrait of oral tale-telling practice. Among other things, such texts—both what was chosen for recording in written form and how that material was presented—are shaped both by economic conditions of publishing and also by the interests, tastes, proclivities, methodologies, and intellectual frameworks that guided specific collectors, translators, editors, publishers, and anticipated readers.

The self-reflexive turn in folklore, ethnography, anthropology, and adjacent disciplines has heightened awareness of the practices, politics, and poetics of various text-making processes that are both essential to analysis of traditional narrative and indicative of the limits of our knowledge about tale-telling, past and present. Considering such factors as the complexities of transcription, the specific contexts of remediation, and the recontextualization of material for new audiences, Richard Bauman and Charles L. Briggs argue that there is "inevitably an intertextual gap between the source text, however conceived, and the text-artifact" (2003,16). What has been left unrecorded, what transpired in oral performance before the advent of field-based methodologies—these are gaps in the written record that are necessarily left open to a degree of informed conjecture. There is much to be gained and much yet to be discovered from careful analysis of the production and reception of such text-artifacts, as I argued in *National Dreams: The Remaking of Fairy Tales in Nineteenth-Century England* (2003). But there are also gaps and silences in the histories of folklore, folk narrative, and the "fairy tale" because rich bodies of material and networks of related forms have been overlooked. This networking of forms and discourses—scholarly and popular, print and performed—is the space in which the present study dwells, and I take my lead from nineteenth-century artifacts themselves.

For example, we can move the historical lens back just a couple of years, to 1876. Field-based collections were proliferating, and *The Times* of London published a review article that focused on three new volumes of this type: Rachel Harriet Busk's *Folklore of Rome, Collected by Word of Mouth from the People* (1874), John T. Naaké's *Slavonic Fairy Tales* (1874), and

Wilhelm Bleek's *A Brief Account of Bushman Folk-Lore* (1875). *The Times'* reviewer seems to anticipate Bunce's rhetorical maneuvers by choosing a one-word title for this article on new folklore books: "Fairyland." The article itself makes use of tropes familiar to anyone who has sampled Victorian writing about folklore, describing the "mythology" that gets "passed from lip to lip, forgotten but not lost, collected like scraps, picked up in fragments amid the dwellings of the poor, the credulous, and illiterate—it is Folk Lore." According to *The Times'* reviewer, the two primary outlets for this burgeoning interest in oral traditions, at least in an England that considers itself modern, rational, and literate, are books and theater: "Folk Lore," the reviewer reflects, "appears in periodical outbreaks of cotton-clad volumes and tinselled pantomimes" ("Fairyland" 1876, 4). Tinsel would make additional appearances as the rhetorical emblem of modern pantomimic stagecraft, but what signifies in the present context is that the cotton-clad folklore tract and the Christmas pantomime were seen as twin forms, possibly at odds with each other but related nevertheless—and both were associated with the Christmas season. As early folklorists developed methodological and critical frameworks for the collection and analysis of oral traditions, they had to contend with the fact that "fairy tales" already had deeply rooted associations with theatricality and artifice, from at least the mid-eighteenth century onward.

In early eighteenth-century England, pantomime represented a kind of "generic monstrosity" (Moody 2000, 10), combining music, dance, and the highly stylized gestures and costumes associated with roles from the Italian tradition of commedia dell'arte. But most early English pantomimes were rather different from those that became standard fare in the Victorian period and those that continue to be performed today. With the implementation of the Theatre Licensing Act in 1737, a select number of theater houses ("patent theaters") had a monopoly on spoken drama. This situation necessitated creative legal maneuvers by the owners of theaters that could acquire only a "burletta" license, and it was in that context that relatively unregulated forms of performance flourished, combining movement, dance, music, and singing in ways that would seem to slip between received categories of state-sanctioned theatrical performance. In this eighteenth-century context, we find the term *pantomime* sometimes being used quite loosely, to indicate a spectacle that was staged in a nonpatent theater, but it also came to be associated with productions that had quite formalized structures—uniting the basic story of a classical myth or popular tale (the basis for the first part of the pantomime, or the "opening") with anglicized versions of stock characters from commedia dell'arte, most notably the lovers Harlequin and Columbine, Clown, and the rival Scaramouche (O'Brien 1998, 492–93). Characters from the opening scene of such a performance would be magically transformed into these commedia figures by a good fairy or "benevolent agent", and a mad, acrobatic, and wordless chase would ensue. This sequence of several scenes was came to be known as the harlequinade, and its action would construct a "parodic analogy" to or burlesque (re)vision of the opening scenes, contrasting its own grotesqueries and physical comedy to the semiseriousness established at the outset (496).

In the words of theater historian David Mayer, by the early nineteenth-century pantomime served as "an unofficial and informal chronicle of the age" (1969, 7). Until fairly recently, conventional wisdom among theater historians has held that the golden age of the English pantomime ends with the relaxation of the theater licensing laws in 1843. As pantomime entered the mainstream of mid-nineteenth-century theater, the emphasis in productions was placed increasingly on elaborate set mechanics and costume design, showiness, and spectacle—anything that might prove a box-office draw for the broadest possible audience (see Lewcock 2003, 136). The extended harlequinade, or sequence of scenes following the transformation of dramatis personae into the stock masks of Harlequin and company, had once been the defining characteristic of English pantomime, but by the mid-nineteenth century the relationship between these sections of the performance was questioned. A columnist for *The Times* wrote in 1869 that Covent Garden's production of *The Yellow Dwarf; or, Harlequin Cupid and the King of the Gold Mines* (loosely based on the popular French tale) offered audiences "a burlesque drama and a harlequinade, either of which might be played separately and the other not be missed" ("Christmas Entertainments" 1869, 3). By the 1870s, the names Harlequin and Columbine often were associated with the faded glories of theatrical history, and by the century's end the harlequinade was offered as a nostalgic novelty rather than as the core of the pantomime structure (Mayer 1974, 62). Nevertheless, the topical humor, social commentary, broad satire, and slapstick comedy associated with the harlequinade have remained central to English pantomime throughout its history.

Pantomime had come to be known for its topical and localized references, but the deep familiarity Victorian and Edwardian audiences, young and old, had with this form of entertainment is clear from examples of self-referentiality and self-parody included in so many productions. This could manifest as metatheatrical commentary: dialogue and lyrics often referred directly and comedically to the specific theaters, neighborhoods, and cities in which specific productions were staged, inviting participation and responses from the audience, referencing and gently mocking a range of theatrical and other social conventions. Their casts of "immortal" characters could include not only fairies, demons, and Greek gods (stock characters for fairy-tale pantomime, if not for our more familiar print versions of stories) but also personifications of theater, pleasure, and pantomime. The "Spirit of Pantomime" is one of these, appearing in pantomimes like the 1884/1885 production of *Jack and the Bean Stalk* at the Crystal Palace, where it was played by pantomime veteran Emma d'Auban. D'Auban's character engaged in playful banter, song, and dance with fellow immortals Father Time and the Spirit of Culture ("Two Pantomimes" 1885, 50). Ten years later, Helen Lee played a particularly glamorous Spirit of Pantomime in a highly successful rendition of *Cinderella* at the Drury Lane theater. Lee appeared in a costume and makeup that signaled indebtedness to seventeenth-century

French fashion as well as Italian commedia dell'arte (figure 1), both of which bear significant relation to British pantomime, as we will see.

These examples of the Spirit of Pantomime as a late nineteenth-century theatrical role indicate pantomime's tradition of self-aware and self-referential comedy, as well as widespread awareness of pantomime as a form with both transnational roots and local cultural currency. These examples also may suggest a degree of nostalgia for a form whose demise was anticipated, whose centrality in English popular culture and in the careers of many individuals whose livelihoods had depended on music halls and pantomimes was in the process of being succeeded by the film industry (see St. Pierre 2009). But for my purposes, it is also worth considering the ways in which pantomime can be approached as a kind of "spirit"—understood both as *essence* and as *specter*—that continues to haunt the history of the fairy tale, deeply connected to forms of performance, spectacle, and embodiment.

By the end of the nineteenth century, the fairy-tale themed Christmas pantomime would be considered "an English institution" to such a great extent that a "Boxing Day without pantomime would be as empty as a Christmas Day without dinner" (Lancaster 1883, 12–13). There is ample evidence of Victorian interest in pantomime audiences themselves, with many depictions of Boxing night at the theater offering a view of a multiage audience of varied economic strata (figure 2). For a remarkably broad audience, pantomime had become a significant medium for the playful transmission and transformation of classic fairy tales. Indeed, a fairly stable set of tales has served as the basis for most pantomime productions of the past two hundred years: these include the perennial favorites "Cinderella" and "Aladdin," but also "Little Red Riding Hood," "Sindbad," "Beauty and the Beast," "Puss-in-Boots," "Dick Whittington," "Jack and the Beanstalk," as well as once-popular, currently obscure pantomime tales of "Bluebeard," "The Yellow Dwarf," and "The White Cat." While some of the tales that were and continue to be reworked in pantomime form are British in provenance, a large proportion of this canon of tales associated with Victorian and modern

MISS HELEN LEE AS THE SPIRIT OF PANTOMIME, AT DRURY LANE.

FROM A PHOTOGRAPH BY ALFRED ELLIS, UPPER BAKER STREET, N.W.

Figure 1. "Miss Helen Lee as the Spirit of Pantomime, at Drury Lane." Cover of *The Sketch: Journal of Art and Actuality*, January 22, 1896. Collection of the author.

Figure 2. "Boxing Night at the Theatre, from Various Points of View." *The Sketch: Journal of Art and Actuality*, December 27, 1893, 484.

pantomime → a different tradition from print – ft canon

pantomime is French in descent. These include stories from *Alf layla wa-layla* (*One Thousand Nights and a Night*) as it was introduced to European readerships by Antoine Galland in the early years of the eighteenth century ("Sindbad," "Aladdin," and "Ali Baba"), as well as *contes de fées* by Charles Perrault ("Cinderella," "Sleeping Beauty," "Puss in Boots," "Little Red Riding Hood," "Bluebeard") and Marie-Catherine d'Aulnoy ("The White Cat," "The Yellow Dwarf"), which took somewhat longer to gain their stronghold on popular musical theater.

Interestingly, many Victorian folklorists and folklore enthusiasts contrasted oral traditional tales (constructed as authentic, innocent, pure) and the literary tales of Old Regime France (which had come to be criticized as inauthentic, artificial, commodified), and they frequently used theatrical tropes to do so. In this sense, folklorists found pantomime to be *bon à penser*, "good to think with" (to borrow Claude Lévi-Strauss's useful phrase), a touchstone in the development of aesthetic, cultural, and communicative categories on which the discipline is founded; this is a theme that runs throughout this book. It is worth noting here that the popular and scholarly significance of Jacob and Wilhelm Grimm's *Kinder- und Hausmärchen* in nineteenth-century Britain (where it was translated, illustrated, and extensively discussed) did not extend to the stage, despite the fact that theatrical versions of tales associated with the collection, such as "Schneewittchen" ("Snow White"), were already being performed in Germany by midcentury.[5] Tales introduced to English-language audiences by way of Grimms' "fairy tales" only made it to the pantomime stage in the twentieth century; in the case of "Snow White," pantomime renditions started to appear after an American musical, a silent film, and the Disney animated feature film had made the story canonical, and "Hansel and Gretel" was adapted as pantomime even later. For the most part, the oral traditional tales popularized by folklorists of the nineteenth century did not expand the pantomime repertoire.

5   According to J. B. Kaufman, Karl August Görner's play *Sneewittchen und die Zwerge* debuted in 1856 (2012, 14).

Figure 3. Frontispiece to Robin Goodfellow's *The Fairies' Repertory, Containing Choice Tales Selected from Mother Bunch, Mother Grim, and Mother Goose* (Edinburgh: Oliver & Boyd, ca. 1820). Courtesy of Toronto Public Library, Osborne Collection of Early Children's Books.

Nevertheless, pantomime and theatricality, more broadly, formed important parts of a shared and recognizable repertoire of "roles and tropes" that permeated cultures of print, performance, and sartorial play in nineteenth-century histories of folklore and the fairy tale. This is evident in book illustrations, including the frontispiece artwork to a little anthology (ca. 1820), whose title has provided inspiration for this introduction: *The Fairies' Repertory* (figure 3). This illustration depicts a scene of music making and merrymaking populated by a motley crew of fairy-tale characters as they had been conventionally illustrated, presumably recognizable from their costuming and body types/sizes, all indications of age, gender, species, and a specific fairy-tale narrative. Interestingly, this frontispiece also resembles a kind of "fancy dress" or costume party, and indeed nineteenth-century fancy dress frequently drew on fairy-tale figures. Either way, this image and the book's title itself are suggestive of the genre's deeply theatrical associations, indicative of the fact that nineteenth-century readerships for tale collections (including the new field-based ones) were familiar with a model of the fairy tale that was fundamentally playful and performative. Such a model forms a backdrop for print and visual representations of fairy tales, as well as for the emergent discourses and theories of folklore study.

For many decades, the print artifacts that have figured most prominently in accounts of fairy-tale history have tended to be ones that resemble dominant popular and scholarly models of the genre: sets of discrete, bounded tales presented in illustrated and/or anthologized form, or tales embedded in larger frame narratives. The field of fairy-tale studies has been reinvigorated in recent years by studies of fairy tales across media, including film, television, dance, fine art, classical music, and manga.[6] Further, recent efforts to map a "new history" of the fairy-tale genre—including Marina Warner's *Once upon a Time: A Short History of Fairy Tale* (2014), Ruth B. Bottigheimer's *Fairy Tales: A New History* (2009), and Caroline Sumpter's *The Victorian Press and the Fairy Tale* (2008), to name a few—have offered productive critical vantage points on the master narrative/s through which the genre's history can be understood. Looking at our contemporary cultural landscape, Cristina Bacchilega offers a powerful analysis of "multimedial or transmedial proliferation of fairy-tale transformations" in recent decades,

---

6   Studies of the fairy tale in film have proliferated since 2010 and include Pauline Greenhill and Sidney Eve Matrix, eds., *Fairy Tale Films: Visions of Ambiguity* (2010); Jack Zipes, *The Enchanted Screen: The Unknown History of Fairy-Tale Films* (2010); Sue Short, *Fairy Tale and Film: Old Tales with a New Spin* (2014); and Jack Zipes, Pauline Greenhill, and Kendra Magnus-Johnstone, eds., *Fairy-Tale Film beyond Disney: International Perspectives* (2015). On fairy-tale television, see Pauline Greenhill and Jill Terry Rudy, eds., *Channeling Wonder: Fairy Tales on Television* (2014). There is a growing body of scholarship focusing on the use of folk and fairy-tale material in a range of art forms. Some examples include dance historian Laura Katz Rizzo's feminist analysis of the production history of fairy-tale ballet in *Dancing the Fairy Tale: Producing and Performing "The Sleeping Beauty"* (2015); Christopher Wood's *Fairies in Victorian Art* (2008); and Richard Taruskin's examination of links among avant-garde music, radical politics, and the study of folklore in *Stravinsky and the Russian Traditions: A Biography of the Works through Mavra* (1996).

focusing on shifts in both the communicative media and their associated audiences (the "fields of fairy-tale cultural production") since the 1970s (2013,16–17). Yet certain stories about the fairy tale's journey in English-language popular culture continue to resonate, in scholarship as in general understandings of fairy tales—whether telling of a movement from orality to print to digital media or of a shift from collective cultural knowledge to authored texts. Such assumptions have obscured or perhaps distracted us from noticing the traces of cross-pollination across forms and media that, I would argue, strongly characterize fairy-tale history. So while a growing body of scholarship promises to challenge the assumed primacy of print material in the mass dissemination of tales across space and time, the conceptual models of both adaptation and remediation presuppose originary forms in ways that are counterproductive for the study of a genre whose history is characterized by multiplicity and remarkable plasticity rather than by singularity and linearity.[7]

Once one is attuned to references to pantomime in Victorian writings about folklore and the fairy-tale genre, they can seem ubiquitous. Such references form a kind of contrapuntal melody that is intimately entwined with the histories of folklore study, folktale collecting, and print fairy tales. Embodying "varying combinations of high spirits, whim, absurdity, grotesquerie, iconoclasm, fairy-tale, scenic splendour, topsy-turveydom, and nightmare," nineteenth-century pantomime "suffered severely in the esteem of critic-historians" (Booth 1980, 150), until very recently. Pantomime is now the object of increased critical attention, in terms of its history as both a popular form of performance and an outlet for subversive social commentary (O'Brien 2004; Richards 2015); its position in Victorian theater culture (T. C. Davis and Holland 2007); its relation to national and regional identities

---

7   Remediation has proven to be a useful framework for folklorists. For example, the foundational work of David Bolter and Richard Grusin (2009) serves as a productive conceptual framework for Richard Bauman's (2011) study of early radio personality Cal Stewart.

(J. Davis 2010; Sullivan 2011); its place in Victorian children's culture and use of child labor (Varty 2008); its resonances with the golden age of children's literature and the Victorian "cult of the child" (Gubar 2009); its intertextual relation to modernist writing (Martin 2006), and its modern performance conventions (M. Taylor 2007). However, recent scholarship on pantomime has tended to rely on outmoded understandings of the fairy-tale genre and its history; likewise, there has been scant attention paid to the specific ways in which fairy tales were (re)shaped, embodied, and performed in pantomime form. In short, pantomime simply has not been brought into sustained dialogue with contemporary folklore and fairy-tale studies. This is what I seek to do in the chapters that follow, focusing primarily on decades in which folklore, children's literature, and fairy-tale pantomime flourished in Britain, roughly from 1850 to 1900. The specific pantomime productions I examine in *Staging Fairyland* are primarily English, with a large number from London theaters. But the case studies that punctuate these chapters are neither strictly chronological nor bound by media and periodization: there are numerous collisions with earlier, concurrent, and future forms that render this history both messier than convenient but also, I believe, more compelling.

As a counterbalance to the "archive" of texts generally privileged in humanities and social scientific scholarship, Diana Taylor has suggested the term *repertoire* to signify "all those acts usually thought of as ephemeral, nonreproducible knowledge," including "performances, gestures, orality, movement, dance, singing" (2003, 20)—in short, the essential ingredients of a successful fairy-tale pantomime. Following Taylor's lead, this study explores ways of approaching particular moments and networks of forms in English fairy-tale history, through attention to textual and visual traces of "milieux and corporeal behaviors" (28). In chapter 1, I argue for a historical methodology and theoretical framework in which the interpenetration of theater studies and a performance-oriented approach to folklore research are key. In a fundamental way, the significance of many artifacts associated with the histories of folklore and the fairy tale resonate only when understood in relation to traditions of live performance. In chapter 2, I consider two such case studies from the early decades of the nineteenth century: one centers on a tale very well known today, "Cinderella," and the other engages a tale that has faded into obscurity but once had broad-based currency—the story generally known by the name of its teller, "Daniel O'Rourke." These early nineteenth-century examples highlight the intersections and overlaps among the domains of sociability and play, theatrical performance, popular print culture (including children's literature and theatrical tie-in products), and what would come to be known later in the century as folklore. Despite the well-documented and oft-cited laments of some Romantic-era commentators—regarding a perceived fairy-tale drought—the genre was recognized as both fashionable and profitable in the early decades of the nineteenth century, largely because of its association with popular theater.

Chapter 3 examines some of the ways in which pantomime and the French fairy-tale tradition (on which it so often drew) haunt nineteenth-century discourses around children's literature and folklore, especially with regard to anxieties about comedy, spectacle, and commerce. One of the ways that this manifests is in folklorists' development of terminology to name and delineate folk narrative genres and to map the boundaries of their discipline. These matters also resonate powerfully in period writings about literature for children, and here I juxtapose pantomime versions of d'Aulnoy's "Yellow Dwarf" with important statements by John Ruskin and Charlotte Yonge—which contain oblique but significant references to theatricality and burlesque humor.

Victorian folklorists generally regarded both the *contes de fées* tradition and fairy-tale pantomime as beyond the purview of their studies; one of the ways these two domains were linked is through the figures of Mother Goose and Mother Bunch—names that became associated with the tales of Perrault and d'Aulnoy, respectively. These English folk figures have lives beyond their association with French fairy-tale writers: each has a performative and cultural history of her own, as I explore in chapter 4. Mother

Goose has ties to early modern traditions of bawdy performance and the-atrical cross-dressing, while Mother Bunch was frequently represented as bold, impudent, sexually knowledgeable, and financially independent. As characters in a variety of nineteenth-century pantomimes, "Mothers" like Goose and Bunch were sometimes cast as managers of commercial domains, including those of the theater and the children's book business, or were rep-resented as governing the realms of childhood imagination and youthful pleasure in a more general and less explicitly commodified way. As we will see, their respective histories across the centuries also cross boundaries of media, culture, language, time, and gender performance.

Cross-dressing itself plays a significant role in the history of panto-mime.[8] In chapter 5, I examine some of the ways in which the cross-dressed parts of "principal boy" and "Dame" could foreground the constructedness and complexity of identity in terms of class, gender, sexuality, and nation-ality. My final case studies draw on pantomime productions of "Little Red Riding Hood" and "Jack and the Beanstalk"—two stories that John Thackray Bunce had identified as among those best known to Victorian children. Of course, "cross-dressing" names social and stage practices, but I argue that it also serves as an apt metaphor for the complex games that involve fairy-tale writers, critics, commentators, performers, librettists, and other individuals who engage in intertextual play and experiment with a variety of identity markers—pseudonyms, invented frame narratives and origin stories, vari-ous forms of disguise—often mobilized satirically and subversively. These are forms of crossing that have motivated *Staging Fairyland* and that can expand and enliven the current repertoire of tales and ideas about the genre. From the perspective of folklore study's history, I argue that they are central to understanding the "fairy tale" in nineteenth-century Britain and are dif-ficult to map within current disciplinary structures.

---

8   For discussions of cross-dressing in pantomime history, see Brandreth (1974), J. Davis (2014), Fletcher (1987), Friedman-Romell (1995), Hollindale (1997), Mayer (1974), and Senelick (2005).

Approached another way, Caroline Levine's repurposing of the notion of "affordances" (adopted by her from design theory) may provide a suggestive model for understanding the fairy-tale genre's persistence as a resonant cultural form. As Levine details, affordance "is a term used to describe the potential uses or actions latent in materials and designs." For example, a book may be viewed primarily as a repository of ideas, or of self-expression, or of facts, or of imagination, and so on; but it is also a material and three-dimensional object whose relatively firm cuboid shape affords its usage as a doorstop, or a seat booster, or a weight for pressing flowers; made from thin, biodegradable, flammable wood pulp, a book affords repurposing as fuel for a fire or as toilet paper; and so on. This notion of *affordance,* when applied to narrative and literary forms, can change the kinds of questions pursued in critical study: "Rather than asking what artists intend or even what forms *do*," Levine writes, "we can ask instead what potentialities lie latent—though not always obvious" (2015, 6). A distinct advantage of this critical framework for the study of the multimedial histories of folklore and fairy tale is that it offers an alternative to the language of purity and contamination that underpins many outmoded models—in which particular iterations of tales are seen as "traditional" or "original" or "authentic" or "valuable" and others as deviant.

Examining the ways in which particular affordances or latent potentialities of the fairy-tale genre, or of a particular tale, are *activated* serves as a reminder of the nuance and complexity of the material being studied, as well as the untapped potential of the genre. Recognition of affordances that have been systematically suppressed is equally valuable. My argument in *Staging Fairyland* consists of more than a plea for expansion of the range of forms considered in the histories of folklore or the fairy tale. Tracing nineteenth-century repertoires across media and in relation to pantomime performance requires a reconfiguration of our thinking about fairy tales—their bearing on questions of identity and sociability, genre and ideology, and also their signifying possibilities, past, present, and future.

1 Intermedial Magic
Text, Performance, Materiality

IN 1749, THE antiquarian, art historian, and novelist Horace Walpole wrote to Sir Horace Mann at his home in Florence, describing a recent visit to the Ranelagh pleasure gardens in Chelsea (figure 4). Walpole had attended "a jubilee masquerade in the Venetian manner," an outdoor entertainment that was both immersive and multimedial, both nostalgic and decidedly fashionable, significant as a site of adult sociability and licentious pleasure, heightened by the possibility of anonymity and the patina of exoticism. As Walpole details, "The whole garden [was] filled with masks and spread with tents," featuring a "Maypole dance with garlands, and people dancing round it to a tabor and pipe and rustic music, all masked, as were the various bands of music [. . .] and a troop of harlequins and scaramouches." Further along, the visitor could find "booths for tea and wine, gaming tables and dancing, and about two thousand persons"; on special nights, the entertainment at Ranelagh culminated in fireworks. Walpole declared the experience "the prettiest spectacle I ever saw: nothing in a fairy tale ever surpassed it" (quoted in Beresford 1920, 103).

How and why was Walpole invoking the fairy tale in this context? His comparison of the London pleasure-garden masquerade to a "fairy tale" invokes experiences associated with a certain category of fantastical story but also those associated with a certain class of performance forms. Walpole's reference

Figure 4. "View of the Rotundo House & Gardens at Ranelagh." Etching by Nathaniel Parr after Giovanni Antonio Canal (Canaletto), 1751. © Victoria and Albert Museum, London.

to a general sense of "fairy tale" (and not to a specific story line) indicates the degree to which these two sets of associations were intimately entwined: the statement makes little sense otherwise. In this case, "fairy tale" denotes spectacular effect and a domain of intensely sensory, sensual, embodied experience in which local and imported customs and styles intermingle. This is a domain with which Walpole, Mann, and others were deeply familiar, and which was largely the province of privileged adults. In this eighteenth-century context, the term *fairy tale* clearly could serve iconically for exotic beauty, physical pleasure, spectacle, and heightened forms of social performance.

Tales (both oral traditional and literary) have frequently been approached as inherently intertextual, each "text" signifying in relation to past tellings in terms of plot, motif, style, or characterization. Important recent work on the intertextual, interdiscursive dimensions of fairy-tale history have inspired radical reassessments of the fairy-tale genre, exploring connections between tales and other forms of discourse (whether literary, medical, scientific, philosophical, anthropological, or political). Studies like Holly Tucker's *Pregnant Fictions: Childbirth and the Fairy Tale in Early Modern France* (2003); Marina Balina, Helena Goscilo, and Mark Lipovetsky's critical anthology of Russian and Soviet tales, *Politicizing Magic: An Anthology of Russian and Soviet Fairy Tales* (2005); and Suzanne Magnanini's *Fairy-Tale Science: Monstrous Generation in the Tales of Straparola and Basile* (2008) have reinvigorated readings of well-known tales and integrated into fairy-tale history texts that had sunk into obscurity.

Nevertheless, one of the challenges of engaging with a sense of "fairy tale" from centuries past, such as this example from the famed Walpole-Mann correspondence, is that it requires imaginative mapping of *intermedial* networks that have long been overlooked, ones that are not exclusively textual and discursive and that are not contained by the methods and theories underpinning current disciplinary formations. Likewise, the fact that the categories of "fairy tale" and "folktale" *currently* carry with them sets of deeply ideological and remarkably persistent associations (with childhood, narrative transparency, moral instruction, etc.) is reflected in commonplace ipse dixit claims about tales—ones that have gone unchallenged, for far too long, both in popular and scholarly discourses. The assumptions made regularly about the "real," "authentic," or "original" nature of tales, oral and literary, often obscure the beautifully complex matters of form, function, meaning, and audience that a more ambidextrous study of fairy tale's multimedial, performative history can unearth—matters that can inform and be informed by the realm of theater. To set the stage for the chapters that follow, I will foreground examples from the history of the English term *fairy tale* and the popular performance traditions in which that genre has played a part—including the realm of play, performance, and costuming that extends from eighteenth-century masquerade to Victorian fancy-dress parties. To do so requires a good deal of movement across temporal and geographic frameworks, with a lens that alternates between historically grounded close reading and one that is much broader in scope.

This chapter also seeks to establish a model for study of fairy-tale history that accounts for performance and materiality, not as interesting side notes but as absolutely integral to understanding the ways in which this protean category has and can signify. Here, as throughout *Staging Fairyland*, I find it productive to draw into dialogue perspectives from folklore and theater. In one sense, there is nothing wholly original in this cross-disciplinary maneuver: a conception of performance is central to contemporary folklore studies, particularly to studies of verbal art that are attentive to the "social interaction between performers and audiences," the creation and (re)negotiation of meaning in discourse in use (Bauman and Briggs 1990, 59). Such perspectives have brought folklorists into fruitful, cross-disciplinary dialogue with theater scholars and practitioners, and these collaborations have been central to much of the (inter-/cross-/trans-disciplinary) work that first fell under the rubric of "performance studies" (see D. Taylor and Steuernagel 2015). But with regard to the study of folktales and fairy tales in/as theatrical performance, there has been a surprising lack of conversation among researchers in these fields. As a result, theater scholars who have considered British pantomime and related forms have had to rely on inherited and often problematic understandings of the "fairy tale." Conversely, most contemporary folklorists have remained largely unaware of the popular theater traditions that would have been in the cultural repertoires of our scholarly predecessors as they engaged in the collection of oral traditions and debated theoretical frameworks for the study of *Märchen*.

Folkloristic perspectives on "performance" have generally extended from and implied an expanded understanding of performance, as both a social mode and a specific communicative register. In terms of the study of folk narrative, this orientation has generated revolutionary studies of tales in and as performance and opens the door to consideration of the interface between narrative and material culture. Notable examples include the studies of the artistry and agency of individual storytellers and careful contextual analyses of specific storytelling events, such as Linda Dégh's fieldwork with Zsuzsanna Palkó (1996), Henry Glassie's with Hugh Nolan (1982), or Donald Braid's with Duncan Williamson (2002). For the most part, the domain of commercial theater has been beyond the purview of such studies, although many have focused on individuals whose uses of storytelling blur the categories of "amateur" and "professional" storyteller, as they do those of "entertainment" and "social commentary."

As Kay Stone has observed, the term *traditional storytelling* often goes undefined and is also frequently employed in a rather vague way "to describe non-theatrical presentations" that are assumed to exist *outside* the realm of commerce—an assumption sometimes challenged by ethnographic work on folk narrative and individual tellers. On the other hand, the early twentieth-century movement to bring "traditional storytelling" into schools and libraries attracted practitioners with theater training and experience, suggesting that the borders between the "traditional" and the professional are, once again, far from clear (1998, 4). In all these ways, the realm of professional "theater" seems to have some relevance to academic folklore study, as well as to folklorists' work in the public sector.

To contextualize nineteenth-century fairy-tale pantomime, specifically, I would like to focus primarily (although not exclusively) on what may seem to be a more conventional notion of "performance" than the one current in folklore scholarship today, turning to the history of fairy tale in theater.[1] The specific story lines currently considered to be "classic fairy tales" have a long and fairly diverse history as theatrical performance, underscoring the centrality of theater itself in the multimedial history of the fairy-tale genre. As always, the term *fairy tale* requires some parsing: if the category of "fairy tale" is taken to encompass a broad range of secular, fantastical narrative traditions, then a study of fairy tale and theater can engage with traditional forms of performance spanning the globe—such as the Prince Panji stories performed in Javanese *wayang topeng* (mask and shadow theater), or the

---

1   Writing from the perspective of performance studies, Richard Schechner has called theater "a subcategory of performance" (1992, 273).

Kabuki treatments of Japanese *bakeneko* (supernatural cat) tales, to name but two significant examples. But even if we limit our scope to the relatively narrow body of story currently considered in the popular imaginary as "classic fairy tale" (predominantly European, dating from the fifteenth through the nineteenth centuries) and use English-language popular culture as a primary vantage point, it remains the case that various transnational forms of theatrical performance play important roles in that history and in the maintenance of the genre's cultural currency. Understood in this way, the fairy tale has figured significantly in the emergence of many forms of performance that remain current in Canada, the United States, Great Britain, and elsewhere—including twentieth- and twenty-first-century developments like improv theater, Theater for Young Audiences, Broadway musicals, as well as the long and dynamic traditions of ballet, opera, and pantomime (see Schacker 2018).

In the eighteenth century, English pantomime was "considered as a form promising sheer entertainment," something that "seemed new and scandalous" (O'Brien 2004, 40), offering a distinctive and popular combination of music, dance, acrobatics, and physical comedy interspersed with some (melo)dramatic story elements (mistaken identities, star-crossed romance, thwarted inheritance claims, etc.). Story and character were conveyed primarily through gesture, movement, and music (including song and recitative) until the relaxation of theatre licensing laws in the mid-nineteenth century. Until that point in time, pantomime also regularly featured commedia dell'arte figures in the distinct section of the performance known as the "harlequinade," when the pantomime's main characters are transformed into anglicized versions of stock characters: Harlequin (figure 5), as well as the familiar Columbine, Pantaloon, and Clown.

At the turn of the nineteenth century, specific characters and story lines currently considered part of the world of "classic fairy tales" became significant parts of the world of English pantomime. These fairy-tale elements continued to serve pantomime's topical humor and slapstick comedy and also

HARLEQUIN.

Figure 5. Engraving of Harlequin, ca. eighteenth century, Harry Beard Collection. © Victoria and Albert Museum, London.

afforded opportunities for social commentary. For example, serious current events resonate in productions from 1830, the year of the "swing riots," in which agricultural workers in East Kent destroyed threshing machines and tithe barns. That December, the Adelphi Theatre's pantomime *Grimalkin the Great* featured actors dressed as Luddite cats whose services are threatened by the new technology of the mousetrap (see Mayer 1969, 256). Beyond London, Christmas pantomime could also speak to local concerns, as did the Manchester Theatre Royal's *Sleeping Beauty* of 1863. Here the spindle traditionally associated with the heroine's enchantment was displaced by stage depiction of a demonic factory, a spinning mill (see Sullivan 2011, 141). Many decades later, in the wake of what was known as Black Week (December 1899), when British forces in southern Africa suffered three successive, staggering defeats, with casualties and injuries in the thousands, the Drury Lane pantomime of *Jack and the Beanstalk* featured a comic and rousing enactment of British conquest—a production to which I return later in this study.

Throughout the century, pantomimes were generally evaluated in terms of innovative costuming and set design, outrageous antics and physical comedy, and novel feats of stage magic, which were both costly and potentially very profitable. These material aspects of stagecraft could serve as more than empty spectacle; nevertheless, the nineteenth century also witnessed many debates regarding the relative cultural value of the related performance genres of "extravaganza," "burlesque," and "pantomime." For instance, the writer and translator J. R. Planché was well known for his fairy extravaganzas based on French tales. These were staged at Madame Vestris's Olympic Theatre as well as at Covent Garden and the Lyceum, from the 1830s through the 1850s. Planché was at pains to distinguish his work from pantomime both structurally (the extravaganzas did not include a harlequinade) and stylistically, priding himself on the creation of "graceful couplets" and sophisticated humor rather than showy displays of technical innovation (see Booth 1991, 194–96). The differences between pantomime and Planché's brand of extravaganza seem relatively minor, in retrospect: at very least, both drew on and played with a repertoire of known tales to feed audiences' "appetite for spectacle" (Richards 2015, 8). Spectacular effects in these related forms of fairy-tale theater had the potential to contribute to a self-reflexive commentary on the dynamics of performance, the performativity of social identities, economies of desire, and the economics of theatrical production—the very processes in which performers and audience alike were engaged and which were established as potent affordances of tales (oral, written, acted) at the turn of the eighteenth century, if not earlier.

As Walpole's eighteenth-century description of the Ranelagh masquerade and spectacle suggests, the fairy tale also has long-standing associations with forms of sartorial play and performance that occur *off*stage. On the one hand, many fairy tales demonstrate a tacit understanding of dress, conduct, and affect as means by which social identities and social status are conveyed and negotiated, both for the viewer and the viewed. Changing into a special kind of clothing (something worthy of note, something meriting description, something "odd," in terms of its deviation from everyday self-presentation) not only alters appearance; within the framework of a tale, it can also effect a change in status, if accompanied by skillful performance—a kind of metamorphosis, an escape from a socially proscribed role, or, in some cases, a revelation of "true" identity enacted through costume. For example, worldwide variants of the tale type ATU 510a, generally known as "Cinderella," frequently draw attention to these potentialities of costume and the transformative affordances of a social event like a ball; in fact, one can easily imagine a variant of that tale type featuring a Ranelagh masquerade. So while costuming is a common plot element *in* tales, it is worth grounding a consideration of fairy-tale theatricality and materiality in an understanding of costuming as a social practice, specifically in terms of masquerade, "fancy dress," or what Americans and Canadians are more likely to call "dressing up." Fancy dress has operated as yet another form of performance in which the genre of the fairy tale has figured prominently, in two distinct ways: there is a long history of costume choices that signal specific fairy-tale characters and types, but there is an equally long tradition of conceiving the experience of fancy dress itself as a kind of magical transformation best understood with reference to fairy tales—"Cinderella," in particular. I turn to one such case study in sartorial play at the close of this chapter; first, let's consider uses of the English term *fairy tale*, an endeavor that lands us squarely in a multimedial web.

The Theatricality of "Fairy Tale"

The origins of the term *fairy tale* are well known and found in print history, specifically the history of translation: the term is generally traced to an elusive 1699 translation of Marie-Catherine d'Aulnoy's *Contes de fées*—rendered in English as "Tales of the Fairies." While that particular book seems to be untraceable, now "regarded as a bibliographic ghost" (Palmer and Palmer 1974, 227), the English term *fairy tale* gained currency from the turn of the eighteenth century onward. In its first two centuries of usage, "fairy tale" was sometimes attached to narratives we might now classify as "fairy legends": stories about encounters with fairies or other supernatural figures. What is perhaps most striking is the fact that early British usage of the term referenced forms of popular theater as often as it did narratives found in book form or in oral traditions. Importantly, no modifier was needed to reference fairy tales on stage: a survey of English periodicals of the eighteenth and nineteenth centuries reveals that use of the term *fairy tale* was as likely to reference a theatrical production (musical, comical or melodramatic) as it was a story to be told or read at hearthside. Apparently the term *fairy-tale play* would have been redundant.

In the 1760s, when giving a subtitle to his abbreviated, farcical version of Shakespeare's *A Midsummer Night's Dream*, the popular dramatist George Colman used the indefinite article, calling it *A Fairy Tale*. Colman took considerable liberties with the play, as he did with several other works by Shakespeare, while adapting them to current theatrical tastes. In *A Fairy Tale*, Colman focused almost exclusively on Shakespeare's fairy characters and the mortal characters known as the "mechanicals" (including the weaver named Nick Bottom), reenvisioning the characters in terms that would have been familiar and appealing to London theatergoers: a "pantomime-inspired farce" (Marsden 1995, 80). The associations between "fairy tale" and spectacle, fantasy, and farce were well established by this early date, both onstage and in print. For instance, fairy tales are one of many comedic forms included in Bickerton's 1745 miscellany titled *The Agreeable Companion; or, An Universal Medley of Wit and Good-Humour, Consisting of a Curious Collection of the Most Humourous Essays, Smart Repartees, Prudential Maxims, Familiar Dialogues, Epigrams and Epitaphs, Tales and Fables, Emblems and Riddles, Shining Epistles, and Beautiful Characters Both Fabulous and Real.* During this early period, appreciation of the fairy tale as a vehicle for humor, satire, and parody spans both print and performance.[2]

By the turn of the nineteenth century, British periodicals increasingly used the term *fairy tale* to reference a host of spectacular and often amusing theatrical forms whose boundaries are fuzzy and whose histories overlap, all deeply influenced by Italian performers and performance styles, particularly those of commedia dell'arte. With its characteristic elements of mask, dance, pantomime, music, improvisatory and slapstick comedy, carnivalesque reversals, and bawdiness, commedia dell'arte left its mark on local theatrical practice in both early modern France and England—where it impacted Elizabethan drama (sixteenth century), the Stuart masque (early seventeenth century), and then English interpretations of the *ballet d'action* by the early eighteenth-century dancing master John Weaver (Grantham 2015, 277–78).

Popular with both mass and elite audiences, performed in both European fairgrounds and at court, commedia dell'arte could be considered "the visual theatre of everyday life" in the sixteenth through the eighteenth centuries, particularly in France and England (Goldsmith 2015, 321). As noted earlier, the most famous of commedia's characters include the cheeky

---

2   Kevin Pask argues that Shakespeare was likewise a key figure in the "fairy way of writing," central to the formation of a British literary canon in the eighteenth century. Pask traces the way this was understood in terms of "a specifically theatrical magic" (2013, 3) and "emblematized in the figure of Puck" whose "engagement with the audience establishes one form of horizontal identification—that between a sophisticated urban audience and the embodiment of rural superstition" (37).

servants and lovers Arlecchino and Columbina (Harlequin and Columbine), the patriarch and wealthy womanizer Pantalone (Pantaloon), and the clownish Scaramucchia (Scaramouche); but commedia dell'arte often featured otherworldly themes and figures such as the *mago* (magician) and *negromante* (necromancer), as well as "astrologers, sorceresses, fairies, oracles, spirits, and ghosts" (Buch 2008, 17–18). David J. Buch dubs this particular mode of theatrical representation of the supernatural as the "comic-marvelous," in which magic is used "not to bedazzle and inspire awe or admiration (a primary goal of the 'marvellous'), but to allow the lowborn to achieve powers that would otherwise be impossible for them." For Buch, the comic-marvelous mode of commedia dell'arte stands in contrast to the use of marvels and magic in "more serious court opera," where magic is the province of the powerful, reinforcing the connection between nobility and divinity (18). It is not surprising to find that commedia served as "the first venue for fairy tales and the newer oriental fantasies adapted in the theaters of the Parisian fairs" (xv). The romance plot and the carnivalesque elements associated with commedia dell'arte—the anarchic combination of comedy and violence, the reversals of power positions, the interrogation of dominant social, cultural, moral, and aesthetic standards—echo in the various performance forms that adopted and adapted commedia conventions and that draw specifically on a repertoire of tales.

The varied and remarkably loose uses of the terms *fairy tale* and *pantomime* in the eighteenth century resonate with the distinct set of performance conventions that would come to characterize the Christmas pantomime: in this period, these two terms did not denote specific story lines so much as they did highly self-aware comedy and social satire, play with gender and sexuality, as well as outrageous costuming and spectacular stagecraft—all of which will signify in chapters to come. Eighteenth-century pantomime also engaged with the broader theater scene in which it was located. As John O'Brien notes, pantomime of this period presented "many of the basic plot elements of the comedies that were simultaneously being offered as mainpiece entertainments," as they "appropriated and condensed the most notable features of the contemporary British stage: the plots of sentimental comedy, the scenery and diegetic material of Italian opera, the physical farce of Continental commedia dell'arte, and the elegance of dance" (2004, 10).

The musical, slapstick, comedic Christmastime performances now known as pantomime are often regarded as being distinctively English, but the variety of theatrical productions that have fallen under the rubric of "pantomime" over the centuries have been unified by their indebtedness to continental forms, styles, and narratives. In fact, very few examples of eighteenth- or nineteenth-century British fairy-tale theater (broadly conceived) drew on British tales and lore. Those stories of local provenance that were performed in this early period tended to be ones that were also well established in chapbook form and which remained part of the pantomime repertoire: examples include 1730 farce *Jack the Giant Killer* at Little Haymarket Theatre (see Burling 1993, 136) and the 1733 opera parody *The Opera of Operas; or, Tom Thumb the Great* at Lincoln's Inn Fields (see Griffel 2013, 357). Fragments of performance history along these lines are familiar to theater historians, but less so to those who work on tales in oral or print form, and thus worth recounting here. In a similar spirit, it is worth highlighting that these chapters in the histories of popular European performance traditions occurred right alongside the development of the literary fairy tale, during the same time periods and through the same transcultural channels.

Tracing the history of literary fairy tales has generally led scholars to consider literary experiments in sixteenth-century Venice (Giovan Francesco Straparola's *Le piacevoli notti* [*The Pleasant Nights*] was published the 1550s), sixteenth-century Naples (Giambattista Basile's *Lo cunto de li cunti* [*The Tale of Tales*] dates from the 1630s), late seventeenth-century France (the output of tales by Charles Perrault, Marie-Catherine d'Aulnoy, Henriette-Julie de Murat, and their fellow fairy-tale writers peaked in the 1690s), and nineteenth-century Germany (Jacob and Wilhelm Grimm's collection of oral traditional tales appeared in various editions between 1812 and 1857).[3] Key moments in this international history are addressed as the present study unfolds. What is noteworthy here is that an effort to trace the history of specifically *theatrical* fairy tales, even when that effort has a focus as seemingly bounded as that of nineteenth-century English pantomime, likewise requires consideration of traditions whose practitioners and conventions extended across national boundaries.

Fairy-Tale Theater across Borders

Carlo Gozzi's series of plays called *Fiabe teatrali* (1761–65) stands as an interesting example of the intersection of oral, print, and theatrical forms, across the borders of language and nation. On the one hand, the history of the Italian term *fiaba* (or *fiabe*, plural) parallels that of "fairy tale": *fiabe* has long been used to designate not only folk and literary tales but also a theatrical form that has close ties to commedia dell'arte traditions. Gozzi's *fiabe* signify both in the histories of commedia-influenced performances as well as those of canonical tales. Most obviously, Gozzi drew narrative inspiration from Basile's "profoundly ludic text" *Lo cunto de li cunti* (Canepa 1999, 251), which by the 1760s had been in print for over a century.

Basile's *Lo cunto de li cunti* is currently considered one of the earliest European published collections of fairy tales, and it includes versions of several tales we now know well. These include some that have entered our current canon by way of late seventeenth-century French writing and English translations, such as "Cinderella" and "Puss in Boots," as well as ones that would later be collected from German oral traditions by Jacob and Wilhelm Grimm and then popularized in English as "Rapunzel" and "Hansel and Gretel." But Basile's book is not a "collection" in the sense that folklorists would later use the word: written in Neapolitan dialect, Basile made no claim that he was documenting oral traditions. Such a paradigm would have been anachronistic in the 1630s, when the narrative repertoire was neither strictly

---

3   For example, see Canepa (1997) and Zipes (2000a).

divided by notions of "tradition" versus "originality," nor the "oral" versus the "written." As his title promises, Basile's text offers a tale loaded with tales, combining styles and registers associated with both court and street, electrifying familiar elements and motifs with his own ingenuity and wit, and interpolating a series of stories of passionate emotion, bodily transformation, and amoral magic into an overarching frame story of mistaken identities, treachery, and desire (see Canepa 2007).

Basile's corpus is richly fantastical and delightfully bawdy, but Gozzi also drew inspiration for his *Fiabe teatrali* from another significant facet of the fairy tale's European history: the wave of "oriental tales" that were fashionable across Europe in the wake of Antoine Galland's French translation/adaptation of *Alf layla wa-layla* (*One Thousand Nights and a Night*). Titled *Les mille et une nuits, contes arabes,* Galland's work had been first to present this medieval Arabic textual tradition (now known in English as *1001 Nights, The Arabian Nights,* or *Arabian Nights' Entertainments*) in a European language, doing so in twelve volumes published in France between 1704 and 1717. Galland's text traveled across borders almost immediately after the publication of the first volume in 1704, and English-language translations from French began to appear as early as 1706 (see Ali 1981, 11–12).

Eighteenth-century audiences were fascinated by the structural and narrative complexity of the *Nights*, in which the well-read, determined, and skilled Shahrazad tells tales nightly in an effort to save her own life but also to quell the misogynistic fury and murderous violence of her husband, the cuckolded king Shahriyar. While accounts of the *Nights* in Europe have tended to give primacy to print, with other expressive and artistic forms positioned as secondary "adaptations," the performance history of the *Nights* in Britain is only a few months shorter than that of the print history. Consider that the frame story of Shahrazad and Shahriyar formed the basis for a popular stage production—Delarivier Manley's *Almyna, or the Arabian Vow*—in London in December 1706, the same year that the first English translation of Galland's first volume of the *Contes arabes* was issued. Manley indicates that she took "something of a Hint from the *Arabian Nights*" (quoted in Krueger 2017, 44), but it is not a stretch to regard this play as a theatrical rendering of the frame story: it tells the tale of a vengeful caliph Almanzor (a stand-in for King Shahriyar) and the narrative art of his vizier's daughter, Almyna (Shahrazad). Manley's play served a significant role in the circulation and popularity of the *Nights* in English, contributing to audiences' sense of the pleasures and challenges offered by the *Nights*—a full decade before Galland had even completed his twelve volumes of *Les mille et une nuits* (see Orr 2008, 108–11). Misty Krueger argues that the *Nights* afforded Manley an opportunity to develop a kind of "female heroic that draws on a rhetoric of reason and virtue," an alternative to conventional narratives of revenge that had shaped much of seventeenth-century drama (2017, 48). From the perspective of fairy-tale history, it is significant that a European tradition of prioritizing female heroism in this iconic story is at least as old as that of female victimization and the spectacle of terror.

In the years that followed the debut of *Almyna*, the specifically theatrical legacy of the *Nights*, "ideologically engaged and technologically innovative," would shape a range of forms of "illegitimate" theater (Orr 2008, 103). These included orientalized melodramas like James Boaden's 1776 recasting of "Beauty and the Beast" as *Selima and Azor* (see Allen 1981, 103; Orr 2008, 111), and afterpiece entertainments like *The Genii . . . an Arabian Nights' Entertainment*, which opened on Boxing Day 1752 and ran for a total of 207 performances at the Drury Lane theater. By the time Gozzi was writing and staging his *fiabe* in the 1760s, the "fantastic apparatus of genii, dervishes, physical transformations, and magical travel" (Orr 2008, 104) of oriental fantasy were fashionable components of both English and Italian popular theater. Gozzi combined these with the stock characters and performance style associated with commedia dell'arte: in the *Fiabe teatrali*, familiar character types (masks) from commedia mingle with characters that were still considered somewhat novel on the Venetian stage, including "witches, wizards, and the King of Hearts, a monarch of an imaginary kingdom costumed like the playing cards" (Griffin 2015, 334). Gozzi mobilized such characters and fantastical settings, and like Manley, he did so in ways that challenged the limits of conventional theatrical practice of his time and also illuminated contemporary constructions of power and identity.

Gozzi's own context was mid-eighteenth-century Venice, and his *fiabe* included some satirical and rather biting treatment of the Venetian theater world. For example, *L'amore delle tre melarance* (*Love for Three Oranges*, 1761) was based on the last tale in Basile's *Lo cunto de li cunti*, but this version featured a comic rivalry between a magician and a fairy—characters who represented Gozzi's own rivals, Carlo Goldoni and Pietro Chiari (see Nicholson 1979, 468). In other of Gozzi's fairy-tale plays, the fantastical elements offer further opportunities for satire and social critique but also "imaginary, formal solutions to unresolvable social contradictions" that arose from Gozzi's position as both a member of the minor nobility and a playwright in need of patronage in a rapidly shifting socioeconomic climate (see Emery 1997, 264–68).

While Basile's seventeenth-century Neapolitan text has such strong links to Gozzi's eighteenth-century Italian *fiabe*, it had no presence on the eighteenth-century London stage. In fact, *Lo cunto de li cunti* would not be translated into English, in print form, until 1848 (Canepa 1999, 29). On the other hand, many French literary fairy tales—which would eventually dominate British pantomime, as I explore in later chapters—echo Basile's Neapolitan text and were likely influenced by its circulation in print form in late seventeenth-century France (see Magnanini 2007). The first of Charles Perrault's tales to gain notoriety on the English stage leads us directly into yet another tangle of transmedial and transnational exchanges: it was the highly orientalized "grand dramatic [and musical] romance" of *Blue-beard, or Female Curiosity!* by George Colman the Younger (son of the Colman who authored the Shakespearean farce, *A Fairy Tale*), with music by Michael Kelly.

Colman's 1798 *Blue-beard* resituated Perrault's sardonic French tale as a romantic melodrama set in Turkey, transforming the lead characters—formerly a wealthy man with an unsettling appearance and a mysterious past, and the daughter of a gentlewoman, seduced by the luxuries and entertainments his money can offer—into the despotic Abomelique and the victimized Fatima. This production was largely inspired by André Grétry's 1789 opera *Raoul Barbe-bleue,* its particular brand of orientalism shaped by the popularity of the *Nights,* both onstage and off. This example of English fairy-tale theater exploits a fantasy of otherness—including the revolutionary undercurrents of Grétry's French opera (see Kuti 2013, 323; Charlton 1992,173)—more than it does magical otherworldliness, resonating deeply with audiences' contemporary concerns and preoccupations (scientific, sexual, imperial).

Early pantomime productions anticipated audience familiarity with a wide range of current performance forms and discourses. In this, they are comparable to the performances of French fair performers who appeared in London in the early years of the eighteenth century, using their plays "to parody and ridicule the establishment repertory" (Scott 1972, 126). Examples of more home-grown metatheatrical satire include the Lincoln's Inn Fields' pantomime *Harlequin Hydaspes; or, The Greshamite* (1719). This pantomime satirized Riccardo Broschi's highly successful opera *Idaspe* (1710) and was likely written by the most famous of all early eighteenth-century pantomime actors: John Rich (stage name "Lun"; see Burling 2000, 64). But once again, the satire is multifaceted and consists of more than a burlesque parody of a familiar plotline, character types, and performance styles. The pantomime's subtitle gestures toward another object of satire: a "pamphlet war" that occurred only weeks earlier between physicians Henry Woodward (affiliated with London's Gresham College) and Richard Mead over the question of "whether purging or vomiting was the sounder approach for the treatment of smallpox." This feud resulted in a duel that rendered Woodward (the Greshamite) "a laughing stock of the London wits" as well as the object of satire on the London stage (63). To comprehend the humor of *Harlequin Hydaspes* thus required acquaintance with pantomime conventions and fashionable operas, as well as London gossip.

Pantomime players themselves have been figures of fame, fashion, and gossip. By the turn of the nineteenth century, England's most popular pantomime player was Joseph Grimaldi, "a London Clown, born, bred," known for his elaborate costumes, nimble footwork and acrobatics, and interactions with the audience (Booth 1991, 154). Grimaldi and his fellow players continued the tradition of local and topical reference, whether in productions for London theaters or elsewhere. The most famous of Grimaldi's fairy-tale pantomime roles was Squire Bugle/Clown in Thomas Dibdin's *Harlequin and Mother Goose; or, The Golden Egg* (1806), which had a phenomenally complicated plot that bore no clear relation to any specific tale; Andrew McConnell Stott characterizes it as "a simplistic rubric intended merely to kick-start the harlequinade" (2009, 172). Nevertheless, elements of the Mother Goose plot as well as the antics associated with the harlequinade became sufficiently well known that they could be referenced in the popular press and the toy theaters made for home use; this is evident in William West's illustration of characters from the production, issued five years after the debut of the pantomime (figure 6).

The 1806 *Harlequin and Mother Goose* secured Grimaldi's position as a star of the Georgian stage and also made the character of Mother Goose a standard in the pantomime repertoire and the full range of ephemera that referenced pantomime. The Clown role in *Harlequin and Mother Goose* also stands as emblem of Grimaldi's significance to the present study: many of his most successful pantomimes were fairy-tale themed—ones that were formative in development of precedents for the pantomimic (re)shaping of well-known plots and roles, including the traditional role of Clown and the emergent figure of the cross-dressed Dame. For example, some of Grimaldi's performance innovations occurred in the earliest pantomime versions of "Cinderella." In the next chapter, I discuss the early history of "Cinderella" in Britain in more detail; what signifies here is that the pantomime debut of this tale in 1804 featured Grimaldi as a newly developed character, the stepsisters' servant, Pedro—a precursor to the now-conventional pantomime role

Figure 6. Print featuring eight characters from the pantomime *Harlequin Mother Goose*. Etching printed by William West, Exeter Street, 1811. Herbert Hinkins Collection. © Victoria and Albert Museum, London.

of "Buttons." A reviewer for *The Times* of London praised the 1804 Drury Lane *Cinderella* for its "striking" transformations, such as the "changes of Cinderella's kitchen-table into a toilette; of a pumpkin into a pavilioned chariot; of the mice into horses," and so on (quoted in Findlater 1978, 102)—feats of stage magic that exploit and expand the varieties of magical transformation associated with the fairy-tale genre and with this tale in particular.[4] As a tale preoccupied with forms of dress and disguise, with familial cruelty and social redemption enacted through dress—up and down the social and

---

4   In 1820, Grimaldi appeared in another "Cinderella" pantomime, *Harlequin and Cinderella; or, The Little Glass Slipper*, this time cross-dressed as the Baroness/stepmother—anticipating what would become the most beloved modern pantomime role: the Dame.

sartorial scale—Charles Perrault's "Cendrillon" (first translated into English in 1729) lent itself brilliantly to forms of theatrical performance, like pantomime, that are known for extraordinary dress, including cross-dressing. It also lends itself to modes of masquerade and fancy dress.

As I suggested earlier, costuming is part of the fabric of fairy tales and a key element in a tale like "Cinderella," but it is also worth grounding a consideration of fairy-tale materiality in an understanding of costuming as a social practice, one that has been popular with both children and adults for centuries. "Costume" can be understood in terms of its association with the theater, a domain that does bear on the history of "Cinderella" but also in terms of the distinct social functions of a form of dress that is not found solely onstage. Folklorist Pravina Shukla differentiates "costume" from clothing, more generally, in terms of the intensification of both materials and communicative power: "When the identity being expressed is singular and significant," Shukla proposes, "the clothing used for that communication is costume," understood here as *special dress that enables the expression of extraordinary identity in exceptional circumstances*" (Shukla 2015, 14; emphasis in original). The title character of Perrault's "Cendrillon" is defined, oppressed, and ultimately liberated by her clothing. In fact, all the outfits by which she is generally known could be considered extraordinary: readers of that tale, whether encountering it in French or English, are offered no information about her "ordinary" clothing. When we first encounter the title character, she has already been demeaned and degraded by her stepmother, and her ash- or cinder-covered clothing become the most potent sign of this extraordinary circumstance. What would the title character have been wearing previously, and what would she have been called? We are left to wonder. Following Shukla, we can acknowledge that Cinderella is in costume from the start of the story.

Cinderella's various outfits have been featured in countless book illustrations, but theatrical and well-publicized fancy-dress figurations of Cinderella *predate* the golden age of fairy-tale book illustration by at least fifty years and become important touchstones for visions of the tale and its title character. Allowing ourselves the luxury of skipping forward in time to the 1870s, before Chapter 2 returns us to the start of the nineteenth century, we can encounter a case study in interfaces among narrative, performance, materiality, and bodily experience.

Dressing the Part

In their study of modern fancy dress in Britain, Anthea Jarvis and Patricia Raine trace the practice to seventeenth-century Italian carnival and masquerade, popularized in eighteenth-century England as public and frequently outdoor events, such as the Ranelagh masquerade with which we began. These practices underwent further transformation, Jarvis and Raine argue, as fancy dress took its place as a predominantly private practice, popular with the social elite, in the nineteenth century (Jarvis and Raine 1985, 4). But Victorian fancy dress was not solely a private practice, as Catherine Hindson demonstrates: fancy-dress balls were also held in theaters like Covent Garden, coordinated by nineteenth-century actresses and theater managers, linking those earlier public practices of fancy dress with an emergent culture of celebrity-endorsed charity (Hindson 2016, 101–24).

While earlier forms of fancy dress were often masked and associated with licentious behavior, sanctioned subversion of social codes and strictures, and carnivalesque reversals, Victorian fancy-dress balls operated somewhat differently. Rebecca Mitchell argues that nineteenth-century fancy-dress events tended to function as opportunities for "participants to negotiate rather than to escape their self-presentation and their milieu: revealing aspects of their character (including, for men, the novelty of sartorial pleasure) by choosing costumes from a prescribed set of identifiable roles and tropes and by choosing often abstract costumes that directly engaged with issues of their day" (Mitchell 2017, 293). The appeal of fancy dress may no longer have been predominantly one of disguise and anonymity (and all the illicit behaviors permitted thereby), but it certainly was an opportunity to exercise creative agency in the adornment of one's body, including exhibition of one's knowledge and cultural literacy—demonstrated through the choice and execution of costume and recognition of the costumes worn by others. Most relevant here is the fact that both the domain of the theater and particular fairy-tale characters formed important parts of a shared and recognizable repertoire of "roles and tropes" that permeate cultures of print, performance, and sartorial play.

Specific fairy-tale characters were part of a shared cultural repertoire, both in the nineteenth century as they are today. They are recognizable even when ripped from their narrative context and are recognizable specifically through the fashioning of their bodies. The frames of reference for doing so *now* are, as we know all too well, indelibly marked by corporatized images, particularly when it comes to Cinderella. The character of Cinderella has proven to be a particularly tenacious costume choice for trick-or-treaters, seemingly inseparable from images of the title character as imagined in the Walt Disney animated feature of 1950 (which itself shaped the costume and design choices of the 2010 Disney live-action *Cinderella*)—specifically Cinderella's grooming and costuming in the palace ballroom scene. The combination of baby-blue-and-white ball gown, yellow-blonde updo, and glass (or clear plastic) pumps is now iconic, the defining features of innumerable commercial Cinderella costumes. These features of the Disney Cinderella's royal fashions were signaled somewhat more obliquely in earlier twentieth-century commercial costumes, such as the vinyl-tunic and plastic-mask costume sets by manufacturers like Ben Cooper and Collegeville, popular from the 1950s through the early 1980s. Those earlier commercial costumes invariably included telltale molded plastic locks of yellow hair and other visual signs of the character's identity (representations of pumpkins, magic wands, or glass slippers) on the vinyl costume itself, against a background of light blue or yellow.

These images are familiar to most North Americans who have participated in trick-or-treat, from either side of the threshold. What is of interest here is the prevalence of fairy-tale fancy dress in an earlier period, during those decades that witnessed the emergence of folklore as a discipline, the proliferation of fairy tales (both literary and oral traditional) as various forms of print culture, and the flowering of fairy-tale pantomime. In the Victorian period, recognizable fashionings of *Cinderella* were to be found onstage, in fancy-dress balls, and in book illustration, and these domains intersect, overlap, and reference one another with remarkable frequency. How did one dress as Cinderella during the height of the Victorian fancy-dress ball? Let's turn now to Ardern Holt's advice for dressing the part.

Holt is best known as the author of the late nineteenth-century costuming guide *Fancy Dresses Described; or, What to Wear at Fancy Balls*, first issued in 1875. Holt notes that the standard practice of fancy dress in the period was to select a costume that was thought to suit the individual, in terms of complexion, age, temperament, and body type. Holt thus begins the 1887 edition with costume recommendations for "fair women," "elderly ladies," "husband and wife pairs," and so on (1887, 2–4). In the general comments and recommendations for specific costumes, Holt repeatedly acknowledges that historical accuracy in fancy dress has always yielded to theatrical effect, current fashion, and current materials: the objective is to spark recognition in the viewer and that requires fluency in current ideas, assumptions, and conventions, first and foremost. A closer look at the fancy-dress options suggested in individual entries from Holt's guide suggests that costume choice (as an expression of self and indicator of cultural literacy) is more complex than Holt's introductory categories and recommendations would seem to indicate.

Holt provides guidelines for Cinderella costumes in each of the editions of the book, and in each case there are two distinct possibilities for dressing as this character: one can dress as the young woman oppressed and ash covered or as the heroine clad in magical finery at the ball. The most extensive entry on Cinderella is to be found in Holt's fourth edition, from 1887:

CINDERELLA. A short cotton dress and tunic, like Lady Adelina Cocks (now Marchioness of Tavistock) wore at the Marlborough

House Ball, with long linen bibbed apron, muslin fichu and cap, a broom in hand, and a glass shoe at side. Another rendering:—Black and white striped short skirt; fish-wife tunic of ash-coloured cashmere; high cambric bodice, V-shape; short sleeves; corsage of red velvet, with black velvet bretelles, crossing in front and attached to tunic; black and white striped stockings; black shoes, silver buckles; short broom and bellows. **Cinderella** at the ball as follows: Train of blue silk; petticoat pink; square bodice; all trimmed with silver lace and roses; wreath on head; the slipper at side of silver perforated cardboard, or satin covered with talc cloth. Dress of 17th century also correct. Or long white satin dress worked in pearls; train from shoulder; high standing collar, wired. Kate Vaughan dressed the character as follows:—Short white satin petticoat embroidered in gold, and low bodice; short sleeves, train from the shoulders, was ornamented with birds of Paradise. Second dress, white satin, elaborately embroidered in silver; the train white, lined with pale blue satin or silk, and large clusters of white ostrich feathers; the hair curled over the forehead, with bandeau of glittering stones; stocking embroidered with silver. For the following, *see* Plate III. Figure 11.—Short plaited skirt; tunic and bodice in one; muslin fichu, loosely knotted; small round velvet or silk cap; bellows at side; broom in hand.

In this lengthy entry, Holt gives primacy to Cinderella *as servant*: costume options along these lines begin and end the entry and are the basis for the one illustration of a Cinderella costume (figure 7). As Holt notes, Adelina (also known as Adeline) Cocks chose just such a Cinderella costume for herself when she was one of five hundred attendees at the Marlborough House ball held by the Prince and Princess of Wales in 1874.

Adeline Cocks was the niece of photographer Julia Margaret Cameron, more of a social activist than a socialite, and was twenty-two years old when she attended this fancy-dress ball. Adeline would become best known for

11. Cinderella

Figure 7. "Cinderella." From Ardern Holt's *Fancy Dresses Described; or, What to Wear at Fancy Balls*, 5th ed. London: Debenham and Freebody, 1887, 11. Courtesy of Toronto Public Library.

her work on prison reform and revitalization of the lace industry and as the eventual namesake for Adeline Virginia Woolf (see "Adeline Duchess of Bedford" 1920, 8–9). But in the 1870s and 1880s, she seems to be noteworthy for her standout fancy-dress appearance at Marlborough House.

The ball itself received thorough and detailed coverage in the periodical press, gaining and maintaining sufficient cultural currency that it could be referenced by Holt, and recognized by Holt's readership, over a decade later. A three-column article appeared simultaneously in the *Illustrated London News* and *The Englishman* on August 1, 1874, and most of the ink was dedicated to description of the Marlborough ball's guests and their costumes. First, "there were all the usual dresses of a fancy ball, Mexicans, Albanians, &c. [The Ottoman ambassador] Musurus Pasha was a splendid Turk in ruby velvet overlaid with gold" while the Princess of Wales "wore a ruby-coloured Venetian dress" whose details of embroidery and construction the writer goes on to describe. Then there were historical costumes, which frequently drew inspiration from portraiture, such as that of "Lord Coville, dressed after a picture at Penshurst of one of Queen Elizabeth's chamberlains" ("Ball at Marlborough House" 1874, 262–63). But of most interest here is the group of attendees the writer calls "the fairy tales," who performed a quadrille.

Resembling the spectacular "processions" included in the final scenes of Victorian pantomimes, a fancy-dress ball quadrille comprised a group of partygoers whose costumes were thematically linked, their initial appearance on the dance floor well choreographed. The Butterick pattern company's 1892 guide *Masquerade and Carnival: Their Customs and Costumes* makes many quadrille theme suggestions, including not only fairy-tale characters but also "a Louis Quinze Hunting Quadrille, in the hunting costume of that period; Kings and Queens of various nations; Army and Navy; Holbein quadrille in Tudor dress; Flowers of the Year; Birds; Pack of Cards; Puritan maidens and Cavaliers; Noah's ark (the animals in pairs)" (8). The success of a masquerade quadrille relies not only on aesthetic effect but also on successful visual referencing of known figures, characters, and types. The noteworthy Marlborough ball quadrille was led by a Miss Graham and the Duke of Connaught, dressed as Beauty and the Beast, and included many other male-female pairs identified by name and costume character in the press coverage. The specific character pairs chosen and reported in the press offer us an interesting perspective on the particular fairy-tale figures that would have been considered recognizable, by way of visual and sartorial cues, to both the ball's attendees and, by way of name alone, to the periodical's readership. These include characters known from English renditions of Marie-Catherine d'Aulnoy's tales (such as Princess Fair Star and Prince Cheri, the Fair One with the Golden Locks and Avenant; the White Cat and the Fairy Prince), the Grimms' tales (the Goose Girl and the King; Red Riding Hood and the Huntsman), nursery rhymes (Bo Peep and Little Boy Blue), and English treatments of Perrault's corpus—including Fatima and Blue Beard, in which case the heroine's name reflects the standard pantomime orientalizing of "La barbe bleue" ("Ball at Marlborough House" 1874, 263). But the most journalistic attention was given to Lady Adelina Cocks and her companion Lord F. Gordon Lennox. This couple was dressed as Cinderella and the Prince.

Of Lady Adelina's "Cinderella," the writer for the *Illustrated London News* notes that she "was a picture, the charm and simplicity of which had a good foil in the surrounding splendour." Adeline's choice to dress as the servant Cinderella and the specific way in which she did so—"in an unbleached linen cap, blue and white overdress, dark blue petticoat, and linen apron"—worked to set her apart from others in her quadrille and from the glamour of the attendees, as a whole; her costume's "charm and simplicity" is truly extraordinary in the context of the Marlborough House ball and is precisely what earned her costume a detailed description and much praise in the papers ("Ball at Marlborough House" 1874, 263). Thirteen years after the ball itself, her fancy-dress choice was still being referenced, as in the Ardern Holt manual, and presumably being emulated as well.

When examining possibilities for dressing as Cinderella at the ball, Holt makes another timely reference: a recent pantomime *Cinderella*. This allusion could easily be lost on a 2018 reader and was not included in subsequent editions of *Fancy Dresses Described*. In other words, the costume details from a single *Cinderella* pantomime had a half-life considerably shorter than that of the legendary Marlborough House fancy-dress ball. But in 1887, all Holt needed to do was mention Kate Vaughan, and it could be assumed that readers would know where and how Vaughan had appeared in such a costume, namely, in the Christmas 1883–84 pantomime at the Drury Lane theater. By this point in time, *Cinderella* had an eighty-year history as pantomime and was one of the most popular pantomime subjects (a status maintained to the present day). Augustus Harris's 1883 production was praised as one of "spectacular comicality with much sumptuousness" ("Drury Lane" 1883, 11). It featured the comedians Harry Nicholls and Herbert Campbell cross-dressed as stepsisters Blondine and Brunette; Minnie Mario cross-dressed as the prince, praised for her singing, dancing, and acting; and Kate Vaughan in the title role.

Vaughan first earned a degree of renown on the music hall stage, as had so many other pantomime players of the era, including the comedy duo of Nicholls and Campbell who were now playing her stepsiblings. Vaughan didn't receive terribly strong reviews for her performance in the pantomime title role, but she did appear in the inventive and spectacular costume designs by William John Charles Pitcher (known as "Wilhelm"). Drury Lane was famous for Wilhelm's costume designs, and star players in costume were immortalized in photographic portraits that appeared in periodicals and could be bought as collectibles; in the case of Vaughan's *Cinderella*, the pantomime's notable costumes included both the ballroom attire (shown on both Vaughan and principal boy Minnie Mario, figure 8) and the title character's trademark cinder clothes (figure 9).

Pantomime costumes for women included those for female players in the part known as the "principal girl" (the youthful female lead and equivalent of Columbine in a harlequinade) and those for players in the role of "principal boy" (the youthful male lead, equivalent of Harlequin, and almost

Figure 8. Photograph of Minnie Mario as the Prince with Kate Vaughan in the title role in *Cinderella*, Theatre Royal Drury Lane (1883–84). Guy Little Collection. © Victoria and Albert Museum, London.

Figure 9. Photograph of Kate Vaughan in the title role in *Cinderella*, Theatre Royal Drury Lane (1883–84). Guy Little Collection. © Victoria and Albert Museum, London.

always played by a woman in Victorian period). These costumes departed from respectable women's wear most notably in terms of skirt lengths and leg exposure, and each of the fancy-dress options described by Holt (even those that are not attached to Kate Vaughan's example) feature tunics or short skirts and tights, in true pantomime style. Where pantomime dress did not carry over into most examples of fancy dress, however, was in the form's iconic examples of cross-dressing: Holt offers no advice to women wishing to dress as Prince Charming, or Jack, or Dick Whittington, all parts routinely played by women in tights. Nevertheless, to dress as Cinderella in this period was to draw on a repertoire of sartorial choices derived from the stage, ones that would not otherwise be considered acceptable in polite society.

Theatricality and costume, playacting and play with clothing, are frequently imagined in terms that are associated with the world of the fairy tale, most especially with "Cinderella." For example, in 1865, theater critic and social commentator George Augustus Sala reflected on the transatlantic tradition of "calico balls," a subset of fancy dress in which costumes are constructed solely or predominantly from cotton—a strikingly humble fabric for evening wear, which many partygoers attempted to counterbalance with the addition of fancy trims. According to Sala's account, "The ladies came in calico dresses, like so many Molly Moggs [sic], and wore them until twelve o'clock; but at midnight the reverse of the transformation scene in Cinderella took place. The cotton-clad belles tripped into their disrobing bower, whisked off their calico frocks, and reappeared in dresses of the most expensive materials, and blazing with jewels" (1865, 194–95). Importantly, Sala is able to assume reader familiarity with "Cinderella," as he is with the barmaid Molly Moggs, immortalized in John Gay's comic ballad of 1710; that these two characters should be conflated reveals how readily fairy-tale characters could be employed in the service of social satire. It may also represent an established precedent for approaching fairy-tale material with irreverence. Sala's description assumes reader familiarity with the conventions of fairy-tale pantomime—in which "the transformation scene" is one that shifts the action from the mundane to the magical, the fairy-tale-themed opening to the harlequinade, and is accompanied by spectacular stagecraft and costume changes.

Sala finds humor in the irony of the calico ball, which was both fashionable but also frustrating to women in an elite social world: many such women, on both sides of the Atlantic, were accustomed to displays of taste, knowledge, and social power through rich and elaborate attire, although Lady Adelina's example suggests an alternative model—one that was the object of praise rather than mockery. The ball Sala describes is imagined as its own kind of theater, and in some sense it works as a kind of pantomime upside down, with wealthy women counting the minutes until they can return to their "ordinary" party clothing: their elaborate ball gowns. Importantly, Sala's ironic touch and foregrounding of this reversal invites us to reconsider "Cinderella," itself—as a story that seems to fetishize ornate dress as both a sign of and essential tool in acquiring social power.

Following in a very old tradition of imagining fancy dress, and specifically the fancy-dress ball, in terms of the "Cinderella" story, Jarvis and Raine likewise draw on fairy-tale discourse in their history of fancy dress. To explain the pleasures of the practice, they reference the familiar role of Cinderella's godmother as the source of clothing for a ball. "What is the age-old appeal of fancy dress?" they ask. "For some, it has granted a wish, like a fairy godmother's wand, enabling a suburban housewife to be Cleopatra, a bank clerk Henry VIII or an eighteenth-century duchess to be a milkmaid." Whether the costume of choice is fairy-tale related or not, fancy dress is imagined as a way of *living* or embodying the world of fairy tale, specifically the role of Cinderella. Not explicitly magical nor even fairy-tale related, another function of fancy dress identified by Jarvis and Raine resonates deeply with Shukla's definition of costume, cited earlier: fancy dress concerns "the casting off of the clothes and conventions of the work-day world," offering participants "the opportunity to be truly themselves" (Jarvis and Raine 1985, 3). This characterization of a second potential function of fancy dress seems equally applicable to the tale of "Cinderella," in which magical dress renders the title character unrecognizable to her own family members but simultaneously *reveals* her "true" identity and agency—revealing that her ash- or cinder-covered clothing was truly the outfit that functions as some kind of disguise, a forced masquerade.

Like the immersive and spectacular forms of sociable entertainment that frame this chapter, theater itself (and not only elaborate stagecraft) has often been constructed in terms of stage magic, representing "that fairy region of muslin, drapery and tin flowers" to which all Britons could be transported with just the price of a ticket ("Christmas Pantomimes and Burlesques" 1851, 3). In some sense, the realm of "fairy" has been as powerfully enmeshed with notions of *artifice* as with those of nature, and yet the definition, significance, and relative cultural value of "artifice" are repeatedly subject to debate. Regardless, to reference the "fairy tale" in centuries past was to rouse a host of associations about which we have since suffered a degree of cultural amnesia: this particular form of fantasy, understood in relation to materialities and embodied experience, in which the ordinary and extraordinary, the mundane and the magical mix freely, lends itself beautifully to social commentary, satire, spectacle, and even farce. These are affordances of the form and ones that have been mobilized for centuries.

The moments of fairy-tale history that I have highlighted so far exemplify points of overlap and intersection between forms and traditions and are particularly resistant to easy, clear, or linear description. Nevertheless, they can serve to highlight the fact that an attempt to study the fairy tale in terms of just one communicative medium, one historical period, and/or one national context is bound to produce a distorted account. Exploration of nineteenth-century British fairy-tale pantomime is necessarily and inevitably a multimedial, transnational, and transhistorical endeavor; and it is to the early years of the century that we now turn our attention.

2 Fairy-Tale Sociability

Print and Performance in Folklore's Prehistory

THE EARLY DECADES of the nineteenth century have long been regarded as a period of infancy in the history of folklore study. For example, Richard Dorson began his study of the groundbreaking folklore research of the Victorian period with some consideration of the antiquarianism that preceded it, searching for traces of field-based research well before such a methodology had been developed for the study of oral traditions. There is no doubt that Dorson's consideration of individuals to whom he granted the hyphenated (and anachronistic) moniker *antiquary-folklorist* was a recuperative measure: antiquarianism and its practitioners had been the targets of widespread "criticism and mockery, from the early modern era onwards," associated with an obsessive but ultimately impossible quest for "the lost glories of the past" (Marchant 2015, 123, 125). Dorson's interest in the work of such generally maligned figures from intellectual history is filtered through his own view of modern folklore study, a desire to grant its lineage dignity and respectability, and an investment in an historical master narrative that moves steadily toward disciplinary maturity. Understood in this way, it is perhaps unsurprising that Dorson paid little heed to the relationships between the proto-folklorists he profiled and Romantic-era popular theater—or commerce, more broadly—but these are the kinds of relationships exemplified

.se studies that constitute this chapter and ones that resonate in the
ᵥᵥ᷂ later scholars.

Along similar lines, there is a long critical tradition in which the turn
of the nineteenth century is regarded as a period of remarkable *inactivity* in
the history of the fairy tale, a time when fairies and their tales were banished
from middle-class libraries and nurseries. Accounts of fairy-tale theater pose
a challenge to received wisdom about the place of the genre in British literature and culture. The examples discussed so far can also serve as remind-
ers that the genre has, for centuries, signified variously and in a variety of
expressive media for diverse audiences—popular and elite, adult and child.

In an oft-cited letter written by Charles Lamb to Samuel Taylor
Coleridge in 1802, Lamb lamented the difficulty he had had in purchasing
fairy-tale books for Coleridge's two-year-old son: "All the old classics of the
nursery" were vanishing from bookshops, he writes, only to be replaced by
"Mrs. B[arbauld]'s & Mrs. Trimmer's nonsense" (quoted in Bottoms 2006,
212). As M. O. Grenby notes, many of the Romantics expressed "wistful
and polemical fears of the chapbook's supersession" in the lives of children
of the early nineteenth century (2011, 107), by which point "chapbook tales
had been incorporated in the new children's literature" and "fairy stories
were also absorbed into the mainstream" of such books (108). Coleridge
expressed similar sentiments, as did William Wordsworth, most famously
in *The Prelude* (1805), where he mourned the apparent loss of "Jack the
Giant-Killer," "Fortunatus," and the *Arabian Nights' Entertainments* from
the bookshelves of children. Of course, there *were* relatively successful
fairy-tale books in print at this point in time, including multiple editions
of Grub Street writer Robert Samber's treatment of Perrault's tales and
the 1802 John Harris edition of stories by French writer Marie-Catherine
d'Aulnoy, as *Mother Bunch's Fairy Tales*—hardly the barren landscape suggested
by some of the Romantics.

This period in fairy-tale history, and the language of loss mobilized by
prominent Romantic poets, has been the subject of vigorous reevaluation in

the past twenty years or so, from nuanced reassessments of fantasy in relation to didactic and evangelical forms of literature for children (for example, see Richardson 1994, 112–27; Tucker 1997; Ostry 2002, 36–38; Bottoms 2006), to studies of print ephemera and periodicals long overlooked as venues for the circulation and discussion of fairy-tale material (see Grenby 2007; Speaight and Alderson 2008; Sumpter 2008). These alternative histories of the fairy tale are serving to expand the range of cultural forms studied and, in so doing, are starting to map the shifting terrain of fairy-tale forms and audiences through periods once considered relatively barren or, at best, ones characterized by the fairy tale's "subterranean survival," to borrow Caroline Sumpter's evocative phrase (15). I would argue that it is the salience of the fairy tale as a form *worth* debating, negating, or even mourning that signals its vibrancy, rather than the movement toward mainstream acceptance as appropriate material for family audiences. As Rita Felski argues, "Artworks can only survive and thrive by making friends, creating allies, attracting disciples, inciting attachments, latching onto receptive hosts. [. . .] The number and breadth of these networks prove far more salient to a text's survival than matters of ideological agreement" (2011, 584). Felski's example of choice is controversial avant-garde artwork that gains as much cultural traction from negative as from positive reviews (see 584). This example has particular resonance for a study of the fairy tale in early nineteenth-century Britain, where the genre certainly had its detractors but maintained a significant place in the popular consciousness nevertheless.

The two case studies in this chapter predate the Victorian materials on which I focus in later chapters, serving as a kind of backdrop for that important period in folklore history, but they also serve to animate more fully what Felski calls the "sociability" of texts. The network of forms that represented the tale of "Cinderella" in 1804, and those connected to the name of "Daniel O'Rourke" in the 1820s, challenge models of "adaptation" and "remediation" that have tended to underpin examinations of fairy-tale material in media like film, and that seem to assume that each tale has a kind of original, traditional, or ur-form. While postcolonial studies and related fields have generated "rich resources" for conceptualizing space, a "language of translation, creolization, syncretism, and global flows" (Felski 2011, 575), there have been fewer challenges to the conceptual vocabulary of temporality. There are exceptions (Felski cites the work of philosophers Michel Serres, Gilles Deleuze, Walter Benjamin), but the seemingly magnetic pull toward linear and progressive conceptualizations of history persists, even in efforts to revise or rethink historical metanarrative. Following Felski, I am interested in approaching my objects of study as "enmeshed in a motley array of attachments and associations" (2011, 589), ones that are of particular significance to folklore's disciplinary history and the emergence of field-based methodologies. As Felski notes, the sociability of texts can be understood in terms of "formal devices that travel beyond the boundaries of their home texts to attract allies, generate attachments, trigger translations, and inspire copies, spin-offs, and clones" (2011, 587)—and connections between fairy-tale "texts" are not necessarily matters of plot and story line. How does a multimedial history of the fairy tale look from this perspective, without relying on comparison of "original" and adapted/reworked texts, freed from the comforting tidiness of linearity? These are questions raised in the previous chapter but explored in greater depth here. The cases I consider foreground the many ways in which print and material artifacts bear traces of complex relations between embodied and performative practices, within networks of texts and networks of people.

Cinderella in London, 1804

Since the early decades of folklore study, versions and variants of what would come to be known as tale type ATU 510A ("Cinderella") have been documented, analyzed, and published in written form. The most famous and enduring of those published in the nineteenth century may be the German tale known as "Ashenputtel," featured in Jacob and Wilhelm Grimm's 1812 *Kinder- und Hausmärchen* and first translated into English by Edgar Taylor in 1826.[1] Nevertheless, the story has tended (then as now) to be framed in relation to the name and story line that dominated British popular culture both when the Grimms started their collecting and publishing efforts and when the term *folklore* was coined more than thirty years later, namely, the 1697 tale "Cendrillon" by Charles Perrault—or, to be more precise, a range of English treatments of that French *conte de fées*.

I will turn shortly to a motley array of "Cinderella"s circulating in London in the year 1804, more than forty years before the coinage of *folklore* as a word and sixty years before the so-called golden age of imaginative children's literature (Green 1962). Taken together, these "Cinderella"s offer some concrete examples of the associations among fairy tale, spectacle, and comedy; they also offer vantage points on the complex relationships between print and theatrical forms. The print versions considered here—namely, an innovative illustrated book sold by T. Hughes and a few other London booksellers, a script with commentary published by John Fairburn, and Benjamin Tabart's Juvenile and School Library version—are all renditions of "Cinderella," but they are linked by an additional factor. It is not, as one might expect, that each claims descent from Perrault's French text (in fact, only Tabart's version does so); nor do they all define themselves in relation to past translations (again, only the Tabart version does so). Rather, they are connected by the fact that all three make claims to cultural value in relation to a successful theatrical production, a pantomime staged in London that year. It is in this multimedial context that a French tale pivoting around relationships among women (whether abusive or nurturing) merges with the commedia dell'arte–influenced romance plot, pitting young lovers against powerful figures who stand in the way of predestined love.

As a point of entry to the tale's complicated history, it is useful to consider the specific name by which the story and its heroine have come to be

---

1   Taylor's version of "Ashputtel" was included in volume 2 of *German Popular Stories, Translated from the Kinder- und Hausmärchen of MM Grimm, from Oral Tradition* (1826, 2:33–46).

known in English. Perrault's first English translator, Robert Samber, established a precedent for the English name we now know very well but with a spelling that will be unfamiliar to modern readers: as Christine A. Jones points out, Samber "opts for the homophone cinder" (rather than "ash") in his 1729 translation of "Cendrillon" as "Cinderilla." In doing so, Samber dilutes the "vulgar and comical" tone of the stepsisters' nicknames for her, as found in the French text, where their aggressive verbal play *amplifies* the insulting quality of the title character's name, slipping from *cendre* (ash) to *cul* (ass) (see C. Jones 2016, 137nn2–3). Punning possibilities did not survive this voyage from French to English. Samber's rendition of the story lacks that particular suggestion of vulgarity, and this is the form in which English-language readers came to know the tale: Samber's version was reprinted more than twenty times in the next ninety years, with just minor variations and alterations (see Blom 1989, 520–21).[2]

Jones traces the now-standard spelling of "Cinderella" to the year I will consider momentarily, 1804, and the illustrated edition of the story published without reference to a specific translator but advertised as "a new and improved translation"[3] by the bookseller Benjamin Tabart (2016, 137n3).[4] Tabart's *Cinderella; or The Little Glass Slipper: A Tale for the Nursery, from the French of C. Perrault*, part of his Popular Stories for the Nursery series (1804–18), is the best known of the early nineteenth-century books to use the now-standard "-*ella*" spelling of "Cinderella," but this spelling actually had been in circulation much earlier than 1804. For example, "Cinderella"

---

2 J. M Blom's bibliography of publications attributed to Samber or based on Samber's work include English editions of Perrault's tales from 1729, 1737, 1741, 1750, 1763, 1764, 1765, 1772, 1777, 1780, 1785, 1791, 1794, 1795, 1796, 1799, 1800, 1802, 1812, and 1817 (1989, 540–47).

3 The relevant page from Benjamin Tabart's 1804 catalog is reprinted in Lissa Paul's study *The Children's Book Business: Lessons from the Long Eighteenth Century* (2011, 44). Tabart also offered a French edition, "with the same embellishments" (44).

4 Iona Opie and Peter Opie have noted that both spellings circulated until at least 1825 (1980, 326–27).

makes an appearance in 1757, in the mock praise poem "An Encomium on Nastiness, Addressed to Young Lady remarkable for dirty Hair, dirty Teeth, and dirty Nails." In this piece of satirical verse, the poet addresses his own "Dear Cinderella," his "Goddess of the dirty hue" (1757, n.p.). In other words, Samber may have made some efforts to mute or tame the tale's tongue-in-cheek qualities and potential vulgarity, but the 1757 example of comic poetry indicates that those qualities persist in a broader history of Cinderella references, ones that are not necessarily evident if one limits the field of study to print editions of Perrault's story. In terms of book history, Tabart's edition of "Cinderella" cemented the modern spelling of the heroine's name, as Jones argues, but throughout the eighteenth and nineteenth centuries both the spelling and the signifying potential of the name "Cinderella" was variable—and the range of media and genres in which it could be invoked was wide.

Closer to the period under consideration here, the name became associated with various forms of equestrian entertainment: "Cinderella" was established as the name of a stud horse in 1793 (*General Stud-Book* 1793, 50) and also as the title of a comedic and musical spectacle performed at Astley's Amphitheatre, located in Lambeth (now central London), an area well known for taverns and entertainment venues. Astley's was famous in the period for its equestrian shows,[5] featuring clowning and acrobatic acts as well as the equitation of impresario and "chief performer" Philip Astley, reputed to be the "handsomest man in England." Astley's is important in the histories of pantomime and the circus, and by the 1790s the shows staged at that venue had moved from a series of "exhibitions and horsemanship" (P. Cunningham 1871, 178–79) to themed and loosely narrative productions.

5   As Henry Green Clarke wrote in 1851, Astley's Royal Amphitheatre of Westminster Bridge Road was "first established about 1767, as an open riding-school, but in 1780 was covered in, and formed into a regular theatre." By the time Clarke was writing in the mid-nineteenth century, Astley's was "one of the best frequented theatres in London" (129).

On August 13, 1794, Astley's advertised "a new Musical Piece, called CIN-DERELLA or the GLASS SLIPPER," which was initially classified in advertisements as a "Pantomime," promising "Various Exercises of Strength" as well as "Tumbling, and Equestrian Performances" ("Last Week" 1794, 1). By the following year, this "Cinderella" show was advertised as a "Musical Tale, consisting of Song, Dance, Recitative, and Spectacle," which *concluded* with "a favourite Comic Pantomime," featuring "new Scenery, Machinery, Decorations, Dresses, and Magic, interspersed with the greatest Variety of Mechanical Changes, Magical Transformations, and wonderful Metamorphoses." The show's "pantomime" even had its own distinct title: "The Fairy's Fantasy; or Enchanted Manor" ("Sixth and Last" 1795, n.p.).

Whatever genre of theatrical performance Astley's 1790s *Cinderella or The Little Glass Slipper* was considered to be, it was without question a form of what Jane Moody calls "illegitimate theatre" (2000), performed outside the circuit of patent theaters and evading royal censors. In this case, we have a generally wordless spectacle that played on audience familiarity with the tale that had been translated from Charles Perrault's *Histoires ou contes du temps passé* and that was already circulating in multiple English editions (see C. Jones 2016, 177–205). It was part of a shared cultural repertoire. The Astley's *Cinderella* also played on established precedents for seeing the story as a potential source of entertainment and comedy, not strictly (or even primarily) as a didactic or moral tale—despite occasional, strategic invocation of such categories by supporters of fairy tales as legitimate forms of entertainment.

While advertisements for the equestrian *Cinderella* do make free use of the term *pantomime*, the "first performance" of the story *as* pantomime is generally dated somewhat later, to the year 1804, when it was staged at the Theatre Royal Drury Lane (for example, see Pickering 1993, xxxiii, 41).[6]

---

6   The production was advertised in *The Times* as early as December 27, 1803, but is generally dated to 1804. The review quoted below was published January 4, 1804, and it announced that the "grand allegorical Pantomime spectacle, called

The pantomime *Cinderella and the Little Glass Slipper* was staged from January through April of 1804, with James Byrne producing and starring as the Prince. It was a musical afterpiece to melodramas offered at the Drury Lane theater during those months, including titles like *The Wife of Two Husbands*, *All in the Wrong*, *The Beaux Strategem*, and *The Country Girl*. The 1804 *Cinderella* would not have been scheduled as the evening's main attraction, but it did generate popular, critical, and commercial interest and spawned multiple items of print culture, as we will see. At this point in time, fairy tales were not yet the backbone of the relatively stable and limited corpus of narrative material used for pantomime, as they would be by midcentury. Nevertheless, some of the contributors to this production already had fairy-tale-inspired work in their résumés. For example, the show's well-known composer Michael Kelly was famous for the score he contributed six years earlier to the hugely successful Drury Lane show *Blue-beard, or Female Curiosity!*

Reviews of the Drury Lane *Cinderella* are able to rely on audience familiarity with "the old fairy tale of the same title"—already entrenched in British popular culture by 1804, its origins in French writing meriting no mention at all. For example, a reviewer for *The Times* assumes that the story, as well as the Roman and Greek mythological characters and settings that appear in the pantomime, are "familiar to every young mind." The reviewer commends the show because "all the groundwork of this pleasant and moral fairy tale is strictly adhered to" and cites as evidence the dispensation of rewards (to Cinderella) and punishments (to her sisters). Here as elsewhere, a reference to the genre as inherently "moral" can be taken with a grain of salt, an indication of a conventional way of characterizing fairy tales but not necessarily the root of their enduring appeal. As the reviewer notes, "There is, indeed, in all this, little or no novelty." Instead, it is the mash-up of fairy tale with classical mythology, as well as the full sensory impact of the

Cinderella, or The Little Glass Slipper, was yesterday evening brought forward for the first time" ("Theatre, Drury-Lane" 1804, 3).

stagecraft, that make the show novel and entertaining. The review notes that it is "the introduction of *Venus, Cupid*, the *Nymphs*, and *Graces*" that "gives an *éclat* to the whole, [and] which renders the effect extremely magnificent. The wonder-working powers of the Fairy are now transferred to the Goddess of Love, who, by her legitimate aids, Cupid and Hymen, accomplishes all the ends of the spectacle, and makes the lovers happy"—and this presumably makes the audience happy, too. What I want to underscore, however, is that this reviewer can count on readers' understandings of the various components of performance and stagecraft that comprise "all the ends of the spectacle": this is what seems to merit review and serves as the mark of the production's success. Aspects of the production like superb costumes and scenery, the grace and agility of the players, and the series of "striking transformations" (such as pumpkin into chariot, and lizards into footmen ["Theatre, Drury-Lane" 1804, 3]), are all foregrounded as feats of stage magic to which the story of "Cinderella" lends itself well, and for which pantomime more generally had become well known.

The association of the "Cinderella" story with memorable transformations and with theatricality, generally, is exploited in a little book that appeared during the Drury Lane pantomime's run in 1804. *Cinderella, or, The Little Glass Slipper* was printed for T. Hughes of Stationers Court and also for a consortium of booksellers that included the innovative John Harris, who in 1801 had taken over the groundbreaking firm established sixty years earlier by John Newbery. This *Cinderella* is an example of an early fairy-tale-themed "movable" book—a kind of lift-the-flap book, also known as a metamorphosis or turn-up book, combining "narrative and visual display" in ways that might be considered proto-cinematic (see Faden 2007, 72). Some movable books have also been referred to as "harlequinades" when the content is based on a late eighteenth- or early nineteenth-century pantomime, as in this case. This toy book consists of four panels of edge-to-edge illustration on which versified narrative is overlaid (figure 10, pages 68–69). The panels can be read sequentially, left to right, but each panel also has an upper and lower flap that can be moved separately, lifted or lowered, to reveal further development of the action in word and picture. It could be purchased "colored" (for one shilling) or "plain" (sixpence), and its subtitle announced its relation to the pantomime under consideration: *As Performed at the Theatre-Royal Drury Lane, with Universal Applause.* As part of a series called the Juvenile Theatre, this movable book and others in the series (including *Goody Two Shoes, or Harlequin Alabaster: As Performed at the Sadler's Wells, with Universal Applause* [1803] and *Mother Goose, or The Golden Egg: As Performed at the Theatre Royal Covent Garden* [1807]) promised "scenic representations, with expositions in verse, of all the most favourite spectacles, pantomimes, ballets, and other grand & picturesque performance at the Theatres-Royal; entirely adapted to the comprehension and amusement of youth" (*Cinderella* 1804, cover).

The prices for these movables in their colored and plain formats, respectively, were equivalent to those of a ticket to the full evening's entertainments at Drury Lane and a late-entry ticket (which would admit one to the pantomime alone), as Jacqueline Reid-Walsh has observed. Whether these movables were seen as a substitute for attendance at the theater, as a form of advertising, or as souvenirs (or some combination of all three), what is most striking is that these books invite the reader to be an active participant in the unfolding of the narrative and theatrical action. As Reid-Walsh argues, such books call on the reader's "print literacy, visual literacy, performance literacy, and a willingness and capacity to play with or interact with the text itself" (2006, 424).

Importantly, the theatrical or performance literacy to which Reid-Walsh alludes appears to have been international in scope: the review of the Drury Lane pantomime cited earlier ends by relating this afterpiece entertainment neither to Perrault's tale nor to the equestrian show of the 1790s but to a treatment of "the subject [. . .] brought forward in no very different way on the French stage, and crowned with no less success than that which promises to attend the performance of *Cinderella*" ("Theatre, Drury-Lane" 1804, 3).

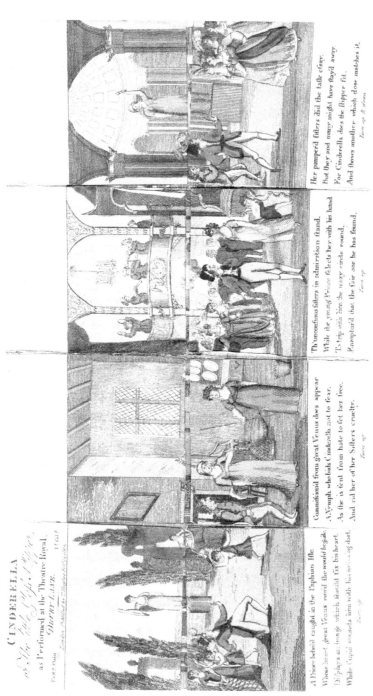

CINDERELLA

or, *The Little Glass Slipper*,

as Performed at the Theatre Royal,
Drury Lane.

Price Sixth.   London, Published by T. Hughes, Ludgate Street.

A Princess and caught in the Paphian Isle,
Whose heart great Venus mov'd the world beside.
Displays an image which should fix his heart
While Cupid wounds him with his winning dart.
Turn up.

Commission'd from great Venus does appear
A Nymph who bids Cinderella not to fear.
As the is first from hate to let her free,
And rid her of her Sisters cruelty.
Turn up.

Th'unconscious sisters in admiration stand,
While the young Prince selects her with his hand
To step into the mazy circle round,
Enraptur'd that the fair one he has found.
Turn up.

Her pamper'd sisters did the task essay,
But they and many might have slav'd away,
For Cinderella does the slipper fit.
And shews another which does matches it.
Turn up & down.

Figure 10. *Cinderella, or, The Little Glass Slipper; as Performed at the Theatre Royal, Drury Lane* (London: T. Hughes, 1804). Movable book: flaps lowered and lifted. Courtesy of Toronto Public Library, Osborne Collection of Early Children's Books.

Then to th'aethereal regions they arise,
In perfect surety of their royal prize,
Who to Diana's castle has homage paid.
But now's deep smitten with the unknown Maid

This pumpkin quick a carriage in a trice.
And twice three barks from these dapper mice.
Thy rags to hurry and these lizards learn
Shall footmen be in livery of green.

Time flys unheeded till the cautioud hour.
Begins to strike most solemn three times four.
At this as if she darted from a trance.
Like lightning flys the Prince & quits the dance.

The Temple
or
VENUS.

One way to find her out he thinks perchance.
That should be that night give a splendid dance.
Among the ladies who will there resort.
He'll see the fair by whom his heart is caught.

But ere the midnight hour the dance forsake.
And to your home quickly yourself betake.
Else thou shalt see thy splendor quickly fly.
And grieve to be beheld in rags and misery.

But drops in haste one slipper on the ground
Which by the amorous Prince is quickly found.
Who now resolves the foot of any fair.
Which fits the slipper shall his kingdom share

The marriage knot in Venus Temple tied.
The Prince enraptured with his charming bride.
Who kind forgives her fathers cruelty
And hopes they'll live together happily.

The Prince
will marry
her who can
put on the
Glass Sliper

It seems likely that the reviewer is referring to a now-obscure ballet panto-mime from 1779, titled *La pantoufle de Cendrillon* (see Buch 2008, 87n85), which in turn was indebted to a comic opera created for the Foire Saint-Germain in 1759. These French theatrical predecessors worked creatively with the plot structure of Perrault's tale by starting the performance with Cinderella's return from the first ball (Anseaume 1759, 3), and in this par-ticular arrangement of plot elements, the injustice of Cinderella's servitude is *not* the focus of the narrative. Whether London audiences circa 1804 would have had this level of familiarity with French performances of *Cendrillon* is impossible to say, but, at very least, *The Times'* reviewer's oblique ref-erence to Parisian popular theater suggests that an 1804 English reader-ship had some familiarity with (or an interest in) Continental performance traditions—even as a distinctive form of fairy-tale pantomime was being crafted on the London stage.

If we dwell for a moment on these earlier French performances of *Cen-drillon*, it is worth noting that the ties between Perrault's tales (published in France in 1697) and Théâtre de la foire are strong, right from the start. For instance, there are theatrical resonances attached to the reference to Mère l'Oye (Mother Goose) in Perrault's *Histoires ou contes du temps passé* (the vol-ume in which "Cendrillon" appeared). The placard reading *contes de ma mère l'oye* appears in the book's famous frontispiece, an image that was copied and adapted for Samber's 1729 English translation (figure 11). On the one hand, this anticipates the many appearances of Mother Goose characters in Victo-rian pantomime, but in its time the visual and verbal references to Mère l'Oye may have operated as a callout to a contemporaneous French theatrical type. As I discuss in chapter 4, French fair entertainments bearing the title *Contes de ma mère l'Oye* have been dated back to 1695 (see Jones 2016, 167n1) and 1694 (Deulin 1878, 29), while a tradition of comic and absurd "goose" and "stork" mothers were popular cross-dressed parts in France. To think about French and English theatrical renditions of a story like "Cinderella" in terms of *adaptation* of Perrault's tale—that is, to frame Perrault's story as a

Figure 11. Frontispiece to *Histories, or Tales of Past Times, with Morals, by M. Perrault, Translated into English* [by Robert Samber] (London: J. Pote, 1729). FC6.P4262.Eg729s. Houghton Library, Harvard University.

print ur-text and then assess pantomime versions in terms of fidelity to the original—starts to look like an oversimplification if not an outright distortion of the dynamic and dialogic relationship between popular performance and popular tale that has shaped the genre, and this specific story, for centuries.

Like the earlier Parisian *opéra-comique* of 1759, the 1804 Drury Lane pantomime plays with the content and narrative structure of the "Cinderella" story. It includes characters not found in Perrault's tale, including figures from Roman mythology as well as a comic servant named Pedro, played by the brilliant and acrobatic Joseph Grimaldi, who was on the brink of nationwide fame (see Stott 2009, 131–56). This pantomime also reworks *established characters and plot elements*, and all this is reflected (or immortalized) in the words and pictures of the movable book. I will return to examples from the Hughes movable book in a moment, but for now it is another print artifact from 1804 that is especially useful to the exploration of the pantomimic (re)shaping of the Cinderella story: *An Accurate Description of the Grand Allegorical Pantomimic Spectacle of Cinderella, as Performed at the Theatre-Royal, Drury Lane: To Which Is Added, a Critique on the Performance and Performers, by a Lover of the Drama. Together with the Story of Cinderella,* published by John Fairburn.

As its lengthy title indicates, Fairburn's publication is divided into three parts (unequal in length): an illustrated rendering of the script, a short "critique" of the production, and a prose version of "The Story of Cinderella." The last of the three resembles the story we currently know so well; in its day, it would have seemed indistinguishable from the versions of the Samber translation widely available in book form. Why it should have been included in this book at all is difficult to ascertain, given that its plot structure differs significantly from that of the script that precedes it.[7] Its inclusion does,

---

7   The script is called a "description," which seems an apt moniker since there is very little dialogue to document: recitative makes up only part of the pantomime and its script, with much of the story conveyed through song, action, movement, and gesture.

however, offer tacit acknowledgment on the part of the publisher that the story was known in at least two quite distinct forms.

Within the covers of the Fairburn book, the pantomime script itself takes center stage, and an initial perusal of the four illustrations that adorn the script in the Fairburn volume would not seem to yield many surprises for the twenty-first-century viewer: the images move from "Cinderella *in the* Kitchen, *ill-treated* by her *Sisters*" (*Accurate Description* 1804, plate 1 [figure 12]), to "*The* Nymph *directing* Cinderella *to return before* Midnight" (plate 2), to "Cinderella *at the* Ball, *dancing with the* Prince" (plate 3), and ending with "Cinderella *fits on the* Slipper, *& produces the* other *from her* Bosom" (plate 4). Reading the script embellished by these four plates, on the other hand, reveals another story, and this is where pantomimic plot points are readily and immediately apparent. Specifically, this theatrical rendition creatively combines established conventions of the tale in print form with those of early pantomime—the latter of which center on young lovers (equivalent to Harlequin and Columbine in the harlequinade) who must overcome obstacles to unite happily at the play's conclusion.

The pantomime does not open, as one might expect, in Cinderella's home. Instead, the first scene is set at the foot of Mount Ida, home to Venus and Cupid. This is what had been depicted in the movable book from the same year, discussed above. This opening setting follows the pantomime convention of introducing the "immortals"—the supernatural characters who shape the actions of the mortals and who include the figure known as the "benevolent agent." In early pantomime, the immortals were less likely to be fairies than gods, nymphs, and sprites (see Pickering 1993, 109). In this case, Venus (the actress Rosemond Mountain) plays the important role of benevolent agent in the pantomime plot, comparable to but also quite distinct from the fairy godmother with whom audiences are now far more familiar. Like the fairy godmother, Venus has an important role to play in human affairs: unlike the godmother of Perrault's tale, Venus's primary concern is romantic love, not familial harmony or justice.

PLATE 1.
See Page 23

Cinderella *in the* **Kitchen,** *ill treated
by her* **Sisters.**

Figure 12. The first of four plates adorning *An Accurate Description of the Grand Allegorical Pantomimic Spectacle of Cinderella, as Performed at the Theatre-Royal, Drury Lane: To Which Is Added, a Critique on the Performance and Performers, by a Lover of the Drama. Together with the Story of Cinderella* (London: John Fairburn, 1804). Courtesy of Indiana University Library.

Eight-year-old Oscar Byrne played Cupid and began the show by lead-ing the corps de ballet through "a fascinating dance, replete with elegance and taste" in homage to Venus. Joined onstage by a chorus of child cupids, bearing silver wings and with wreaths of fabric roses on their tiny heads, the effect was reported as one that "combined [the] luxuriance of dance and scenic effect," firmly establishing Drury Lane as "the first stage in the British Isles" (*Accurate Description* 1804, 5). Pleased with the opening spectacle, the character of Venus moved quickly to establish her primary concern in the mortal realm: she does not focus her attention on the pantomime's title character but rather on the Prince (James Byrne)—a "vain" and "proud trai-tor" to the goddess of love, a man who has displayed more devotion to Diana than to Venus. In short, it is the Prince's preference for warfare and hunt-ing over romance, not Cinderella's unjust treatment by her stepmother and stepsisters, that is the "problem" Venus seeks to resolve with the assistance of Cupid and the Nymph.

In the pantomime, it is Venus's duty to ensure that a preordained romantic pairing is achieved. There will be no surprise, as far as the title character's romantic destiny is concerned, even if her domestic and famil-ial dilemmas seem incidental to the pantomime's opening scene. It is the path taken to that marital destiny that promises novelty and spectacular effects. This particular way of imagining and telling the story of "Cinderella," including the cast of immortal characters who have the Prince's fate as their primary concern, becomes part of the print history of "Cinderella" by way of such texts as Fairburn's *Accurate Description* and the movable book version published by Hughes—where the action at Mount Ida takes up the first of the book's four panels. Of course, the initial situation created in the panto-mime (and circulating in the Fairburn and Hughes texts) runs counter to the story as we currently know it, as it did the many print versions based on Samber's translation (including the prose "Story of Cinderella" appended to the script). In the pantomime, it is evident from the outset that Cinderella's union with the Prince is prescripted. It will not be a reward for her goodness, nor does it seem to stand primarily as an attempt to restore her rightful social position. Instead, the marriage will be the realization of a romantic plan that Venus herself has ordained from the start. The Prince's yearning for Cinderella and ultimate marriage to her represents Venus's correction of *his* behavior, not that of Cinderella's stepsisters. At the same time, this romantic pairing also fulfills a generic expectation of pantomime, inherited from commedia dell'arte: the quest of a young couple to outwit the oppressive forces and controlling characters that stand in the way of their pleasure and prosperity.

The first glimpse the Drury Lane audience would have had of Cinderella herself (played by Maria Theresa DeCamp) is in the form of a statue, a "figure [that] arises on a pedestal, in a seductive position, correspondent in dress to the same which Cinderella wears at the ball." As Prince and audience alike gaze upon this statue, Cupid delivers his arrow and the Prince is enraptured (*Accurate Description* 1804, 7). As the setting shifts to the mortal realm, the performance moves quickly to the delivery of invitations to the Prince's ball and then to a kitchen interior featuring the now-animated character of Cinderella (in tatters, not a ball gown) with servant, Pedro. This shift in setting is depicted in panel two of the movable book, which dwells in and around Cinderella's house: a lift of the flaps brings the viewer/reader from inside the kitchen to the exterior of the house, where Cinderella's magical carriage awaits. The particular (re)configuration of plot elements I have described, beginning with the immortals who seek to redirect the Prince's passions, invoking an image (a statue) of Cinderella at the ball for that very purpose—and well before Miss DeCamp has appeared as Cinderella the servant—has not been documented in earlier print iterations of the tale. Importantly, it presumes audience acquaintance with the general contours of the story, its key characters, and the items of clothing that will signify *only* as the plot unfolds. It also implies an audience ready, willing, and able to appreciate playful reconfiguration of the story's established thematic concerns and plot elements. The opening sequence of scenes would be disorienting and objectionable if this were not the case.

Similarly, the "Critique on the Performance and Performers" included in the Fairburn volume calls on a general understanding of the story's moral thrust that would have had to be learned somewhere other than Drury Lane and which suggests a disconnect between the performance of *Cinderella* and popular discourse about the story's form, function, and meaning. In the critique, the writer does not seem to share Venus's concern with the Prince's priorities and choices but focuses instead on Cinderella's virtues and her sisters' misdeeds—even though the pantomime gives these matters cursory treatment at best. After discussion of the production's "beautiful scenery," tasteful dresses, "pretty and appropriate" music, "light and elegant dances," and Grimaldi's "comicality," the critique retreats to a reminder of "how Cinderella, amidst all her sufferings, yet was happier in her mind than her fine dressed sisters," recommending that audiences aim to be "like her, [and] return good for evil" (*Accurate Description* 1804, 20). This serves as a bridge (both thematically and formally) between the pantomime script and the prose "Story of Cinderella" that rounds out the Fairburn publication. These two distinct approaches to "Cinderella"— one that focuses on domestic exploitation, in which magical forces offer the heroine social opportunities that she had been denied, and another that focuses on the marriage plot, with magical forces directing the hero to realize a romantic destiny—coexist. They are referenced within the covers of a single text.

M. O. Grenby has observed that the growing popularity of French fairy tales on the nineteenth-century English stage was intimately connected to the popularity of the tales in the English book trade. Grenby notes, for instance, that both Benjamin Tabart's series Popular Stories and rival publisher/bookseller John Harris's series Popular Tales (1810) drew heavily on English traditional tales and French *contes de fées* and exploited their readership's perceived familiarity with tales in pantomime form. Both publishers thus "routinely advertised their fairy tales as being inspired by current theatrical productions" (Grenby 2006, 1–2). Tabart's range of "entertaining" books included "myths and legends, biographies, histories, and science books" (Paul 2011, 42), as well as fairy tales. Those tales Tabart chose were drawn either from a repertoire of English chapbook stories (like "Whittington and His Cat" and "Jack and the Beanstalk") or from French ones, principally tales of Perrault and d'Aulnoy, including "Little Red Riding Hood," "The Sleeping Beauty," "Cinderella," "The White Cat," and "The Yellow Dwarf." Each of these tales was also in the process of entering the pantomime repertoire at this time.[8]

The most canonical of the works considered here, Tabart's 1804 *Cinderella; or The Little Glass Slipper*, does not signal a theatrical connection on its title page. Instead, the subtitle of this book—*A Tale for the Nursery, from the French of C. Perrault*—traces provenance through a history of print translation and an emergent association of the fairy-tale genre with publications made specifically for children. When the first advertisement for the book appeared in the *Morning Chronicle* on January 14, 1804, it announced that the publisher "has the honour to acquaint all the Masters and Misses of the Metropolis" with "a new Edition, price 6d., of the famous Romance of CINDERELLA," in the small format he called a "Liliputian folio, embellished with three coloured Engravings." Tabart's little book represents an effort to produce cheap editions of individual tales; in terms of price, it offers an alternative to the six-shilling bound volumes of Popular Stories also sold by him at twelve times the price (see Paul 2011, 64). The lilliputian *Cinderella* would seem to be in direct competition with the "plain" version of

8   David Pickering cites the interest George Colman (the Elder) had in staging "Little Red Riding Hood" in the mid-eighteenth century but notes that the first pantomime version of the story, *Red Riding Hood; or The Wolf Robber*, appeared at Sadler's Wells in 1803 (1993, 126). The first "Sleeping Beauty" pantomime dates to 1806 (186), and d'Aulnoy's once-popular tales "The Yellow Dwarf" and "The White Cat" made their pantomime debuts in 1807 and 1811, respectively (217, 212; see also Bolton 2000, 160, 157).

the movable book published by Hughes, which likewise sold for sixpence, although Tabart's *Cinderella* had the advantage of color in its illustrations. These two books can also be seen as competing in terms of what they promised to depict: advertising this book just eleven days into the run of the Drury Lane pantomime, Tabart claimed that the colored engravings in his own *Cinderella* were not illustrations of Perrault's tale per se but rather representations of "the three principal scenes of the piece, as performed at the Theatre Royal Drury Lane" ("Cinderella" 1804, 1).

It was the copper-plate illustrations to his *Cinderella*, specifically, that Tabart advertised as links to the Drury Lane production, but those illustrations also lack clear markers of theatrical depiction. Despite Tabart's claim, there is no Venus, no Cupid, no Mount Ida, and no statue of Cinderella to be found anywhere in his "new edition" of the well-known tale. Likewise, the engravings give no sense of action taking place on a stage (no visual suggestion of a proscenium arch, no detail indicative of Drury Lane or any other theater). What the illustrations *do* offer is a depiction of a character who was proving to be phenomenally popular onstage, although he is wholly absent from the written narrative as it was published by Perrault in 1697, as it had been translated by Samber in 1729, or as it was presented by Tabart in 1804: namely, the character of Pedro, servant to the stepsisters, played at Drury Lane by Grimaldi. In fact, the plate captioned "The Sisters going to the Ball," which features Pedro, was bound at the front of the volume, serving as frontispiece (figure 13).

While the Drury Lane pantomime would seem to have little to no bearing on the *written* portion of Tabart's *Cinderella*, its author(s) was undoubtedly familiar with that popular production. The text of Tabart's *Cinderella* is believed to have been penned by Mary Jane Godwin or possibly William Godwin, both of whom are known to have attended the opening night of the *Cinderella* pantomime at Drury Lane on January 3, 1804. Somewhat ironically, William Godwin's diary entry for that day indicates that his activities also included a visit with Charles Lamb (Myers, O'Shaughnessy, and Philp

Figure 13. "The Sisters going to the Ball." Frontispiece from *Cinderella; or The Little Glass Slipper: A Tale for the Nursery, from the French of C. Perrault* (London: B. Tabart, 1804). Courtesy of Toronto Public Library, Osborne Collection of Early Children's Books.

2010). Without a doubt, the Godwins and Lamb himself were well aware of this popular and successful production—as were the great majority of Londoners, given the breadth and diversity of theatergoing audiences circa 1804.

In the face of a virtual chorus of Cinderellas, all competing for a share of the popular audience, laments like those of Lamb, Coleridge, and Wordsworth, cited at the outset, start to ring strangely hollow. But as Janet Bottoms argues, they do "point to a widely held belief at the time that there was an 'opposition' [to fairy tales]" and that this was manifesting itself as a dearth of "old classics" for children (2006, 212). This has continued to resonate in late twentieth- and twenty-first-century scholarship. For example, Tabart bibliographer Marjorie Moon expresses her admiration for "the way in which [Tabart] challenged the anti-fairy-tale brigade, those stiflers of imagination and suppressors of fantasy by launching in 1804 his delightful series of Tales for the Nursery" (Moon 1990, 5; see also Paul 2011, 62). In fact, it would have been in Tabart's best commercial interests to assert that good versions of fairy tales were increasingly hard to find.

In a preface to the collected *Popular Fairy Tales* (1818), Tabart differentiates his compendium from extant versions of the well-known stories, which he characterizes as "so obsolete in their style, so gross in their morals, and so vulgar in their details, as to be altogether unfit for the purpose to which they seem to be adapted"—that is, as books for children (Tabart 1818, iii; see Paul 2011, 64). In this, Tabart echoes rhetoric associated with writers like Anna Letitia Barbauld and Sarah Trimmer. When it came to advertising certain titles in his fairy tale line, Tabart did not emphasize differences from extant print versions of the stories, such as his attempt "to elevate their language and sentiments," as detailed in his own preface (1818, iii). Instead, he highlighted their fashionable relationship to current or very recent theatrical productions, as we have seen. This would seem to align with Tabart's representation of his own bookshop: publications like Tabart's *Visits to the Juvenile Library* (1805) and *A Visit to London* (1808) offered portraits of his own business and storefront as thoroughly modern and fashionable, a place to see and be seen—from the shop's design and extensive inventory to the stylish dress of the clientele (Paul 2011, 33–35). At least part of what this "improved" and improving rendition of "Cinderella" seems to offer readers is cultural capital, akin to theatergoing and to shopping itself. While Romantic-era laments about a fairy-tale drought have endured, the genre's historical positioning as fashionable and profitable has tended to be overlooked.

The centrality of the Drury Lane pantomime to the varied print forms of "Cinderella" circulating in 1804, and discussed here, could inspire a kind of reversal in historical study: no longer do we need to focus on the adaptation of print fairy tales to renditions in other media, like theater. Instead, one could argue that the movement from stage to page is equally significant. Indeed, this is the framework suggested by the very few critics who have mentioned the impact of early pantomime on the world of print. As noted earlier, Grenby suggests that publishers began to recognize the profitability of fairy-tale materials (and particularly theatrical tie-in products) because of the success of fairy-tale pantomimes at the turn of the nineteenth century. For his part, the late George Speaight, best known as an expert on British toy theaters, argued in one of his last articles that "pantomime's penetration of the world of children's books, their composition and publication" is a phenomenon that merits much more attention (1946, 92). But there are problems inherent to the essentially linear nature of an adaptation paradigm of fairy-tale history, even when conventional nodes in that linear model are reversed. Taken together, these varied "Cinderella"s are suggestive of the rich network within which fairy tales were being produced and received, within a web of interpenetrating forms and discourses.

Daniel O'Rourke, "From His Own Lips"

Like the "Cinderella"s of 1804, the case of "Daniel O'Rourke" moves across genres of print and performance, but it does so in ways that foreground the strange coalescence of folklore discourse with an earlier tradition of cultural ventriloquism and literary imposture. The history of "Daniel O'Rourke," a tale of supernatural adventure, is closely associated with the career of antiquarian Thomas Crofton Croker and offers more evidence of the "sociability of texts"—ones that are seemingly disparate but deeply connected. Importantly, the name "Daniel O'Rourke" refers not only to a story but also to an iconic Irish storyteller, a person Croker claimed to have met and from whom he reportedly heard the eponymous tale, "from his own lips" (T. C. Croker 1825, 277). Sociability in its more conventional sense, in terms of interpersonal connections and encounters, clearly matter here. Indeed, it is revealing to map out Croker's position in relation to fellow antiquarians/ proto-folklorists, on the one hand, and within a social and creative network of individuals working in London in the 1820s, on the other. Croker's claims to particular forms of encounter with Irish storytellers like Daniel O'Rourke and the implications of specific iterations of the story bearing O'Rourke's name—both print and theatrical—are illuminated in relation to these complex and overlapping social networks.

This case study requires movement through time and across media, but October 20, 1826, is a useful starting point. That morning, Sir Walter Scott breakfasted at the London home of his daughter Sophia and her husband, *Quarterly Review* editor John Gibson Lockhart. Guests identified by name in Scott's journal entry for the day include fellow Scotsman Allan Cunningham, the poet who first gained renown after contributing "old songs" of his own devising to Robert Hartley Cromek's *Memoirs of Nithsdale and Galloway Songs, with Historical and Traditional Notices Relative to the Manners and Customs of the Peasantry* (1810); Daniel Terry, the Scottish actor, playwright, and theater manager renowned for his stage adaptations of Scott's novels and ability to impersonate the novelist himself; Canadian-born artist Gilbert Stuart Newton, who was then establishing his reputation as a painter of literary scenarios and characters, and who had already drawn Scott's portrait; and a relatively new acquaintance, Thomas Crofton Croker—"author of the Irish fairy tales," as Scott describes him in his diary entry from that October day, "[l]ittle as a dwarf, keen eyed as a hawk and of very prepossessing manners" (Anderson 1972, 217). An Anglo-Irishman who had lived in London and worked as a clerk in the Admiralty since 1818, T. Crofton Croker had already contributed to a growing body of writing on Ireland and the Irish with his first book, *Researches in the South of Ireland, Illustrative of the Scenery, Architectural Remain, and Manners and Superstitions of the Peasantry with an Appendix, Containing a Private Narrative of the Rebellion of 1798* (1824). But it is what Scott calls "the Irish fairy tales"—Croker's *Fairy Legends and Traditions of the South of Ireland,* published anonymously in 1825 by John Murray—that has earned him a place of honor in the history of folklore research and seems to have earned him a place at Scott's table.[9]

9 Croker described this breakfast meeting in a letter to his sister, reporting the "flattery" he received from this most admired man: "He mentioned my *Fairy*

The *Quarterly Review* praised *Fairy Legends* for a style that "seems to stamp a certain authenticity upon the narrative" ("Fairy Legends" 1825, 198), and the book was a commercial and critical success. Publisher John Murray issued both a second volume and then a second series of the book, for which Croker received the handsome sum of £300 (Smiles 1891, 2:152). In addition to a degree of (much-needed) pecuniary benefit, the first edition of *Fairy Legends* had also garnered Croker admiring letters from and ongoing correspondence with Sir Walter Scott and Wilhelm Grimm.[10] By the time of the October 1826 breakfast at the Lockhart home, the second edition of the book had been released, now bearing Croker's name as author, and the Grimm brothers had published their own German translation of it, extensively annotated and titled *Irische Elfenmärchen*. Croker had been brought out of the shadows of anonymity and into contact with some of the leading figures in the world of arts and letters. As Dorson notes, "Friendship and exchange of information with the Grimms and Scott were a fruitful by-product of *Fairy Legends*" (1968a, 47); they also seem to offer Croker a kind of legitimacy by association in terms of intellectual history.

An understanding of the role of sociability in scholarly work, and especially in the formation of a new discipline, underpins Dorson's 1968 study of the "great team" of Victorian folklorists, as it does his considerations of the antiquarians of earlier decades whose work anticipated the emergence of folklore study later in the century. It may not have served Dorson's purposes in *The British Folklorists* to examine the many points of overlap and intersection

---

Legends, and hoped he should soon have the very great enjoyment of reading the Second Volume. 'You are our—I speak of the Celtic Nations (said Sir Walter)—great authority now on Fairy Superstition, and have made Fairy Land your Kingdom; most sincerely do I hope it may prove a golden inheritance to you'" ("Sir Walter Scott and Mr. Crofton Croker" 1854, 452).

10   Scott's first letter to Croker dates from April 27, 1825; it is reproduced in full in *The Letters of Sir Walter Scott*, ed. Sir Herbert Grierson (1825–26, 9:94–97). Scott's letter was reproduced with permission in subsequent editions of *Fairy Legends and Traditions of the South of Ireland*.

between this (emergent) domain of scholarly enterprise and the world of popular entertainment; nevertheless, Croker's multiple and multimedial iterations of a single tale, and that tale's own points of connection with forms of narrative imposture and stage mimicry, offer us a sense of the complex web of discourses and forms underpinning the emergence of folklore study.

Researchers generally agree that *Fairy Legends and Traditions of the South of Ireland* was, in one or another, the product of several hands, including those of fellow antiquarians Thomas Keightley and Joseph Humphreys. The authorship of the volume was challenged even in its own day (see Hultin and Ober 1983, xxiv–xxv, and Hultin 1986, esp. 289–93), but many features of this text imply a master voice and perspective. There is, of course, the very fact that the book was attributed to T. Crofton Croker shortly after its initial anonymous publication (and has been ever since), but there is also the fact that the text refers repeatedly to "the Compiler" (singular) in prefatory and concluding remarks and uses first-person narration to describe encounters with particular tellers and tale-telling events. Importantly, *Fairy Legends* invites as much, if not more, contemplation of the Irish storytellers whom the Compiler describes as it does the fairy folk who populate their tales, as much delight in storytelling events as it does in supernatural story itself.

The way in which the Compiler describes encounters with named tellers suggests a field-based methodology—or at least it has done so for modern folklorists, reading through what may be the rose-colored lenses of our own preferences and proclivities: *Fairy Legends* has been deemed "the first field-based collection to be made in Great Britain" (Dorson 1968a: 45).[11] This is certainly something that would have been ahead of its time in 1825. While the text's first-person descriptions of places, people, and storytelling events may seem to invoke visions of the "field encounter," they also extend a tradition of humorous portraiture and literary imposture that would have resonated deeply with Croker's readership and social circle. As we will see, Croker makes use of storytelling

---

11   This distinction is one that has been echoed by Henry Glassie (1985, 11), Eileen Fitzsimmons (1978, 14), Francesca Diano (1998, xxiii), and others.

strategies in his first-person narration, playing with the trope of face-to-face encounter to invoke English stereotypes and exemplify Irish humor.

As I have argued elsewhere, the book's textual strategies complicate the portrayal of Irish tellers to English readers and (in many ways) anticipate later theorizations of performance and the entextualization of oral traditions (see Schacker 2003, 46–77). Some of the most modern-seeming of these strategies are narratological and concern matters of voicing. Consider that several of the narratives that compose the collection are presented as quoted speech, embedded in a first-person account of meeting a particular man or woman and hearing a tale. Information about a tale-teller or performer is detailed in such examples of framing narration, which one assumes to represent the voice and perspective of the anonymous "Compiler." For instance, the story "The Crookened Back" begins with a narrative sketch of Peggy Barrett and the details of a specific performance situation: Peggy's abilities are compared to those of "all experienced story-tellers," and she thus "suited her tales, both in length and subject, to the audience and the occasion." In particular, the Compiler foregrounds Peggy's ability to tell tales that traverse the spectrum of believability, both stories that were "brief, very particular as to facts, and never dealt in the marvellous" and those others, told "round the blazing hearth of a Christmas evening" and "when the winds of 'dark December' whistled bleakly round the walls, and almost through the doors of the little mansions, reminding its inmates that the world is vexed by elements superior to human power, so it may be visited by beings of a superior nature." At such moments "would Peggy Barrett give full scope to her memory, or her imagination, or both; and upon one of these occasions she gave the following circumstantial account of the 'crookening of her back'" (T. C. Croker 1825, 296–97). The text then presents as quoted speech Peggy's narration of her frightening May-eve encounter with the shape-shifting *phooka*, many years earlier.[12] Likewise, in "Linn na-Payshta" (later retitled "The Hidden Treasure"),

---

12 See Schacker (2003, 55–56) for a fuller discussion of "The Crookened Back."

the text begins with a description of an exchange between the landlady of an Inn at Sligo and the first-person narrator. The text invites us to assume that this is the voice of the Compiler or Croker himself: the landlady reportedly addresses him as "a gentleman" of "*teeste* and *curiosity*" (T. C. Croker 1859, 303). Convinced to take a tour of Connaught, the Compiler ventures forth and encounters "an old cowherd." Aware that the stranger/narrator/Compiler is interested in "ould stories about strange things" (1859, 305), the cowherd proceeds to narrate the legend of Manus O'Rourke's Halloween encounter with the eel-like *payshta*, supernatural guardian of treasure.

These examples of named tellers' tales embedded within stories of personal encounter—that is, legends embedded in stories of encounters between the collector and specific folk narrators—is not used consistently in *Fairy Legends*. Some texts lack framing commentary by the Compiler altogether; others shift from the Compiler's description of a named individual to omniscient narration of that person's supernatural experiences. Nevertheless, the localization and contextualization of what we may retrospectively call the "field encounter," evident in stories like "The Crookened Back" or "The Hidden Treasure," grants the Compiler's first-person narration the same kind of veracity that is characteristic of legends themselves. The "Daniel O'Rourke" tale would seem to epitomize this tendency, going so far as to name the specific day on which the eponymous teller told this version of his tale. It opens thusly:

> People may have heard of the renowned adventures of Daniel O'Rourke, but how few are there who know that the cause of all his perils, above and below, was neither more nor less than his having slept under the walls of the Phooka's tower. I knew the man well: he lived at the bottom of Hungry Hill, just at the right hand side of the road as you go towards Bantry. An old man was he a the time at the time that he told me the story, with gray hair, and a red nose; and it was on the 25th of June 1813, that I heard it from his own lips, as he sat smoking his pipe

under the old poplar tree, on as fine an evening as ever shone from the sky. I was going to visit the caves in Dursey Island, having spent the morning at Glengariff. (T. C. Croker 1825, 277)

While O'Rourke's story is reportedly known by many, the first-person narrator (presumably the Compiler) claims to have know the man well and is familiar with his physical appearance and the location of his home—here described as if by and to a local, both English speakers, individuals for whom landmarks on a well-traveled road would be recognizable. The account the Compiler is going to offer of Daniel's performance would seem to have claims on our attention outpacing those of any other reports of these "renowned adventures." As the text shifts to Daniel O'Rourke's own voice, the status of the tale as oft told is underscored: "I am often axed to tell it, sir," said he, "so that this is not the first time" (T. C. Croker 1825, 278). It is tempting to see these rhetorical maneuvers in terms of the Compiler's validation of his project, establishing O'Rourke as yet another experienced tale-teller in his community, like Peggy Barrett, and also framing an English person's experience of *reading* this book as being akin to entering O'Rourke's local community, sitting alongside the men under the old poplar tree.

In *Fairy Legends*, O'Rourke's quoted account extends for over ten pages, with no return to the first-person narration of the Compiler. It is in Daniel's quoted speech that readers hear of his tipsy exit from a Lady-day dinner; his stumble into a nearby ford; his desertion on an island and isolation in a bog; his rescue by a talking (and vengeful) eagle who flies O'Rourke to the moon, where he is left clinging to a reaping hook and begging for mercy from the (merciless) man in the moon; his fall toward earth when the man in moon gives the reaping hook a great *whap* with his kitchen cleaver; his rescue by an old gander, who tried to fly O'Rourke to Arabia; and finally, Daniel's tumble into the sea and encounter with a whale—at which point he awakens and finds himself doused with water, a familiar voice cursing him for falling asleep beneath the haunted "ould walls of Carrigaphooka"

(T. C. Croker 1825, 290). Like O'Rourke's wife, the audience for this story-telling suspects that the adventures are induced by drink and possibly by sleeping in an enchanted locale; the experiences Daniel recounts are not presented by the Compiler as true and incontrovertible fact. The framing narration, on the other hand, makes different kinds of truth claims. As we have seen, before presenting this story as O'Rourke's quoted, first-person narration, the Compiler of *Fairy Legends* went so far as to specify the date on which he purportedly encountered this man and heard his story of supernatural encounter from that his "own lips": June 25, 1813. From a twenty-first century perspective, this gesture toward temporal specificity seems to signal an authentic field encounter with O'Rourke.

In fact, readers of the 1820s would have had quite a different perspective on the Compiler's claims, the name "Daniel O'Rourke," and the story that O'Rourke ostensibly told to Croker. On the one hand, the fact that Croker would have been only fifteen years old in 1813 adds a touch of irony to O'Rourke's use of the honorific "sir" and throws into question the reliability of Croker's claims to close friendship—and even the veracity of the report. On the other hand, when we consider forms of popular print and performance that circulated in the wake of *Fairy Legends*' 1825 publication, as well as those that set the stage for its reception, these claims actually reverberate as something *understood* to be fictional, even comedic; or, to use our current frame of reference, they suggest that this narrated encounter is something like a fieldwork fiction or perhaps legendry about legend-telling.

The story Croker tells about his relationship to and encounter with Daniel O'Rourke has had particular staying power, as has the tale attributed to that gray-haired, red-nosed old man. Interestingly, O'Rourke's narrative had gained enough cultural currency in mid-nineteenth century England that it could be referenced in shorthand. For instance, in Lady Georgiana Fullerton's 1846 novella about a Catholic woman in England, *Ellen Middleton: A Tale*, one evening's entertainment consists of singing ("Irish melodies," "Jacobite songs," and "English ballads"); impassioned political discussions;

and tale-telling—including "the wonderful history of Daniel O'Rourke, who held on to the moon by its horns" (1846, 192). A decade later, the narrator of Elizabeth Gaskell's novel *North and South* compares the attempts of the main character, Margaret, to govern her own thoughts to O'Rourke's comical and hopeless exchanges with the man in the moon, from whom Daniel had sought and failed to find refuge: "Margaret poured out the tea in silence, trying to think of something agreeable to say; but her thoughts made answer something like Daniel O'Rourke, when the man-in-the-moon asked him to get off his reaping-hook. 'The more you ax us, the more we won't stir' " (1855, 2:29). Gaskell doesn't reference Croker by name, but the quoted speech in her novel is drawn word for word from "Daniel O'Rourke" as the story appeared in *Fairy Legends and Traditions of the South of Ireland.*

Much more recently, a picture-book version of the story by Caldecott-winning American writer and illustrator Gerald McDermott was published as *Daniel O'Rourke: An Irish Tale* (1986). Choosing to delete references to O'Rourke's drunkenness—actually an important part of the tale, as presented in *Fairy Legends*—McDermott prefaces his picture book with accounts of the *phooka* (fairy creatures with whom a modern North American readership may be unfamiliar) and of the source of this story, echoing Dorson by tracing it to Croker's collection efforts in the early nineteenth century. This provenance apparently serves McDermott's and his publisher's marketing needs and echoes Dorson's account of Croker's significance to the history of folklore research, but that particular lens fails to bring into focus some of the subtleties of Croker's various entextualizations of and comments on the "Daniel O'Rourke" story. In O'Rourke's quoted words, this was not the first telling of the tale, nor would it be the last. But the tangle of print and performative iterations of this story that precede the appearance of *Fairy Legends and Traditions of the South of Ireland* is far more intricate than one might suspect. O'Rourke's adventures include not only a trip to the moon, into the sea, and back home again, but they also took him to the stages of London theaters and the pages of a wide range of print forms.

In the 1825 endnotes that follow the tale in *Fairy Legends*, Croker writes that the story is "a very common one, and is here related according to the most authentic version" (T. C. Croker 1825, 291). It may not be surprising to discover that the understanding of authenticity activated in this case differs significantly from those valued in current scholarship on oral tradition. But even taken on its own terms, such a statement does more than provide further scaffolding for the text as both well known and a reliable representation of a particular people and place. The rhetorical strategies employed in this instance are both more subtle and more playful than they may appear.

In a fundamental way, Croker's notes to the tale undermine the picture of field encounter established in the tale text itself: rather than discussing a personal interaction with a man named Daniel O'Rourke, on June 25, 1813, Croker establishes very clearly that the story and Daniel himself had much more than a local reputation. First he traces the appearance of a "pleasantly versified" rendition of the story "in six cantos" by Mr. S. Gosnell of Cork, published in Blackwood's Magazine, in 1821 (T. C. Croker 1825, 291). He then turns to the venue that had made English audiences well acquainted with the character of O'Rourke and his misadventures: the "lively entertainments" of "that inimitable imitator" Charles Mathews (293). In these notes, Croker highlights the history of the story as it had appeared in periodicals and as stage comedy.

Mathews was an English theater manager, comic actor, musician, singer, and ventriloquist well known for his Irish impersonations and his "table entertainments"—multicharacter, one-man musical comedies he called "Mathews at Home." From 1808 to his death in 1835, Mathews performed these enormously popular shows, sold simultaneously in print form where they often were illustrated by caricaturist Isaac Robert Cruikshank (brother to George Cruikshank, illustrator of the first English edition of Grimms' fairy tales, Edgar Taylor's *German Popular Stories*, in 1823). Mathews earned himself a reputation as "the great mimic" (Berg 1884, 187) and created a host of stock characters that drew on racial, national, and class stereotypes: these included ballet master Monsieur Zephyr, Major Longbow, Dr. Prolix, the apothecary Mr. Sassafras, Monsieur de Tourville, Hezekiah Hulk, and Daniel O'Rourke. The character of O'Rourke was introduced by Mathews as an Irish ship's steward, featured in an 1819 show Mathews called *A Trip to Paris* (Yates 1860, 241–42) and another in 1821, called *Adventures in Air, Earth, and Water* (figure 14). It was in the 1821 show that Mathews's "Daniel O'Rourke" had "his Dream" and "his Visit to the Man in the Moon" (Mathews 1839, I. 113). As Croker acknowledges in his notes, O'Rourke was, by 1825, already established as one of Mathews's personae. Albert Ellery Berg claimed in 1884 that Mathews's characters were "almost comedies in themselves" but that they also "perished with their creator" (1884, 187). Quite to the contrary, Mathews's stage personae became familiar to audiences on both sides of the Atlantic, emulated early in the career of African American actor, singer, dancer, and choreographer James Hewlett. In 1824, Hewlett staged an "homage to Mathews," combining "characters from various 'at homes,' including a stage Irishman named Daniel O'Rourke" (MacAllister 2011, 64).

Like Hewlett, Croker seems to have understood that his invocation of a character with the name of "Daniel O'Rourke" signaled indebtedness to Mathews, but it also signaled involvement with a world of impersonation and comedy, a popular theatrical milieu in which the art of imitation was celebrated. Beyond a shared use of this particular character type, Charles Mathews's life and career are further enmeshed with those of Croker—and also with those of other people in Croker's circle. Mathews knew both Scott and Terry, and he leased the Adelphi Theatre for "his series of inimitable 'At Homes'" from 1828 to 1831 (P. Cunningham 1871, 188). Three years after his death in 1835, his son, Charles James Mathews, married the theatrical innovator, theater manager, and performer Madame Vestris; he also became a regular player in J. R. Planché's fairy extravaganzas, acting roles like Riquet from *Riquet with the Tuft* (Richards 2015, 82). To complicate matters further, Croker's son, T. F. Dillon Croker, moved in the same

Figure 14. "Mr. Mathews: In His 'At Home' of 1821." Etching by (Isaac)
Robert Cruikshank, ca. 1821. NPG D5229 © National Portrait Gallery,
London.

Main point of book! ✳

social and professional circles as Mathews's son: Dillon Croker had known
Planché since childhood, and in 1879 he would coedit Planché's collected
extravaganzas, which were sold in print form, as were the vast majority of
popular entertainments discussed so far.

Most significant to the current discussion is the fact that print and performance are entwined in this as in other chapters of the tale's history, and
the relationship is anything but unidirectional or linear. In 1826—the same
year that witnessed publication of the second edition of *Fairy Legends* as
well as the publication of the Grimms' German translation—Croker's own
theatrical version of "Daniel O'Rourke" was staged at the Adelphi Theatre
in London. While Daniel O'Rourke was already established as a "stage Irishman," there doesn't seem to have been a precedent for using an Irish supernatural legend, specifically one presented textually as a personal experience
narrative (or memorate), as the basis for a pantomime. But *Harlequin and
the Eagle: Or, The Man in the Moon and His Wife*, was indeed the pantomime
staged at the Adelphi in the 1826 Christmas season, and it was revived for
a short run in 1871.[13]

According to Croker's son, it was Sir Walter Scott who suggested that
"the adventures of Daniel O'Rourke" would make an apt and lively "subject for the Adelphi pantomime"; this reportedly happened at that October
1826 breakfast (T. F. D. Croker 1859, vii). In fact, the seeds of this idea
were planted somewhat earlier. Consider, for instance, that Croker's 1825
endnotes to "Daniel O'Rourke" in *Fairy Legends* contained a similar observation: in the notes he writes that it is "surprising that [actor and theatrical machinist Charles] Farley, the magic genius of Covent Garden, should

13 The writer and Victorian pantomime librettist E. L. Blanchard notes in his diary
    that *Man in the Moon* was staged at Drury Lane on April 11, 1871, and "goes
    off moderately." Blanchard's biographers refer to this pantomime as a " 'Freak
    of Fancy,' " which was "founded on 'Daniel O'Rourke,' one of Crofton Croker's
    fairy legends of the South of Ireland" and "was the medium for introducing a
    very beautiful panorama by [designer] William Telbin, illustrating Irish scen-
    ery" (Scott and Howard 1891, 2:396n4).

have so long overlooked a story so well calculated for pantomimic effect" (T. C. Croker 1825, 293–95). Scott's commendatory letter to Croker, sent on April 27, 1825, also connects the dots, commenting on "the extreme similarity" of "[Irish] fictions to ours in Scotland," and expressing admiration for the "interest of the stories and the lively manner in which they are told." But it was a distinctly Irish supernatural being, the Cluricaune (which makes no appearance in the rambling story of Daniel O'Rourke as it appeared in *Fairy Legends*) that struck Scott as "an admirable subject for a pantomime" (Grierson 1932–37, 9:94). Croker's note and Scott's letter seem to anticipate the project that had come to fruition by the time of the breakfast gathering that October morning. By the time of this breakfast, Croker was already in the process of transforming the story known as "Daniel O'Rourke" into a pantomime.[14] *Harlequin and the Eagle* was commissioned for the Adelphi Theatre, which recently had been purchased by Scott's close friend Daniel Terry, with significant financial backing from Scott (who was in the midst of his own money problems owing to the economic crisis of 1826).[15] All three of these breakfast companions were deeply invested in the success of that production.

A review in *The Times* on December 27 indicates that the new pantomime "founded on the popular Irish story of *Daniel O'Rourke's Journey to the Moon*, was produced at [the Adelphi] with the most perfect success." The review commends the production's stagecraft, including "tricks and changes" that were "well conceived, and managed with great facility." It then mentions the pantomime's "creditably executed" scenery, including that

14 As per Scott's suggestion, the story line now included a good-natured Cluricaune, who transforms into the eagle from an already-established version of the story.

15 As Louis Jennings writes, a "period of wonderful prosperity after the great wars" ended abruptly in the autumn of 1825, when the speculation that had fueled the economy led to an "inevitable crash which over took so many country banks and commercial houses towards the close of the year." As Jennings notes, the fortunes of many prominent people were impacted, and the "most memorable of the sufferers was Sir Walter Scott" (1885, 1:313–14).

which offered "a view of the old and new London bridge" ("Adelphi Theatre" 1826, 3). The review is relatively brief, as compared to those of the Adelphi pantomime's competition at Covent Garden, Sadler's Wells, the Surrey Theatre, and Drury Lane (where that season's pantomime stole a little of *Daniel O'Rourke*'s thunder by featuring another man in the moon ["Theatres" 1826, 3]). Beyond the initial reference to the well-known story on which the pantomime was based, the reviewer makes little to no reference to plotline and characterization; nevertheless, a few such details are of particular relevance to the present discussion.

The pantomime of *Harlequin and the Eagle* opens in the realm of the immortals, at the waterside home of Puck and a fairy. As the pantomime begins, these two immortals emerge from the rainbow-arced waterfall to discuss human revelry and "one fellow reeling toward the bog, / A drunken dog, / By far the drunkest fellow in the parish." He is Daniel O'Rourke, a "buffoon" who will, Puck predicts, soon experience a series of misadventures sure to "puzzle all your humdrum antiquaries" (T. C. Croker 1826, 4)—providing a lovely example of self-mockery on Croker's part. The satirical undercurrents of the scene are compounded by the fact that the home of the immortals is not just any waterfall but that known as Powerscourt Waterfall (*Harlequin and the Eagle* 1826, 3), Ireland's highest waterfall. This site had been in the London news a few years earlier when the falls had been temporarily dammed in order to provide an impressive spectacle to King George IV during his 1821 visit to Ireland. The plan had been to give the king a view of the falls' release from a specially built bridge below, but that event never came to pass; this proved to be a blessing in disguise, given that the force of the released waters destroyed the viewing platform on which the king was to have stood.[16] In the pantomime, the stage representa-

---

16   See Aoife O'Driscoll, "Learn More about the Highest Waterfall in Ireland! Did You Know . . . ?" The Powerscourt Blog, May 6, 2014, accessed June 29, 1017, blog.powerscourt.ie/blog/bid/182243/Learn-more-about-the-Highest -Waterfall-in-Ireland-Did-you-know.

tion of this iconic site of natural power serves double duty, operating simultaneously as an emblem of failed attempts by Irish nobility to impress the English monarch.

As the pantomime continues, it references several additional legends and legendary figures from Croker's collections. For example, when the action returns to a waterside location in scene 5, set at the Lake of Killarney, Croker works in a plot twist that allows him to draw on and combine figures from several legends he had included in *Fairy Legends and Traditions of the South of Ireland*. In the pantomime, this lake is ruled by several ghosts: Fior Usga, the drowned princess from the legends of the same name, and O'Donoghue and his legendary white horse, from a story Croker had referenced in *Researches of the South of Ireland* (1824) and then developed into a full-blown narrative for *Fairy Legends*.[17] In the harlequinade, O'Rourke (rather predictably) is transformed into Clown, and in scene 5 we are introduced to the lovers who soon will be transformed into Harlequin and Columbine (T. C. Croker 1826, 16). The legend of "Daniel O'Rourke" as it had appeared in *Fairy Legends* has no romantic subplot, but the pantomime grafts one onto the story, drawing on the ballad of "Cormac and Mary"—also featured in *Fairy Legends*—to do so. In short, this pantomime invited London audience members to draw on their familiarity with current pantomime structure and devices; their familiarity with antiquarianism and the interests of antiquaries, who were frequently caricatured, most famously by Walter Scott himself;[18] and their familiarity with a range of Irish legends Croker himself had helped to popularize. The production mobilized Irish stereotypes for comic effect and was one of many in the period that

---

17   On the contrast between Croker's treatment of this legendary figure in his two books, see Schacker (2003, 66–67).

18   Kenneth McNeil notes that the character of Oldbuck in Scott's 1816 novel *The Antiquary* "allowed Scott to poke fun at his early antiquarian preoccupations and the career he might have had, had his ambition not moved him into a literary realm offering freer creative rein" (2012, 23).

depicted Irish characters onstage as "amiable but unredeemable boors or rascals" (Mayer 1969, 254). Croker's engagement with the emergent conventions of pantomime can be seen as indebted to the comic performance tradition exemplified by Charles Mathews's cabinet entertainments, running parallel to Croker's own engagement with the emergent conventions of the tale collection—all of which could serve as venues for representing the Irish to English audiences.

As was the case for the 1804 Drury Lane *Cinderella* and other successful pantomimes of the era, the script for *Harlequin and the Eagle: Or, The Man in the Moon and His Wife* was a print commodity unto itself, for sale during the run of the pantomime and priced at ten pence. Two years later, the script from the Adelphi pantomime was repackaged, accompanied by a critical introduction by Croker, as *Daniel O'Rourke; or, Rhymes of a Pantomime* (1828). By this point in time, the name "Daniel O'Rourke" had become firmly linked with Croker's, as reviews of the book indicate. For example, a review of the 1828 book appeared in the *Mirror of Literature, Amusement, and Instruction*, where it was approached both in terms of versions of "O'Rourke" already known and available and also in terms of the perceived distinctiveness and superiority of Croker's new rendering of "the well-known story," now presented "in a series of pantomime rhymes." This review praises *Rhymes of a Pantomime* for providing "an abundance of fun and moonshine"—and a version of the story that "soar[s] far above the common run of such versions." Croker's treatments of the story and the character of O'Rourke are widely acknowledged to be neither the first nor the last of such (re)tellings, but the innovations and contributions of a performer like Mathews now seem to merit little discussion. The reviewer then pauses to wonder why it was "that the Majors [Drury Lane and Covent Garden] have not yet adapted this story for their stages" as the Adelphi Theatre had for its own. Readers of the *Mirror of Literature* are also reminded that they "are already familiar with the story of Daniel O'Rourke, as narrated by Mr. Croker" because the *Fairy Legends* version of the story had appeared in the periodical a couple of years earlier ("The Editor's Album" 1828, 149). The link between the book called *Rhymes of a Pantomime* and the pantomime of *Harlequin and the Eagle*, staged at the Adelphi Theatre, is readily apparent; less obvious is the perceived link between this new little book and Croker's *Fairy Legends*, which would seem to represent quite different forms of print culture—drawing on distinct sets of rhetorical, stylistic, and discursive strategies and anticipating distinct sets of audience expectations. But the connection is one that this reviewer highlights and that Croker also foregrounded.

A short prefatory note positioned at the beginning of *Rhymes of a Pantomime* states that this book was designed "to accompany the Irish Fairy Legends" (T. C. Croker 1828, 3). The sense that these books could be paired on a bookshelf, or read in tandem, is echoed in the periodical *La Belle Assemblée*, where a reviewer writes of the delight already provided by Croker's work and asks readers to recall "the admirable story of Daniel O'Rourke, which has been dramatised at two or three of our theatres"—but which also will "be recollected by every reader of the first series of the Fairy Legends. For smartness and for breadth of humour," the review continues, "it has rarely been surpassed" ("Poets" 1828, 300). This review, like the one from the *Mirror of Literature*, makes oblique reference to the story's *multiple* iterations, above and beyond those attributed to Croker and against which Croker's versions stand out as particularly "smart." What may appear from a twenty-first-century perspective to be a diverse set of performance events and print artifacts were *not* seen as incompatible at the time; far from it, they were seen as complementary, of interest to the very same audiences. "Good readers," instructs another reviewer of the 1828 *Rhymes*, "buy *Daniel O'Rourke*, and bind it up with your copy of the *Irish Fairy Legends*" ("Daniel O'Rourke" 1828, 116).

One way to approach the pantomime, the printed script, and this book called *Rhymes of a Pantomime* is in terms of early experiments in cross-marketing: these print and performance forms were seen as mutually supportive ventures, and in that context the performances and print commodities associated with Croker alone are the ones that would seem to matter. But the 1828 *Rhymes of a Pantomime* is of further interest here. In the preface, Croker offers an alternative account of the story's possible origins and sources, echoing, in some regards, the endnotes to the tale as it had appeared in the 1825 *Fairy Legends*, but departing from them in others. For instance, in both publications, Croker draws attention to parallels between O'Rourke's adventures and those of Astolpho, from Ariosto's early modern epic *Orlando furioso*—a comparison that the 1828 reviewers seem to have found unconvincing. But in the 1828 *Rhymes*, now that Croker has ventured into the world of popular theater, he no longer mentions Mathews's theatrical "At Home" shows as significant venues for the persona of Daniel O'Rourke. Given the fact that Croker and his various reviewers anticipate audience familiarity with "Daniel O'Rourke" as the story had appeared in *Fairy Legends and Traditions of the South of Ireland*, it is striking that one source for the story that is *never* mentioned in the footnotes is that of a face-to-face encounter between Croker and his "good friend" Daniel O'Rourke on that June day in 1813. That is understood to be a fictional conceit, one that requires no further discussion.

Croker describes the development of the persona of Daniel O'Rourke in terms of a tradition of comedic impersonation *outside* the domain of commercial theater. Croker thus cites a legend about "a Mr. Doyle, a surgeon, who moved in the very pleasant and intellectual society of Dublin some seventy years since" and who on one occasion and for the amusement of his peers was "dressed in the proper costume of the character he was to personate": a "mock rustic" who then proceeded to "tell the story of Daniel O'Rourke." This is yet another origin story, one that traces the story and persona to an example of cross-class ventriloquism—a kind of pranking disguise carried out among Dublin's elite, sustained through time as an amusing anecdote. "Whatever the source of the story [of O'Rourke] may have been," Croker writes, "it became orally very popular, and was a particular favourite in the south of Ireland," where the tale of the iconic O'Rourke made an appearances in miscellanies and the popular press (T. C. Croker 1828, 6–7). The story about Doyle's impersonation of a "rustic" raconteur likewise gained some traction and was repeated in some of the reviews of *Rhymes of a Pantomime* (see, for example, "Daniel O'Rourke" 1828, 115). It appealed to audiences familiar with forms of mimicry, impersonation, and imposture, on and off the stage, who understood theatricality to be an essential component of sociability, in the present moment as it had been in Doyle's time.

This brings us full circle, back to the group gathered for breakfast in October 1826. Scott's diary entry for Friday, October 20, invites consideration of Croker himself as a character type, one increasingly familiar in English drawing rooms, in English print culture, and on the English stage: the odd and charming Irishman, alternately canny, comical, and sentimental. Scott compares Croker to fellow Irishman Tom Moore, who was most famous as author and frequent performer of *Irish Melodies* (Anderson 1972, 217); but Moore was also a satirist and librettist, collaborating with composer and singer Michael Kelly, who wrote the score for the 1804 pantomime *Cinderella*, discussed earlier. Obviously, the domains of sociability within which Moore circulated, as well as the ones represented by this breakfast gathering, implicate the world of theater in a fundamental way. In Lockhart's home, we witness a meeting of the librettist, producer, and financier of the upcoming Adelphi pantomime; but it is also worthwhile to consider the varieties of performance, theatricality, and cultural ventriloquism represented and appreciated by Scott and his breakfast guests.

Walter Scott, Allan Cunningham, and T. Crofton Croker shared a fascination with verbal art of various kinds, and all were interested in orality and its bearing on "literature." Each engaged, in one way or another, with the process of "collection," as it was then understood, and the publication of traditional material (ballads, folktales, legends) long before the methodological aspects of this kind of work—as distinct from literary (re)creation—had been established. This was occurring in the wake of the "ballad scandals" of the late eighteenth and early nineteenth centuries (Stewart 1991, 102–31). Each of these men also has been subject to criticism for degrees of inauthenticity and fabrication, both in terms of the material collected and published, and the representation of their own respective positions vis-à-vis that material and the communities from which it originated. For instance, Walter Scott's work is often approached in terms of his "'genial play' with writerly guises," and his antiquarian efforts in *Minstrelsy of the Scottish Border* (1802–3) have been seen as "simultaneously an invention of tradition, an imaginative recounting of the historical and regional parameters that defined the author's own community; and an (in)authentic (auto)ethnography in that it forges, in both sense of the word, a historical and genealogical continuity that is set against the disruptive forces of modernization" (McNeil 2012, 24). As Andrew Lynch notes, Scott's "'shadow play' with minstrels, oral informants, manuscripts, editors and commentators" makes it challenging "to find a 'truth-voice' in his narration" (2014, 172). And perhaps Croker was engaging in a kind of performance, both in his social life and in his writing: within a tradition of cultural impersonation and ventriloquism, the measure of "authenticity" here may be *in* the performance—that is, something understood by the audience *as* performance and appreciated as such. In this case, we have a story of drunken misadventures, told through two constructed personae: Daniel O'Rourke, who had an established and varied history by 1825, and the Compiler/collector/antiquary.

Croker's own work and his authorial claims can be understood in terms of folklore's disciplinary history and the kinds of antiquarian research being done in his day, but they can also be contextualized in relation to discursive traditions of imposture used widely in a variety of forms of eighteenth-century literature and which continued to resonate in the early nineteenth century. Decades before the term *folklore* was coined and well before fieldwork methods and standards were conventionalized, these rhetorical maneuvers extended discursive traditions characterized by play with extant genre conventions, complicating notions of "fiction" and "nonfiction." In addition to scholarship on the ballad, there is a rich body of critical work on the history of the novel to attest to this, especially in terms of categorical instability between genres we now see as fictional and those we regard as factual (see, for example, McKeon 1984). For such critics, the novel has long been viewed "as an ambiguous form—a factual fiction which denied its fictionality" through a variety of discursive maneuvers (L. Davis 1983, 36).

An exploration of folklore's history requires engagement with similar forms of discursive play and "spurious truth-claims" (Loveman 2008, 3). This case study certainly challenges assumptions about categorical and generic stability, especially regarding these kinds of truth claims—ones that inspired Richard Dorson to declare Croker's *Fairy Legends* to be the first field-based folklore study in Great Britain. The perspective I am suggesting here may point to reading practices quite different from Dorson's, or our own for that matter, but they are highly relevant to an understanding of these early chapters of our disciplinary history: what Kate Loveman characterizes as "active and sociable forms of reading" (2008, 6). As Loveman argues in her own study of early novels, "One of the motivations for the sociable reading of [such texts] was [. . .] an abiding interest in *discussing* their truth-status." Along those lines, "skilled interpretation of narratives" could be viewed as "an exercise in detecting falsehoods and avoiding deception. Such interpretive practices were applied to a range of genres and, as writers responded to readers' common habits, shaped those genres" (2008, 2). Situated in a web of theatrical, print, and oral forms, toying with matters of voicing, authorship, and representation, the tale of "Daniel O'Rourke" seems to invite exactly this kind of playful engagement from its readership.

As Jason Scott-Warren suggests, contemporary readers find it all too "easy to forget that a printed book [in the eighteenth- and early nineteenth-centuries] presents a facade, a public surface that can be radically at odds with the reality that lies beneath it—although tell-tale cracks might lead us to suspect that all is not as it seems" (2016, 225). Both the cases of "Cinderella" and "Daniel O'Rourke" suggest that our present-day repertoire of reading strategies can prove woefully inadequate to the reading of nineteenth-century discourse about fairy tales. The gaps, self-contradictions, and elisions one detects when tracing a tale through its multimedial history do indeed signal that there is more being communicated than what is apparent on the surface. The "cracks" Scott-Warren pursues in his own work concern claims about sources, methods, and authorship—all of which can be situated in "an intricate web of agents and interests" (252) and all of which would come to be of heightened significance in the development of folkloristic theory, method, and textual practice later in the century.

3 Disciplining the Fairy Tale

The Unruly Genre in Folklore and Children's Literature

VICTORIAN WRITINGS ABOUT fairy tales—both oral traditional tales and literary ones—routinely reference pantomime; conversely, commentary on pantomime has tended to include claims about fairy tales, past and present. At the end of the century, the forty-nine-year-old actor, playwright, and theatrical biographer T. Edgar Pemberton looked back with fondness to "recollection of a stage on which the prototypes of the fairies that Grimm and Gammer Grethel and Hans Christian Andersen had taught me to believe in gaily and realistically tripped" (1896, 25). Pemberton sees the flow of influence moving from English stage to German and Danish literature, implying that the theatrical fairy tales already well established in the Britain of his childhood *prefigured* and shaped responses to the stories made popular by the Grimms and Andersen. He is able to assume that his readership will recognize that the long-standing tradition of fairy-tale pantomime was a relevant frame of reference for English-language readers encountering the work of the Grimms and Andersen for the first time in the mid-nineteenth century. Importantly, Pemberton draws a connection between what might appear, from a contemporary critical perspective, to be distinctive textual phenomena: Grimms' fairy tales (framed as a pure, authentic representation of oral traditions and first translated into English in the 1820s), Gammer Grethel (a fictive narrator created by Grimms' translator Edgar Taylor for an 1839 edition of *German Popular Stories*),[1] and the literary tales of Hans Christian Andersen (first introduced to English readers in the 1840s).

As he continues, Pemberton notes that the stage fairies remembered fondly from his childhood were themselves drawn from earlier forms of English print culture: a corpus of "dear old familiar nursery stories" (1896, 27) that includes Perrault's "Little Red Riding Hood," a production of which serves as a case study in chapter 5, and d'Aulnoy's "Yellow Dwarf," of which more will be said shortly. These stories had been transformed into what were, for Pemberton, pantomime's distinctive combination of "sustained sentiment and well restrained fun" (25). Pemberton may stand as a lonely voice in his casting of sentiment and restraint as hallmarks of pantomime, but the ease with which he traces fairy-tale history across varied forms of performance and print proves to be remarkably commonplace. The close association of French tales with the English stage—pantomime, in particular—and the complex relations of print and theatrical cultures evident in these examples merit closer attention. These associations and entanglements inform early writing about folklore and the fairy tale, and I would suggest that they are key to critical readings of folklore's disciplinary history.

(Re)naming

Nineteenth-century writings about the "fairy tale" or "popular tale" raise some fundamental questions about genre. At a surface level, such texts can prove frustrating to the twenty-first-century reader because they engage terminology—specifically, genre designations—in ways that seem almost cavalier and certainly are at odds with modern usage. But when approached as experiments in discursive and disciplinary practice, such writings can prove to be important sites for exploring ideologies of genre, some of which resonate in popular and scholarly discourses today. In this chapter, I bring into dialogue some key statements from the tangled histories of folklore,

---

1   On the invented figure of Gammer Gretel, see Schacker (2003, 41–43).

children's literature, and the fairy tale, highlighting tacit assumptions regarding generic coherence, stability, and transparency.[2]

To begin, we can consider an oft-cited moment in that disciplinary history: August 22, 1846. This date marks the appearance in *The Athaneum* of a now-famous letter by William J. Thoms, dated August 12 and signed under the pseudonym of Ambrose Merton. The primary concern in Thoms's letter is the need for rigorous collection and documentation, directing his comments to the reader who "has made the manners, customs, observances, superstitions, ballads, proverbs &c., of the olden time his study," or who might aspire to do so (1846a, 863). In a parenthetical aside, Thoms coins the compound word "Folk-lore,—*the Lore of the People*," as an apt alternative to the then-current terms *popular antiquities* and *popular literature*. Interestingly, in his short catalog of folklore forms, Thoms neglects to name the one genre that was already and would continue to be most popular with English-language audiences: the folktale, or what was then likely to be called the popular tale, nursery tale, fireside tale, or fairy tale. For Thoms and many of his contemporaries, popular tales were powerfully associated with old women—even Taylor's invented figure of Gammer Grethel served to reinforce this connection—and they were valuable to (predominantly male) scholars insofar as they contained evidence of customs, manners, and beliefs, imagined as living relics "of the olden time," subjects that were clearly Thoms's primary areas of interest. Thoms's apparent oversight may indeed signal that the fraught status of the "fairy tale" in folklore study is evident from the very beginning, but the tremendous body of tale scholarship produced by Victorian folklorists indicates that the genre was to become central, even if left unnamed in the discipline's founding statement and debated for many decades to come.

2   This endeavor is informed by ethnographic and literary reconceptualizations of genre, specifically, the work of Charles L. Briggs and Richard Bauman (1992) in combination with the reception theory of Hans Robert Jauss (1982) and the analysis of genre and ideology offered by Thomas Beebee (1994).

In his proposed renaming and definition of an intellectual field, Thoms rejected the Latinate "popular antiquities" in favor what he called "the good Saxon compound, Folk-lore" (1846a, 862); this is a maneuver that was colored by "more than a hint of nationalism," as Alan Dundes suggested decades ago (1965, 4). This move also signaled an implicit rejection of a *French* tradition that in the previous century had established an English readership for fairy tales: specifically, the literary *contes de fées* of late seventeenth- and early eighteenth-century France, which became enormously popular in Britain. Thoms's 1846 letter can thus be regarded as not only nationalistic but also subtly anti-French—or, to borrow Linda Colley's term, francophobic (1992)—seeking to distinguish modern English interest in the science of folklore from the Britons' enthusiastic reception of earlier French experiments with the literary tale.

While fairy tales were already firmly ensconced in both British print and theater culture by 1846, Thoms avoids reference to contemporary theater in both his letter and the Folk-Lore column he published the following week. He does, however, use Elizabethan drama as a point of reference, identifying William Shakespeare as "the best and most beautiful expositor" of "the Fairy Mythology of England" (1846b, 886). He then invokes the model of the Brothers Grimm, Jacob Grimm in particular, in his call for an Englishman who "shall do for the Mythology of the British Isles the good service which that profound antiquary and philologist has done for the Mythology of Germany" (1846a, 863). Importantly, a readership for this new breed of field-based tale collections—collections of narratives explicitly framed as print representations of oral tradition—had already been established by this point in time: in 1823, Jacob and Wilhelm Grimm's *Kinder- und Hausmärchen* (what we know as *Grimms' Fairy Tales*) had been translated into English by Edgar Taylor as *German Popular Stories*. The book was a publishing success, generating a second volume in 1825 and multiple editions throughout the century. In the decades that followed the initial appearance of Taylor's *German Popular Stories*, a string of new tale collections making similar claims to oral, field-based authenticity captured the interest of English-language readers, shifting the terms of critical conversation about the genre and broadening the corpus of "nursery tales" available in print form.

The history of the fairy tale in England is marked by these kinds of semiotic, linguistic, and cultural border crossings, including both the transformation of field-based collections into popular folklore books (a distinctly nineteenth-century phenomenon) and that of seventeenth-century French literary tales, repeatedly reshaped and repurposed in various forms of English print and theater culture. Delineations of the "real" or "traditional" fairy tale abound in writings by early folklorists, as they attempted to regulate the boundaries of the emergent discipline of folklore and also those of a narrative genre undergoing some radical reevaluation. Such musings are also found in popular writings of the 1840s onward: then, as now, everyone had an opinion about the form, function, meaning, and value of fairy tales. Many constructions of the "authentic" fairy tale reflect anxieties about a number of binary oppositions—the domestic and the foreign, the oral and the written, male and female, adult and child, art and commerce—and French *contes de fées* are frequently invoked as negative examples. Although such statements sought to contain and regulate the production and reception of the fairy tale as a popular genre to the exclusion of the French literary tales, they tell only a partial story. In the pages that follow I argue that the rowdy, bawdy, and satirical stage genre of English pantomime suggests an alternative and frequently overlooked medium for the transmission of *contes de fées* during these formative decades in the history of folklore studies. This chapter culminates with a fuller consideration of a Victorian pantomime treatment of d'Aulnoy's popular *conte* known as "The Yellow Dwarf," but our journey begins somewhat earlier.

By the time Thoms christened the discipline of folklore, there was burgeoning interest in oral traditions and field-based tale collection but also well over a century's worth of print culture and nearly fifty years of pantomime dominated by literary tales from France. French tales in a variety of English guises formed a significant part of the horizon of expectations that would orient the production and reception of later nineteenth-century discourses around the fairy tale, both oral and literary. As is well known, the term *fairy tale* is itself associated with the French tradition: the term entered English parlance with the translation of Marie-Catherine d'Aulnoy's *Les contes de fées* as *Tales of the Fairies*, and translations of French *contes* flooded the eighteenth-century literary marketplace, especially toward the fin de siècle. Counter to previously accepted histories of the fairy tale in England, which have tended to take at face value the most vocal and vociferous of the genre's critics, scholars such as Christine Jones (2016), David Blamires (2008), M. O. Grenby (2006), and Ruth B. Bottigheimer (2002) have demonstrated that the late eighteenth century witnessed no waning in the popularity and profitability of French tales. Blamires cites twenty-two English editions of d'Aulnoy's tales published between 1699 and 1799 (2008, 69), a number that exceeds Melvin D. Palmer's count of fourteen editions in the same period (1975); given the challenges of bibliography in this field, that number was likely even higher. Focusing on the last two decades of the eighteenth century, Grenby cites at least fifteen London editions of the tales of d'Aulnoy and Perrault, in addition to those released in Dublin, Edinburgh, and the provinces and as chapbooks (2006, 5). Jones's detailed bibliographic account of early translations of Perrault's tales documents at least five editions published before the 1760s (2016, 177–78), when the tales began what Bottigheimer calls "their spectacular commercial ascent" in English print culture (2002, 14), a rise that would be sustained and magnified in the nineteenth century.

At the turn of the nineteenth century, the tales of both Perrault and d'Aulnoy were firmly entrenched in popular print culture and were soon to become favored plotlines pantomime, as discussed in chapter 1. Certain Perrault tales that have remained pantomime standards were among the first to be staged as pantomimes in London theaters: a "Little Red Riding Hood" pantomime debuted at Sadler's Wells in 1803 (*Red Riding Hood; or, the Wolf Robber*), the "new grand allegorical spectacle" of "Cinderella" was produced at Drury Lane in 1804 (as we have seen), and the same venue offered a pantomime of "Sleeping Beauty" in 1806. Other pantomime plotlines derived from fairy tales by Perrault include "Bluebeard," notorious from the George Colman 1798 melodrama and parodied in the 1811 pantomime *Harlequin and Bluebeard* (see Booth 1976, 30), and "Puss-in-Boots," which flourished later in the century despite an inauspicious debut as pantomime: the 1818 Covent Garden production of *The Marquis de Carabas; or, Puss in Boots*, whose opening-night performance ended in a riot (Stott 2009, 249). The fairy tales of d'Aulnoy and other French women writers of the *contes de fées* tradition provided James Robinson Planché with a tremendous amount of story material for his fairy extravaganzas, a burlesque form that engaged playfully with mythological and fairy-tale elements, closely aligned with pantomime but also regarded as more genteel and restrained (see Richards 2015, 65–123). Of d'Aulnoy's tales, a couple were more broadly popular as pantomimes in the nineteenth century: "The White Cat," which was first staged at Drury Lane in 1811 (*The White Cat; or Harlequin in Fairy Wood*) and "The Yellow Dwarf," whose history as pantomime I discuss later in this chapter.

Noisy, boisterous, and playfully risqué, pantomime was and continues to be considered family entertainment, often serving as children's introduction to the world of theater and forming a significant (if frequently overlooked) part of a cultural repertoire of fairy tales. As we have seen, the popularity of French *contes* on the English stage is intimately connected to the popularity of the tales in the English book trade. Grenby notes, for instance, that both Benjamin Tabart's series Popular Stories for the Nursery (1801–18) and John Harris's Popular Tales (1810) drew heavily on English traditional tales as well as French *contes de fées* (particularly those of d'Aulnoy and Perrault) and exploited their readership's perceived familiarity with tales in pantomime form, evident in publishers' advertising strategies (Grenby 2006, 1–2; see also Paul 2011, 44).

Within such a landscape, constructions of folk creativity as spontaneous, natural, pure, effortless—as modernity's "silent Other" (Shuman and Briggs 1993, 109)—resonate with a host of contemporaneous anxieties about industrialization, artificiality, mechanical reproduction, commodification, and theatricality. Burgeoning interest in folklore can thus be recast as one of many discursive iterations of the "Victorians' investments in characterological naturalness," responses to what Rebecca F. Stern calls concerns about "mechanized behavior" and "manufactured" identities (1998, 425–26). As Roger Abrahams has suggested, the early decades of folklore's disciplinary history are marked by profound "ambivalence" on the part of scholars who "saw newspapers, magazines, broadsides, and chapbooks as carrying cultural viruses into the process of oral transmission" (1993, 381). If we could recapture the perspective of a nineteenth-century reading public intimately familiar with both *contes* in translation and pantomime, the field-based collections of the Grimms and their followers might appear fresh and new, their perceived "purity," "naturalness," and authenticity attributable, at least in part, to the fact that they could be cast as yet untouched by the commercial worlds of publishing and theatrical production. As we have seen, John Thackray Bunce used children's knowledge of fairy-tale pantomime to whet their appetites for folklore research; for his part, Pemberton slid with apparent ease between the work of the Grimms and Christmas pantomimes based on French tales; and many of Bunce's and Pemberton's contemporaries also brought such cultural phenomena into dialogue, even as they sought to draw sharp distinctions between them—a trend that carried well into the twentieth century, and beyond.

The fact that academic folklorists, past and present, generally distance themselves from both the term and the category of "fairy tale" often comes as surprise to those outside the field, but ambivalence about the fuzzy genre of the "fairy tale" is related to attempts to clarify the boundaries of disciplinary concerns, a rejection of the particular literary tradition with which the term has long been associated. In that literary tradition, orality is frequently invoked for complex ideological and aesthetic reasons, as a trope that is mobilized strategically and not as a primary medium for narrative creativity nor as the object of serious study. Nevertheless, our Victorian scholarly predecessors had remarkably elastic notions of genre and of the narrative forms that fell within the purview of "folklore." The term *fairy tale* is thus used with some frequency throughout the nineteenth century to designate not only the literary tale traditions of French writers like d'Aulnoy, Perrault, Jeanne-Marie Leprince de Beaumont, and others but also the oral traditions introduced in field-based collections. In Joseph Ritson's 1831 book *Fairy Tales, Legends and Romances; Illustrating Shakespeare and Other Early English Writers*, genre distinctions are left implicit. Ritson draws on a wide range of literary traditions, legends about fairies, folk customs and beliefs—despite the fact that he was a fastidious antiquarian and a highly vocal critic of the (then-accepted) practice of giving a literary "polish" to traditional tales, exemplified in the work of Sir Walter Scott, Allan Cunningham, and many other celebrated writers of the early nineteenth century.

As late as 1887, Folk-Lore Society members like William Clouston evince a striking level of generic flexibility. In his two-volume tour de force, *Popular Tales and Fictions: Their Migrations and Transformations*, no space is given over to genre definitions and distinctions. Instead, Clouston mobilizes a range of terms, interchangeably and without distinction, including but not limited to folktale, popular fiction, popular tale, fireside tale, and fairy tale. In Edwin Sidney Hartland's *The Science of Fairy Tales*, published four years later, the "folktale specialist" of the Victorian "Great Team" (Dorson 1968b, 1:360) addresses issues of genre more directly and in doing so demonstrates that a remarkable transformation in terminological usage has taken place. Hartland explains that his concern is with what are "vaguely called Fairy Tales," now understood as "traditionary narratives not in their present form relating to beings held divine, nor to cosmological or national events, but in which the supernatural plays a part" (1891, 3–4). Hartland argues that "Literature [. . .] of whatever kind, is of no value to the student of Fairy Tales" whose interest is more properly located in issues of "purity" and lack of "any outside influence" (1891, 4). By 1900, Hartland seems to have rejected the term *fairy tale* altogether: in his *Mythology and Folktales* the genre has been renamed, with the work of the Grimms central to the performance of a kind of disciplinary origin story. It is "to the Grimms we are indebted," Hartland writes, "for first discerning the importance of folktales, and for inaugurating their systematic collection and comparison" (1900, 14). Nevertheless, when it comes time to define *Märchen*—which Hartland does in terms of function ("told merely for amusement" [1900, 36]) and content ("narratives embodying marvelous occurrences" [1900, 37]) —he retreats without explanation to the decidedly unscientific term "Nursery-tales" (1900, 37). A list of "Aids to the Study of Folktales" is appended to this slim volume; it includes such foundational studies as Marian Rolfe Cox's *Cinderella*, Max Müller's *Chips from a German Workshop*, and Hartland's own *The Science of Fairy Tales*, as well as an 1888 edition of *Perrault's Popular Tales* (see Hartland 1900, 41–43). The *conte de fées* tradition thus lurks in the background not only as the source of that most durable of all the genre terms rehearsed during the period but also as a point of reference for emergent scholarly distinctions between the literary tale and the oral traditional tale.

Possessing Traditions

Distinctions between the folk and the literary, the traditional and the novel, the authentic and the artificial, continued to shape folklore discourse, scholarly and popular, in the decades following Thoms's naming of the discipline. This is evident in key statements from two Victorian arbiters of taste, namely, John Ruskin's 1868 introduction to the reissue of *German Popular Stories* and Charlotte Yonge's 1869 series of articles for *MacMillan's Magazine* on the history of children's literature. By refocusing attention on the discourse of generic "authenticity" and "artificiality" apparent in each of these Victorian essays, we can begin to uncover some of the attitudes and anxieties that shaped the discursive practices and popular reception of our discipline in its early decades —specifically those regarding mass literacy and the marketplace, children and commodity culture, and art in an age of industrial capitalism. These two essays are positioned at sufficient temporal remove from milestones like the initial publication of the *Kinder- und Hausmärchen* and Thoms's first articles on folklore that they can take for granted their audiences' familiarity with a *range* of fairy-tale forms and media that includes international oral traditions.

Like Pemberton and many other commentators, Ruskin articulates his fairy-tale preferences in relation to memories of childhood. Ruskin begins his 1868 introduction to "the good old book" of his own early library (what had been, in 1823, the first English treatment of Grimms' fairy tales) by acknowledging its status as a commodity that links past and present and is imbued with cultural value. With a familiar rhetorical flourish, Ruskin uses devices associated with fairy-tale narration in order to sketch the contours of the genre's history and mark his current contribution to it. He begins, "Long ago, longer ago perhaps than the opening of some fairy tales, I was asked by the publisher who has been rash enough, at my request, to reprint these my favourite old stories in their earliest English form, to set down for him my reasons for preferring them to the more polished legends, moral and satiric, which are now, with rich adornment of every page by very admirable art, presented to the acceptance of the Nursery" (1868, v). In response to the publisher's request, Ruskin argues that the value of Edgar Taylor's translations (or, more accurately, his adaptations)[3] from the German is best understood in terms of a series of contrasts. The association of the genre with the past (including Ruskin's own youth) and with children, generally, is taken for granted here; in fact, Ruskin has nearly as much to say about the ideal child

---

3   For consideration of Taylor's approach to translation, see David Blamires, "The Early Reception of the Grimms' *Kinder- und Hausmärchen* in England" (1989) and Jack Zipes, "*German Popular Stories* as Revolutionary Book" (2012).

and the ideal fairy as he does the ideal fairy tale. He sketches a highly roman-
ticized vision of childhood that actually bears little resemblance to his own
privileged youth and education, asserting that *German Popular Stories* is
valuable because it is free from the "taint" that results when authors address
"children bred in school-rooms and drawing-rooms, instead of fields and
woods—children whose favourite amusements are premature imitations of
the vanities of elder people, and whose conceptions of beauty are dependent
partly on costliness of dress. The fairies who interfere in the fortunes of these
little ones," he continues, "are apt to be resplendent chiefly in millinery and
satin slippers, and appalling more by their airs than their enchantments"
(1868, vi). Like Bunce, Ruskin blurs the line between fairy-tale character and
child reader, fantasy and reality, bringing children into direct contact with
fairies, whether homely or not. Once again, fairies (beloved or despised)
signal their quality of character sartorially: as with books themselves, splendor in outward appearance is suspect. The degraded ("tainted") status of
the richly clad fairy also seems to be potentially contagious, as she herself
is likely to "interfere with the fortunes of little ones"—and here Ruskin's
choice of verb suggests a degree of transgression, the possibility of sexual
violation, or, at the very least, a disregard for social boundaries.[4] All this
grants a particular moral urgency to the selection of fairy-tale material as
part of children's entertainment and education.

Ruskin's comments emerge from a report of a professional and commercial exchange: a conversation he reportedly had had with his publisher
about the value of reprinting a book that had been one of Ruskin's own childhood favorites. Nevertheless, in this introductory essay Ruskin disavows
pecuniary motives. In fact, he seems to suggest that materialism, featured

---

4   4.b. in the *Oxford English Dictionary's* entry for "interfere" (v.): "Of persons:
To meddle *with*; to interpose and take part in something, esp. without having
the right to do so; to intermeddle. Also with indirect passive." The verb's more
explicitly sexual usage (4.d. "Const. *with*: to molest or assault sexually") only
develops in the twentieth century.

here as a kind of commodity fetishism that confuses aesthetics and monetary value, is potentially ruinous for the fairy tale as well as for its child reader. Tapping into constructions of children and the folk as straightforward, unself-conscious, unpretentious, and fundamentally "pure," Ruskin seems to position crass materialism as a threat to the "cult of cleanliness and purity that was central to Victorian moral sensibility" (Herbert 2002, 186). A preoccupation with materialism and consumer culture characterizes many of the "fairylands" of the pantomime stage, as successive chapters of this study will explore. This critique of children's culture circa 1868 is shaped by Ruskin's profound concern for the moral, social, and aesthetic ramifications of Britain's worship of that false God: money.

By establishing the value of *German Popular Stories* in these particular contrastive terms, Ruskin also invokes a set of peculiarly mid-Victorian anxieties regarding children's perceived capacity for imitation or mimicry, on the one hand, and the relation between artistic value (aesthetics) and monetary value (commodification), on the other. As Rebecca Stern has suggested, Victorian constructions of the child are ideologically conflicted,[5] invested in childhood as a state of primal innocence and truth, the "most 'natural' period of life" (1998, 440) but also in the child's dangerous "propensities for mimicry" and artifice (438). Children and child behavior thus could be conceived of as natural, straightforward, and transparent *or* as potentially duplicitous, unruly, even unreadable—a set of internal contradictions and ideological conflicts that echo contrasting visions of the fairy-tale genre and which Ruskin may be trying to stabilize and discursively contain.

"Children should laugh," Ruskin concludes, "but not mock; and when they laugh, it should not be at the weaknesses or faults of others" (1868, vi).

---

5   Marah Gubar has argued that many Victorian ideas about children and childhood stem from "competing—and incompatible—conceptions," namely, "the relatively new concept of the child as an innocent, helpless Other" which "clashed most dramatically with an older vision of the child as an adult in the making" (2009, 155).

As opposed to the artifice of both explicitly didactic "moral" tales and those employing "fine satire, gleaming through every playful word" to attract "the old" as well as "the young," Ruskin finds in *German Popular Stories* the fairy tale restored to its "proper function"—namely, to exemplify "the simplicity of the sense of beauty" that is, for Ruskin, the treasure of childhood and the province of the true fairy tale. In his discussion of George Cruikshank's illustrations, this takes a gendered turn: Ruskin praises Cruikshank's artwork for its "harmonious light and shade, the manly simplicity of execution, and [its] easy, unencumbered" sense of design (xiii–iv). These echoes of the Grimms' own aesthetic ideals are understood in opposition to satire, artifice, vanity, materialism, represented metonymically by the fairies' "millinery and satin slippers," all of which sully and taint the genre and are here implicitly feminine. Less obviously, Ruskin's privileging of a "manly" aesthetic—simple, direct, and pure—resonates with earlier Romantic constructions of English national identity, as analyzed by Linda Colley,[6] while aligning the ideal child with ideals of (adult) masculinity. By the late eighteenth century, Colley argues, "The British conceived of themselves as an essentially 'masculine' culture—bluff, forthright, rational, down-to-earth" (1992, 252). On the eve of the French Revolution, Britons became deeply invested in this potent admixture of national and gendered identities. What remains absent or perhaps repressed in Ruskin's praise of the "good old book" and its manly illustrations is the realm of the feminine, the indirect, the impure, the irrational—qualities Britons had often projected onto French art, culture, and politics.

Ruskin's own resistance to the fairy tale as a modish commodity and, by extension, to children's literature as big business, is brought into clear

---

6   I do not mean to suggest that a nationalist rhetoric and ideology have subsumed Ruskin's individual voice and distinctive aesthetic sensibility. Detailed consideration of Ruskin's "masculinist" ethos and aesthetics is beyond the scope of this book but is one of the central concerns of the collected chapters in Dinah Birch and Francis O'Gorman's *Ruskin and Gender* (2002).

relief as he connects the appeal of the genre to nostalgic visions of preindustrial social life. In stark and, I would argue, purposeful contrast to the
salonnières of Old Regime France and the realities of his own nineteenth-
century context, Ruskin proposes "that in genuine forms of minor tradition,
a rude and more or less illiterate tone will always be discernible; for all the
best fairy tales have owed their birth, and the greater part of their power, to
narrowness of social circumstances." Ruskin indulges his vision of "healthy
and bustling town life, not highly refined" surrounded by "the calm enchantment of pastoral and woodland scenery" reflecting on the connection
between this utopian setting and the instinctual invention of stories by its
inhabitants. The resulting narratives are, Ruskin imagines, characterized by
"wildness and beauty" but "restrained and made cheerful by the familiar
accidents and relations of town life" (1868, xii). The ideal or "genuine" fairy
tale thus defined emerges as part of a nostalgic vision of past social stability
and cultural containment, and an implicit critique of modernity, materialism, and industrial capitalism.

As an avid theatergoer and a fan of pantomime, Ruskin had great
admiration for those child actors who performed with apparent ease and
"innocence," but he was not pleased by all he witnessed on the pantomime
stage. In 1867, he wrote a letter to his friend Thomas Dixon[7] (printed in the
March 1 edition of the *Pall Mall Gazette*), in which he reflects on his generally unpleasant experience of Covent Garden's current pantomime, *Ali Baba
and the Forty Thieves*. Ruskin begins with lengthy reflections on varieties of
labor, pleasure, and amusement (both "base" and "noble") and ends with
a report of his revulsion at a sight that seemed to delight his fellow audience members: "the forty thieves," all played by cross-dressed young girls,
"who proceeded to light forty cigars." This particular image of children as
thieves likely would have resonated with contemporaneous representations

---

7   Ruskin included this letter in *Time and Tide, by Weare and Tyne: Twenty-Five
     Letters to a Working Man of Sunderland on the Laws of Work* (1867). See Sharon
     Aronofsky Weltman (2007, esp. 29–35).

of the notorious "Forty Thieves" gang of London's East End, although Ruskin makes no direct reference to them in his letter to Dixon. Regardless, the image of girls cross-dressed as grown men, cigars in mouth, is what seems to linger in Ruskin's mind, troubling him, and comparable to "an ugly and disturbing dream" (1867, 4).[8]

Not all professional acting and performance by children inspired such a reaction: in contrast, Ruskin writes admiringly of the action that took place moments before the cigar-smoking thieves took the stage, when "a little actress" of about eight years of age "danced a *pas-de-deux* with the donkey" (the pantomime's so-called skin part, played by two actors in shared costume); he reports that she "does it beautifully and simply, as a child ought to dance." As Ruskin details, his sense of her beauty is linked to her ordinariness, the quality of her education, her representation and representativeness of childhood (not necessarily girlhood), and apparent lack of self-awareness: "She did nothing more than any child well taught, but painlessly, might easily do. She caricatured no older person, attempted no curious or fantastic skill. She was dressed decently, she moved decently, she looked and behaved innocently, and she danced her joyful dance with perfect grace, spirit, sweetness, and self-forgetfulness" (1867, 4). In children and fairy tales alike, Ruskin seems to prize *naturalness* above all else, a quality he associates with "self-forgetfulness"—a quality to which satire, mimicry, reflexivity, and self-parody are anathema. The irony, as Ruskin realized, was that fairy tales of both the satirical and "authentic" varieties circulated in the same cultural spaces simultaneously, just as the child Ruskin considered most innocent shared a stage with those he found so distastefully self-aware. The healthy, bustling, and *sheltered* village life Ruskin imagined as the birthplace for the fairy tale and its child audience was a fantasy. In the modern city, narratological and characterological "naturalness" required monitoring, protection, and even cultivation: like the swagger and cigar-smoking of the child

8   This letter is a touchstone for Marah Gubar (2009, 157) and is quoted extensively by Katherine Newey and Jeffrey Richards (2010, 155–58).

thieves, the sweet grace of the child dancer was still a form of performance, a stylization of the body that required education and rehearsal, as Ruskin acknowledges.

Writing in 1869, one year after the reissue of *German Popular Stories*, prolific children's writer and essayist Charlotte Yonge also adopted a nostalgic tone as she traced English children's literature through the decades. Yonge constructs an historical narrative that begins with the origins of literature for children in a "wholesome" period of "comparative neglect," when children read whatever was available in their households, to one of *excessive* literary production (1869, 229–30). Unlike Ruskin, Yonge is direct in her condemnation of French literary fairy tales. "The spontaneous manufacture of the little books of mere amusement," she writes, had by the mid-eighteenth century "received a great impulse from France, by the translations of [. . .] d'Aulnoy's and Perrault's adaptations of the old mythic lore common to all nations" (230). Like the Grimms, Yonge evaluates French fairy tales anachronistically, in terms of their apparent adherence to or departure from generic conventions that would only emerge later—in nineteenth-century folklore theory and folklore books. Topping this list are the matters of formal coherence and a particular narrative style taken to be markers of authenticity, antiquity, and universality. On both fronts, Yonge finds d'Aulnoy's *Tales of the Fairies* (published in England in 1699) to be "a queer book, indeed." She identifies the writer's distinctive narrative structure and style as an encumbrance to reader enjoyment of "the immortal fairy tales." In d'Aulnoy's hands, these tales "stand imbedded in a course of lengthy romances of the Italian or Spanish order, but where predicaments occur in which the heroes and heroines sit to tell and hear their tales with exemplary patience" (230)—a patience with the odd, the deviant, and the queer that, Yonge implies, the modern English reader would or should lack. To Yonge's eye, only Perrault's imported tales have remained "unbroken," representing examples of "real" fairy tales. Yonge proceeds to trace the work of English editors to rework French tales to accommodate generic and formal expectations as they "judiciously" edited out d'Aulnoy's framing dialogues and "clarified" Perrault's concluding morals (230). Editors' deletions of some of the most distinctive features of these *contes de fées* are thus understood by Yonge as part of a process of textual improvement, necessary to restore the tales to their "true" status as folklore.

Yonge shares Ruskin's enthusiasm about Taylor's forty-five-year-old *German Popular Stories*, casting it as "the first real good fairy book that had found its way to England since 'Puss in Boots' and Co." For Yonge, Taylor's treatment of the Grimms' collection offered "once again the true and unadulterated fairy tale"—not because she believed the text to be closest to oral storytelling, but because it was a "safer and better weeded" form than those collections available previously or than the translations of the *Kinder- und Hausmärchen* that had followed Taylor's. "[H]appy [was] the child who was allowed to revel" in *German Popular Stories*, Yonge reflects, "perhaps the happier if under protest, and only permitted a sweet daily taste." Yonge notes that it "has become the fashion to speak of children and fairy tales as though they naturally belonged together, and so they do, but it is the genuine—we had almost said authentic—fairy tale, taken in moderation, that is the true delight of childhood" (1869, 306). Yonge's account thus implies hierarchies of delight and of pleasurable, entertaining pastimes and genres. But if the fairy tale in its "proper" form is pure, transparent, homely, and straightforward, why must the presentation of fairy tales be carefully tended ("weeded"), and why must the reading of fairy tales—or, to extend Yonge's metaphor, the consumption of stories—be guarded and regulated by adults?

Like Ruskin, Yonge expresses disdain for the "trumpery, arbitrary moral fairy [who] only spoils the taste of the real article"; but she reserves her harshest judgment for "the burlesque fairyland" and "its broad fun, slang, and modern allusion," all of which "destroy the real poetry and romance of childhood and foster that unnatural appetite for the facetious which is the bane of the young" (1869, 306). Both Ruskin and Yonge thus hint at a need to regulate children's reading and the fairy tales to which they are exposed; to weed out the tainted, queer, unnatural, vulgar, and excessive potentialities of the genre. For Yonge, these unsavory undercurrents are associated specifically with satirical and spectacular forms of theater: burlesque and pantomime, terms and forms that were closely linked in the 1860s, when burlesque treatments of classical myth mirrored the playful pantomimic recasting of well-known fairy tales. For Yonge, these theatrical forms bear directly on trends in literature for children: "The burlesque has found its way into children's literature," she concludes, "and is fast vulgarizing every sweet nook of fairyland, which has come to be considered as a mere field for pantomime." While fairy-tale pantomime was of undisputed monetary value, a topic to which I return in chapter 5, it is the perceived cultural value of a book like *German Popular Stories*—with its elements of restrained levity—that figures into Yonge's calculations. "A real traditional fairy tale," Yonge proclaims, "is a possession" (306).

Encounters with "The Yellow Dwarf"

These accounts of the history of children's literature and, more specifically, of the fairy tale in England, represent the kinds of Victorian writing that have shaped twentieth- and twenty-first century perspectives, contributing to a master narrative that situates the English translation of Grimms' fairy tales as a seminal work, the first to take root in an otherwise hostile environment for fairy tales. But this is clearly only a partial and slightly skewed perspective, as a rereading of these essays—one attuned to theatrical references—can reveal. The essays hint at deeply rooted anxieties about literary production and monetary profit, childhood and comedy, with the British Christmas tradition of fairy-tale pantomime standing either as the prime example of generic perversion or, for a pantomime fan like Ruskin, "a matter of intense rapture" (quoted in Weltman 2002, 160) that could readily turn nightmarish.

As a counterbalance, it is worth considering one of the highly successful fairy-tale pantomimes that was actually onstage when Ruskin's introduction and Yonge's essay were newly printed. While Ruskin and Yonge were contemplating the nature of the true unadulterated fairy tale, Henry James Byron's pantomime *The Yellow Dwarf; or, Harlequin Cupid and the King of the Gold Mines* was entertaining audiences at Covent Garden. This was one of approximately thirty nineteenth-century productions of "The Yellow Dwarf" staged across Britain and in New York City (Bolton 2000, 160–67) and one of at least eighteen mounted by century's end in London alone (see Pickering 1993, 217). Statements like Ruskin's and Yonge's are frequently cited in studies of Victorian children's literature and fairy-tale history, while this popular pantomime is generally overlooked, despite the fact that it drew significant audiences over the holiday season of 1869–70. It likely reached many more Britons in its day than did the essays discussed above, and it was lauded—not criticized—for being a production "of the costliest kind," offering "the most gorgeous of spectacles" ("Theatres: Christmas Pantomimes" 1870, 27).

By 1869, there were already precedents in place for "The Yellow Dwarf" *as* pantomime, and these provide important context for what was happening on the stage of the Covent Garden *Yellow Dwarf; or, Harlequin Cupid and the King of the Gold Mines*. Like "Cinderella," the English performance history of "The Yellow Dwarf" includes an early production at Philip Astley's Royal Amphitheatre. In April 1807, the former light-horseman, riding instructor, and entertainer advertised "an entirely new Ballet Spectacle, in which will be introduced a Panoramic View of the City and Bay of Naples" (the main attraction being a performance called "The Neapolitan Pirate"), followed by "an entirely new Pedestrian and Equestrian Comic Pantomime, called MOTHER BUNCH and the YELLOW DWARF; with its dependent splendid Stage Spectacle, new Scenery, Machinery, Dresses, Music, &c." ("Royal Amphitheatre" 1807, 1). This equestrian spectacle seems to have achieved some success and was revived at Astley's the following year. The status of *The Yellow Dwarf* as a pantomime standard, beyond the equestrian show circuit, can be traced to its next theatrical iteration: the 1821 Covent Garden pantomime of *Harlequin and Mother Bunch*, written by Charles Farley and featuring Joseph Grimaldi in the part of the Yellow Dwarf and the harlequi-nade role of Clown.[9] Like Astley's afterpiece of 1807, Farley's pantomime added and featured in its title a character not to be found in the French text: both of these early *Yellow Dwarf* productions drew on an association between d'Aulnoy and the English folk figure of "Mother Bunch," to whom English print renderings of d'Aulnoy's tales had been attributed since 1773. Mother Bunch has a complex history in legend, in print, and onstage, as I explore in the next chapter, but she also makes appearances as an important character in these first two theatrical productions of *The Yellow Dwarf*, play-ing the part of the benevolent agent or good fairy and played as a cross-cast part by "Master Longhurst" in Farley's pantomime.

Unlike many of the tales I refer to in this book, the story of "The Yellow Dwarf" has not maintained the popularity it enjoyed in the eighteenth and nineteenth centuries, so some plot summary is in order. In d'Aulnoy's hands, "Le nain jaune" told the story of the vain and restless Princess All-Fair (Toute-Belle) who, to the dismay of her mother, finds no suitor to her liking. The Queen seeks the council of the Desert Fairy (*la fée du désert*), but on her way she stumbles into the territory of the tricksterish Yellow Dwarf (*le nain jaune*). At the foot of an orange tree, the dwarf saves the Queen from ferocious lions but demands her daughter's hand in return. Distraught, the Queen withholds this information from All-Fair, who in turn seeks out the advice of the Desert Fairy, only to find herself in the same location and the same predicament as her mother: personally indebted to the Yellow Dwarf, with one of his hairs wound magically and symbolically around her finger. Hoping to escape this matrimonial fate, All-Fair returns home and accepts a proposal from the most

---

9   For Stott, this pantomime is notable because Grimaldi's son, who played the part of Guinea Pig (an attendant to the King of the Gold Mines) was censured by the press for "indecency upon the stage" (2009, 255). Neither Stott nor the pantomime's review in *The Times* offer any detail regarding these indecent acts, but the latter does refer to "certain gross vulgarities in which he indulged last night, and for which he received at the time a gentle hint from his audience" ("Covent-Garden Theatre" 1821, 2).

powerful of her royal suitors, the King of the Gold Mines (*le roi des mines d'or*). Somewhat ironically for our heroine, marriage to one of her original suitors—the fate that so repulsed her at the beginning of the tale—becomes key to the promise of "freedom," that is, freedom from bondage and a demeaning marriage to the dwarf. But the story does not end there. Kidnapped at the altar, All-Fair and the King of the Gold Mines both find themselves to be objects of desire (the Desert Fairy lusts after the King) and attempt to battle the combined magical powers of the Desert Fairy and the Yellow Dwarf. The hero and heroine are killed in the battle.

At the basic level of plot and tone, d'Aulnoy's ironic tale would seem to require some radical readjustment to conform to the conventions of "fairy tale" as we now know it. But it also required significant reworking to conform to the conventions of the nineteenth-century pantomime opening (which generally concerned obstacles to two young lovers' desired union) and the harlequinade (in which dramatis personae from the opening are transformed into stock characters). Perhaps unsurprisingly, pantomime versions of d'Aulnoy's cynical and tragic tale of unlikable royals tended to foreground love against the odds and move toward a happy ending.

One review of the 1821 pantomime notes that the story on which *Harlequin and Mother Bunch* is based "is taken from the popular Fairy Tales of Mother Bunch," which would seem to imply reader familiarity with a body of work derived from d'Aulnoy's writing, but associated in England with the invented pseudonym of Mother Bunch. Indeed, the ease with which the pantomime reviewer slides from references to Mother Bunch as stage character to Mother Bunch as authorial persona is remarkable. And like the well-traveled figure of Mother Bunch, the Yellow Dwarf was to become part of a flexible repertoire of pantomime characters—making appearances in productions that have little or no association with d'Aulnoy's tale, well into the twentieth century. For example, there is a Yellow Dwarf character in Seymour Hicks's *Bluebell in Fairyland* (1901, revived 1935 and 1936 [Wearing 2014, 492, 573]) and also in Robert Nesbitt's *The Queen of Hearts* (1933

[331]). As far as the English-language legacy of the story of "The Yellow Dwarf" is concerned, much of its currency in the nineteenth century may be attributable to its growing success onstage.

Nevertheless, in 1821 a reviewer of *Harlequin and Mother Bunch* notes that "The Yellow Dwarf" is "not one of those [story lines] most generally known" and so offers his readers a "brief outline" of it ("Covent-Garden Theatre" 1821, 2). While we might assume that the reviewer's citation of story lines "generally known" refers to a corpus of fairy tales in print (of which "The Yellow Dwarf" was certainly one), the plot the reviewer actually details departs significantly from the tale as had been circulating in English book form for a full century (Opie and Opie 1980, 83). Instead, the summary offered within the review is that of the pantomime's plot—and there is no effort made to distinguish between print and theatrical domains, despite the quite significant differences in characterization, tone, and theme. For example, in both d'Aulnoy's French text and in early English print translations, the Queen (All-Fair's mother) lacks a name and plays a minor role in the story, but in the 1821 pantomime and in the reviewer's summary of the story, the Queen's role is amplified considerably: she is referred to as the Queen of Golconda. This name would have resonated with an audience who knew of the Golkonda diamond mines, legendary in Britain since the seventeenth century and a symbol of India's riches and resources. Giving the Queen a much greater role in the story also would have served the emerging conventions of pantomime casting. Nearly forty years before the cross-cast role of the Dame became standard fare in every Christmas pantomime, the Queen in the 1821 *Harlequin and Mother Bunch* was played to much acclaim by James Barnes and was actually one of two such cross-cast parts in that production: this early pantomime *Yellow Dwarf* created a tidy symmetry by repositioning the Desert Fairy as the Yellow Dwarf's mother and cross-casting that part as well.

Perhaps most significantly, the 1821 *Times'* reviewer of *Harlequin and Mother Bunch* describes the story's central dilemma as one of courtship, but no longer is All-Fair a character resistant to marriage. On the pantomime stage, All-Fair is a "principal girl"—a female lead who will serve as Columbine in the harlequinade and who is therefore *desirous* of union with her true love, the King of the Gold Mines (played by the acrobatic former circus performer, Thomas Ellar; see Stott 2009, 218). In true pantomime fashion, an older adult stands in the way of this pairing: Princess All-Fair's mother, the Queen, whose choice of a suitor for her daughter is none other than the Yellow Dwarf, played by the enormously popular Grimaldi. As the "favourite lover," the King of the Gold Mines is transformed predictably into Harlequin; the Yellow Dwarf becomes Clown ("The Drama" 1821, 825). Key plot elements from d'Aulnoy's French fairy tale—such as those concerning All-Fair's vanity and independence, her total lack of interest in choosing a husband until it becomes expedient to do so—are omitted from the pantomime. But they are also omitted from the summary of the story as it was presented in the 1821 review. In effect, the story of "The Yellow Dwarf" became synonymous with its treatment *as* pantomime. This happened surprisingly early in the history of this story on the English pantomime stage, and a similar conflation occurred for numerous tales that had been popular in both print and pantomime form, long before Ruskin and Yonge launched their critiques of a burlesque fairyland.

Importantly, pantomime productions of this period were not evaluated based on fidelity to extant fairy tales in print. Instead, the appeal and value of an early nineteenth-century production tended to be assessed in terms of the novelty of its spectacle, stagecraft, acrobatic dance, physical comedy, and topical humor. For example, *The Literary Chronicle and Weekly Review* reported that the opening night of *Harlequin and Mother Bunch* was notable for the "ample gratification" provided lovers and audience alike "of fun and laughter; while the more sedate part of the audience were delighted with the ever-varying brilliancy of elegant, tasteful, and splendid scenery" ("The Drama" 1821, 825). In fact, d'Aulnoy's French text contains several spectacular settings, which would seem to be well suited for this kind of theater, from Toute-Belle's home palace to the fantastical steel castle of the Desert Fairy;

from the orange grove where Queen and Princess first encounter the Yellow Dwarf—perhaps reminiscent of the Versailles Orangerie, but certainly indicating something exotic and quite valuable in a European context—to the seaside where the despairing King of the Gold Mines encounters a helpful mermaid. The original story is also peppered with highly dramatic incidents, including kidnapping, bondage, battles to the death, and entrances and exits marked by thunder. It features a number of physical transformations and uses of disguise, including the Desert Fairy's metamorphosis of herself into a beautiful nymph and of her attendant bats into swans. But the 1821 *Harlequin and Mother Bunch* pivots around a scene of metamorphosis that is particular to pantomime as a form: the "transformation" that links the production's opening and the harlequinade.

The stage character of Mother Bunch instigates the transition, when "the escapes, changes, tricks, transformations, and whims of pantomime are then called into full operation, and do not cease until *Columbine* [formerly All-Fair] has lost her speed, *Harlequin* [formerly King of the Gold Mines] his wand, and the *Clown* [formerly the Yellow Dwarf] an individual upon whom to bestow his cuffs or commit his robberies" ("Covent-Garden Theatre" 1821, 2). Exploiting the comic possibilities of "gadgetry" (Mayer 1969, 214–16), Harlequin engages in further transformation, wielding the bat (or "slapstick," after which that brand of physical comedy is named) and changing an onstage rendering of the Margate tollhouse into a steamship. As David Mayer notes, pantomimes of the 1820s and 1830s frequently made a mockery of new transportation technologies and "Grimaldi's Covent Garden steam packets tended to blow up." Not to be outdone by Harlequin's acquisition of a steam-powered ship, Grimaldi's Clown delighted the audience by transforming a seemingly random set of everyday items—a bathtub, a barber's pole, a woman's dress and bonnet, a meat cleaver—into a speedier sailing vessel than the modern steamship (214). On the pantomime stage, sheer inventiveness or absurdity generally wins out over possession of cutting-edge inventions. Whether finding "magical" possibilities in familiar objects or creating spectacular effects from "exotic" goods, pantomimes like this one created richly material worlds onstage. Tales from the French tradition proved to be remarkably adaptable in this regard: despite significant differences in form, tone, and style, much of the "magic" in the *contes de fées* resides in characters' abilities to control the world of things—to access social, familial, economic, or sexual power through the manipulation of physical appearances and sensory perceptions[10]—and this resonates deeply with pantomime conventions.

Forty-eight years and one disastrous fire later, the rebuilt Covent Garden theater offered another "Yellow Dwarf" pantomime, the one to which I referred at the outset: H. J. Byron's *The Yellow Dwarf; or, Harlequin Cupid and the King of the Gold Mines*. Byron was praised by *The Times* for his selection of material, which offered "both character and good working material" and with which he worked "skilfully, adhering to the spirit of pantomime while constructing a sufficiently intelligible plot" from a now-familiar story. The review continues, noting that "the writing (in verse, as usual) is smart without the easy freedom which is the happy privilege of such compositions being abandoned, that the 'puns' are many and as bad as may be desired"; but as is the norm in reception of fairy-tale pantomime, no specifics of the versified dialogue are deemed reportable. Instead, this review echoes those of four decades earlier, turning to description of "the successive scenes, or 'tableaux'" that make this "one of the most gorgeous and brilliant pantomimes" ("The Christmas Entertainments" 1869, 3). Battles and adventures are set before the "pictorial effects" of tableaux depicting the banks of the Thames and the Crystal Palace, icon of Victorian consumerism and industrialization.

---

10   This is magic rendered practical, brought down to the material plane. For example, d'Aulnoy's "Le nain jaune" features a queen who is willing to get her hands dirty, to knead and bake cakes made of ingredients whose value and "magic" resided in their association with distant locales—millet, sugar candy, crocodile eggs—and these cakes are needed in order to request favors of the magical Desert Fairy.

Even the pantomime's opening two tableaux, set in enchanted realms, have distinctly modern and, in this case, mundane counterparts: the domain of the evil characters is presented as a kind of demonic public house and that of Cupid resembles a bank or accountancy office ("Theatres: Christmas Pantomimes" 1870, 27). Rather ordinary social, commercial, and economic transactions are thus set against fancifully rendered backdrops. The curtain arose on a "subterranean cuisine" (27), where comedian J. D. Stoyle, playing the Yellow Dwarf, was seen "carousing at a table," singing and drinking with "gnome waiters in attendance" (Byron 1869, 5). These activities were interrupted by the dwarf's godmother, the Desert Fairy—known here as Siroccotina and played by veteran pantomime actor William Henry Payne—who enters the underground pub with a clap of thunder.

Declaring herself in want of a husband, Payne's Siroccotina has links to pantomimes of the past, particularly the tradition of cross-casting the part of Desert Fairy. This particular characterization of the Desert Fairy also anticipates pantomimes yet to come: since the 1860s, lustiness has served as one of the defining characteristics of the popular pantomime Dame, no matter what fairy tale underpins the production. In Byron's Yellow Dwarf, the Desert Fairy's attempts at seduction—including her crowd-pleasing dance in the "abode of enchantment" in scene 5 (Byron 1869, 14)—are given an added comic twist: the object of her affections is the invented part of All-Fair's servant, Twitterino, "represented admirably" by W. H. Payne's son, Fred, who was already a very successful pantomime player in his own right, primarily in Harlequin roles ("Theatres: Christmas Pantomimes" 1870, 27). But the opening scene of Byron's The Yellow Dwarf also establishes a rationale for the dwarf's pursuit of Princess All-Fair: in this pantomime treatment of d'Aulnoy's tale, the dwarf has been granted his magical powers by the pantomime's supreme villain, Bogie, and needs to prove that he is making good use of that "certain power for evil." Clad in a highly orientalized costume ("tight and light and bright"), with a comical version of a Phrygian cap (dotted and striped) perched on his head (figure 15), the Yellow Dwarf

Figure 15. "Scene from 'The Yellow Dwarf' at Covent Garden Theatre" (J. D. Stoyle in the title role). *Illustrated London News*, January 1, 1870, 29. Collection of the author.

imagines that in his "fashionable togs" he will be irresistible to a beautiful princess (Byron 1869, 7). No longer is this a tale of a fiercely independent and vain princess or of royal promises made and broken: now it is a story in which the plot (from the opening tableau onward) is shaped by overlapping and conflicting attempts at courtship and seduction, some cast as legitimate, others as absurd.

As the action moves to the second tableau, "Le bureau de cupidon," fairyland romance is imagined in terms of economic transactions in ways that are sustained throughout the pantomime and that resonate, perhaps surprisingly, with d'Aulnoy's ironic treatment of courtship and marriage. For example, the production's benevolent agent, Cupid ("attractively personated by Miss Maria Harris" ["Theatres: Christmas Pantomimes" 1870, 27]) is met sitting at a desk, "keeping the Hearts ledger" and surrounded by little cupids/clerks. Cupid is alerted by Mercury's one-shilling telegram that

Princess All-Fair has rejected all suitors, and "to raise some interest" (pun intended), he departs the office by Hansom cab (Byron 1869, 8). Unlike earlier pantomime representations of Princess All-Fair, the principal girl in this production shares with d'Aulnoy's character "an obstinate dislike of matrimony" ("Christmas Entertainments" 3). In this particular pantomime, however, that aversion to marriage is associated with an extreme childishness: All-Fair prefers her dolls to men. Only Cupid's arrow can cure her.

Ultimately, the conventions of pantomime's romance plot require the marriage of principal boys and girls, the expected "happy ending," but elements of satire and irony persist in this production. For example, the pantomime seems to mock any aspiration to patriarchal power that may be held by All-Fair's father, the invented character of King Kammomile the Kantankerus. On the one hand, he bears a comically alliterative name with a sedating wildflower as his namesake. His authority is also undercut by his inability to control the actions of his subjects, his daughter, and his wife. Constant bickering between the King and the Queen, played by husband and wife duo Mr. and Mrs. Aynsley Cook, presents a highly satirical view of married life. As one of All-Fair's suitors concludes, "From what I see, / I don't think matrimony'll do for me. / I prefer liberty and a latch-key, / Snug chambers where a chap can sport his oak, / And never ask to be allowed to smoke" (Byron 1869, 15). On the surface this speech would appear to undermine the tidiness of the romance plot's expected narrative arc while also representing a fairly conventional and misogynist celebration of bachelor life. When delivered with gusto and a wink by the raven-haired beauty Nelly Harris, the actress cast as freedom-loving Prince Pet, it resonates otherwise, with the potential to gently subvert dominant and heteronormative visions of marriage as the primary path to adult fulfillment, and contented bachelorhood as the sole province of men.

D'Aulnoy's French text describes Toute-Belle's many suitors and their gifts, and in pantomime terms this serves as a prime opportunity for a procession. As Edward Ziter has observed, the procession often operated as an "allegorical world tour," with members of the chorus representing "the armies, industry, crafts, or history of 'all' nations" (2003, 193). The scope and sweep of global representation could also be delimited in a specific way, as it was in an 1886 production of *The Forty Thieves*, when the procession "depicted Great Britain and her colonies" (194). In the case of the 1869 *Yellow Dwarf*, the procession was a parade of cross-dressed suitors including our hero, Prince Dulcimer (Julia Mathews, Monarch of the Gold Mines), the worldly Prince Pet (Nelly Harris) and also the orientalized secondary roles of the Prince of the Pearl Island (Miss Love), the Little Great Mogul (Miss A. Cook), the Persian Prince (Miss Lee), and the Chinese Prince Ching-a-ring-ching (Miss Craven), who speaks in gibberish that becomes a running gag: "Chew, cherry chop stick, ring a ting ring," the Chinese prince declares when introduced to King, Queen, and Princess (Byron 1869, 9). Here we find the conventions of Victorian pantomime intersecting with emergent paradigms for tale collection in an unexpected way: both were deeply invested in conceptions of "national character," domestic and foreign, and in both media this could slip readily into stereotype and racism—which was played for comic effect on the pantomime stage. As Michael Ragussis has documented, "ethnic, colonial, and provincial character types" multiplied on English stages of the late eighteenth century (2010, 2), and these types became staples of popular and comedic theatre throughout the nineteenth century. This particular procession was considered so run-of-the-mill that it didn't even warrant commentary by any of the production's reviewers.

Once again, newspaper ink was reserved for description and illustration of the pantomime's spectacle and scenic design: in the weekly periodical *The Graphic*, the focus is on the climactic scene of *The Yellow Dwarf*—"the gem of pantomimic action, decoration, and arrangement." The scene depicted is located outside the dwarf's Castle of Steel. The castle's exterior wall and gateway gleam with metallic foil and dominate stage left, linked visually to the steel (foil-covered) dogs that guard the entrance and the dwarf's troop of amazons, a chorus of dancers described as "beauties clothed in a combination of attire of steel and skirts." Against a tropical backdrop and with the sun setting over the water and distant mountains, the dwarf's forces have just been defeated by Dulcimer, Cupid, and their attendant "regiment of lovely young Cupids in fair wings and pink shapes." The stage is full, the amazons and cupids have danced their ballet—"enabling the ladies concerned in it to make so attractive an appearance" as that depicted in Simon Durand's engraving ("Covent Garden Pantomime" 1870, 148)—and the dramatic action has reached its climax.

With the lovers happily reunited and villains reformed, the players gather onstage. The Yellow Dwarf himself leads a final chorus of pantomimic rhyming couplets that will conclude the fairy-tale opening and then usher in the harlequinade that served as a "parodic analogy" to or burlesque (re)vision of the opening scenes (O'Brien 1998, 496). "Oh say a good word for our Pantomime," he implores the audience. "It's not sublime?" Cupid joins in, reminding the viewers that "at Christmas time, / It's scarcely the thing to be hard on rhyme" (Byron 1869, 25). Venus enacts the transformation of the tableaux and characters from the "The Yellow Dwarf" into those of harlequinade, speaking that metamorphosis into being:

> Our fairy opening finished, quick appear
> Forms welcome at this season of the year,
> With grace and elegance that's sure to win,
> Appear blithe, nimble, tricksy Harlequin. [HARLEQUIN *appears.*]
> Without companionship you wouldn't shine,
> So to your aid I call fair Columbine. [COLUMBINE *appears.*]
> That specimen of persecution queer,
> Ill-treated, tottering Pantaloon appear, [PANTALOON *appears.*]
> Whilst all the efforts of the night to crown,
> Last but not least, bright, jovial, Christmas Clown, [CLOWN *appears.*]
> With bump and thump, with laugh and merry jest,
> To please the public, each now try his best.

Final pleas for crowd-pleasing antics from the performers and a "good word" uttered once the performance has come to an end remind the audience of the fact that this take on d'Aulnoy's tale will play itself out onstage nightly, through New Year's Eve, at the very least. They also remind the audience of their role in the theatrical transaction, including the fact that the financial success of a theater's pantomime was, and continues to be, absolutely vital to its solvency. From at least the turn of the nineteenth century to the present day, pantomime has been "the cornerstone of the British theatrical economy" (Holland 1997, 195; see also Lewcock 2003, 135–36). In cases like this, the potential profitability of fairy-tale pantomime is acknowledged and integrated to performance conventions, a topic to which I return in chapter 5.

Most accounts of fairy-tale history indicate that the earliest English translators of French tales effectively stripped the texts of subtext, innuendo, and, it would seem, encoded social critique (for example, see Warner 1994b, 15–16). In eighteenth-century print translations and print adaptations, the imported "tales of the fairies" had been beloved by English readers for their fanciful imagery and attention to material details, including d'Aulnoy's descriptions of fantastical palaces, elaborate costume, and exotic foods in tales like "Le nain jaune." While the genre of the fairy tale has since come to be associated with hegemonic, heteronormative, patriarchal, and capitalist fantasies, the tales of d'Aulnoy and Perrault can be considered, from the outset, fundamentally nonessentialist, remarkably modern in their capacity to explore not only the performativity of identity but also the vagaries of sexual, political, and material desires. Although transformed significantly, some of the complex and unstable representations from the French tales— issues of identity and social power, fantasies of costume and disguise, ambition and desire—were placed center stage in English theaters, depicted as both "queer" and "jovial," conveyed with pantomime's characteristic comic touch and spectacular style.

In their considerations of fairy tales past and present, both Ruskin and Yonge had found themselves addressing forms of fairy-tale humor and children's laughter, distinguishing between comedic impulses that they consider authentic and wholesome and those associated with some form of generic and moral degradation—generally labeled as "burlesque." Importantly, the signifying power of "burlesque" (like that of "queer") is predicated on a notion of a pure, genuine, authentic, originary form, one whose cultural status as well as conventional subject matter can be the object of parody (see Dentith 2000, 134–37). Part of the cultural work achieved by nineteenth-century theories about fairy tales was the construction of a model of the pure and authentic fairy tale. In the work of Victorian folklorists and cultural commentators like Ruskin and Yonge, such authentic tales were associated with particular social formations (isolated, preindustrial) as well as with certain publications of the past; they were seen as a rare treasure, to be nurtured and protected in the present.

The paradigms introduced by field-based tale collection and Victorian folklore theory link purity and authenticity specifically to oral tradition, which was itself understood as a repository of information about national character and cultural history. The impulse toward self-awareness, self-parody, and burlesque, on the other hand, were increasingly seen as outgrowths of decadent cosmopolitanism, the domain of mass communication and commerce. This binary still reverberates in fairy-tale studies, where satire, reflexivity, and metafiction are often assumed to be both postmodern invention and the unique province of literary fiction. Seen another way, the notion of a pure form of fairy tale, free from self-parody and reflexivity, can be regraded as an *invention* of the period under consideration here, one that served an ideological agenda and continues to shape interpretive practices. In fact, a burlesque impulse can be traced through the history of the literary fairy—and is a dormant potentiality in oral traditional forms as well. As Barbara Babcock suggested forty years ago, the performance of oral narrative always entails elements of metanarration—a variety of communicative techniques employed to draw attention to contexts of social interaction, establish narrative authority, engage interlocutors, establish links to prior discourse and events, and so on (see Babcock 1977). This is especially true of *Märchen*, which not only allow for the suspension of natural laws, social rules and constraints but also afford a certain amount of play with narrative rules. They invite reflexivity, in terms of both sociocultural norms and narrative ones.

United in their efforts to delineate, describe, and champion the "true" fairy tale, nineteenth-century commentators often found themselves defining the genre by a series of exclusions, by addressing everything the true tale *was not*: not trivial, not burlesque, not materialistic, not modern, not worldly, not adult. And yet, to assume that generic (re)negotiations like those of the Grimms, Clouston, Hartland, Ruskin, and Yonge represent fully the framework within which "the fairy tale" was received and interpreted would be a mistake. The enduring popularity and centrality of the fairy-tale pantomime—a theatrical genre whose history itself can be seen as a parodic analogy to that of folklore—suggests an understanding of the genre as always potentially unruly, self-aware, satirical, and timely.

4 Fluid Identities

French Writers and English Fairy Mothers

WHILE H. J. BYRON'S *The Yellow Dwarf; or, Harlequin Cupid and the King of the Gold Mines* was playing at Covent Garden, just a short stroll away at the Drury Lane theater the pantomime of the 1869–70 season drew inspiration from yet another French fairy tale: *La belle et la bête* (Beauty and the Beast). E. L. Blanchard's *Beauty and the Beast; or Harlequin and Old Mother Bunch* (figure 16) featured a cross-dressed Mother Bunch character, serving as the performance's good fairy or benevolent agent; this much it had in common with earlier pantomime versions of d'Aulnoy's "Le nain jaune" ("The Yellow Dwarf"), as well as earlier pantomime versions of "Beauty and the Beast." As noted earlier, by the 1860s there was already a long-standing tradition of British publishers attributing d'Aulnoy's fairy tales to Mother Bunch, an obfuscation of authorship and provenance that seems to have been modeled after the conflation of Charles Perrault with Mother Goose—and I will turn to both these phenomena shortly. For the present, it is worth noting that the matter of authorship of "Beauty and the Beast" in print has its own complications: the tale made its first appearance as a 1740 French novella by Madame Gabrielle-Susanne Barbot de Gallon de Villeneuve, while the better-known version of the story is the one published simultaneously in French and English by Madame Jeanne-Marie Leprince de Beaumont in 1756. But this particular tale does not, in fact, have a history of misattribution to d'Aulnoy,

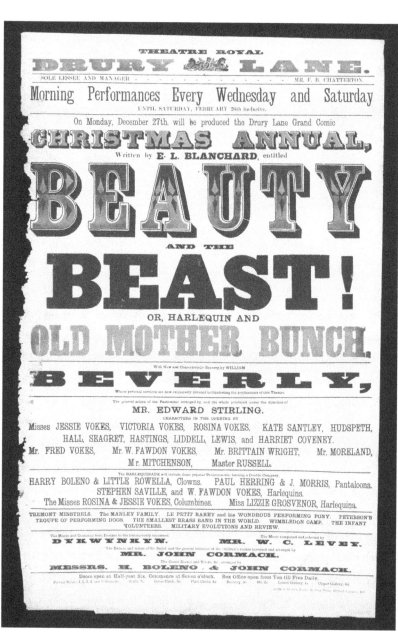

Figure 16. Poster advertising morning performances of *Beauty and the Beast! or, Harlequin and Old Mother Bunch*, the Christmas pantomime at the Drury Lane theater, December 27, 1869. Letterpress. Printed by Judd and Glass, London, 1869. Harry Beard Collection. © Victoria and Albert Museum, London.

nor to Mother Bunch. So what are we to make of Bunch's starring role in the Drury Lane pantomime?

Beauty and the Beast; or Harlequin and Old Mother Bunch reinforces an association between Mother Bunch and the broader worlds of fairy tale, generally, and fairy-tale pantomime, more specifically—blurring the lines between storytelling and capitalist consumption, tradition and modernity, in ways that are characteristic of midcentury productions. In the penny *Guide to the Pantomimes of 1869*, summary of this particular production begins with description of Mother Bunch as a kind of mistress of curiosities and novelties, as both "custodian of a number of ancient relics brought to her by Old Custom" as well as "the exhibitor of a series of modern improvements" (1869, 7). As a reviewer for *The Times* reports, "The curtain rises upon Mother Bunch's 'juvenile repository' for the sale of toys, story-books, &c, where a small boy [. . .] is recounting to his mates a fairy tale." Not content to be a passive audience, the boy's mates argue about the tale's details, and Mother Bunch appears—as the shop's proprietress, an expert on all things fairy tale, and "a representative of the good old times." After Mother Bunch sings a song about "the good old nursery lore" and summons a flock of lady-birds, the audience and the young players are escorted through a parade of "representatives of modern improvement," from London and beyond: these include the "Embankment, Viaduct, Blackfriars Bridge, Thames Tunnel (as a railway station), Electric Telegraph, and Suez Canal" ("Christmas Entertainments" 1869, 3). Bridging "old times" and modern times, traditional lore and technological innovation, this iteration of Mother Bunch possesses and trades in fairy tales, available for children's consumption and associated with all these particular border crossings and blendings.

In 1857, the opening scene of T. L. Greenwood's *Harlequin and Beauty and the Beast; or, Little Goody Two-Shoes and Mother Bunch's Book-case in Baby-land* had made similar connections, set in the bookshop identified in the pantomime's title, where several well-known "mothers" of print and stage—including Hubbard, Shipton, and Goose—were seen stirring a "huge cauldron" on which was "inscribed, 'Mother Bunch's Infant Food'" ("Christmas Pantomimes and Entertainments" 1857, 9). In this case, nourishment and business are entwined. For writers like John Ruskin and Charlotte Yonge, who saw fairy tales as a natural source of childhood pleasure but also bemoaned the degrading influence of commerce and capitalism, the witchy work of these fairy-tale mothers might seem a potentially toxic stew. The ways in which Mother Goose and particularly Mother Bunch came to have long-standing associations with the French *contes de fées* tradition as well as the highly profitable fairy-tale pantomime—two domains that were regarded with some skepticism by folklore enthusiasts of the nineteenth century—is the tangled history that this chapter seeks to explore.

As we have seen, Victorian fascination with oral traditional narratives ("popular tales") often set the new breed of field-based tale collections in opposition to extant editions of fairy tales imported from France, about which many English commentators had become increasingly critical. Nineteenth-century critiques of French tales on the grounds of their artificiality, superficiality, and decadence have long been attributed to the fact that in translation the texts had been "progressively infantilized, stripped of subtext and innuendo until they indeed appeared to be the 'artificial' and empty extravagances" disdained by a new wave of folklore enthusiasts (Schacker 2003, 7). Before I turn to the discursive strategies that characterize the French *contes de fées* tradition, and then to the complex intertextual fields within which Mothers Goose and Bunch circulate, *infantilization* itself merits some attention. The term is often used to designate two seemingly connected processes, one concerning content, style, and meaning, and the other concerning audience.

In terms of the histories of folklore and the fairy tale, infantilization generally has been seen as a form of degradation or diminishment of cultural material that has been (re)cast as children's entertainment or for pedagogical use (see Bacchilega 2012, 450). These processes extend the logic of nineteenth-century models of folklore and fairy tales, underpinned by theories of cultural evolution, in which folk culture was regarded as inherently childlike, a living relic of earlier points in the development of civilization. Within such a paradigm, the popular tale or folktale could be cast as an early formation in the evolution of literature—"the childhood of fiction," to quote the title of Scottish folklorist John Arnott Macculloch's 1905 study of "folk tales and primitive thought." For Macculloch, these "old world stories" could simultaneously offer modern children with reading pleasure, while providing the adult scholar with an endless source of "wonder," both distinct from and yet reminiscent of that remembered from childhood (viii). This model and the ideological assumptions that underpin it continue to shape much children's literature and popular culture based on fairy tale and world folklore, despite decades of recuperative critical work.

What is signaled by the figure of the child reader, viewer, or listener is no less variable than ideas about children and childhood. For instance, it doesn't necessarily follow that the (re)casting of folklore and various folk narrative traditions as being suitable "for children" indicates that those narrative traditions are unsophisticated; likewise, the reworking of such cultural material for young audiences does not necessarily *require* formal, stylistic, and semiotic simplification, a stripping away of subtext and innuendo. So while one cannot underestimate the changes wrought in the process of making French *contes de fées* into English children's literature and popular entertainment, a more nuanced approach to French fairy tales, both in terms of their subtle stylistic and narrative strategies and also in their numerous English guises—pantomime, in particular—can complicate this master narrative.

Crafting *Négligence*

From the earliest decades of folklore's disciplinary history, the form, content, and style of French literary *contes de fées* have haunted tale collectors and folktale enthusiasts, whether held up as the epitome of literary artifice and aristocratic posturing (as have been the tales of d'Aulnoy) or regarded as well intentioned but seriously flawed attempts to document popular lore (as with the tales of Perrault). In 1888, folklorist Andrew Lang—best known today for his Rainbow series of illustrated fairy-tale books—declared that Charles Perrault's tales had been granted "full fairy citizenship" in England ([1888] 1977, xii). By this point in time, Old Regime *contes de fées* had had a significant impact on English theater and print culture. Critical reassessments of French tales by English readers and scholars of the nineteenth century drew on this multimedial repertoire and were also fundamentally connected to discursive constructions of the folk, folk style, and folklore. Early folklore enthusiasts led the way in their rejection of many popular literary texts or, as in William J. Thoms's case (discussed in the previous chapter), their virtual erasure.

Critiques and, more often than not, misrepresentations of French narrative style, form, content, and audience have frequently served as a yardstick against which the authenticity and cultural value of the oral traditional tale was measured; this particular legacy can be traced to the 1812 publication of the first volume of the Grimms' *Kinder- und Hausmärchen*. Elizabeth Harries notes that the book's introduction includes praise of Perrault for his "naïve and simple manner," a style that grants his tales "the flavor and purity of the true folktale" (2001, 22). "The merit of [Perrault's] work," the Grimms continue, "rests on his refusal to add things and on his decision to leave the stories unchanged, aside from minor details" (translated and quoted in Tatar 1987, 209). The fundamental and, at that point in time, nascent paradigms of field-based research informed the Grimms' praise of Perrault's *Histoires ou contes du temps passé*: the underlying assumption was that the stories in Perrault's volume represent oral traditional (folk) tales, imperfectly transmitted, which the Grimms associated with children.

The German equivalent of the term *children's tales* is one the Grimms used in the title of their own collection, and which has its counterpart in the English usage of the term *nursery tales*. Such narratives, the Grimms suggest, exist in a pure oral form, there to be discovered, preserved, reproduced. The value of Perrault's volume, according to this logic, is measured in terms of its success at representing these ideal forms—and the Grimms' comments imply that it is Perrault's style that indicates closeness to oral tradition: value is evident in the "naïve and simple manner" of the stories' narration. Despite d'Aulnoy's status as initiator of this literary vogue, she and fellow *conteuse* Mme de Murat earn only a parenthetical mention in the Grimms' revisionist history, which uses the idea of child as audience as shorthand for cultural authenticity and purity. It was Perrault alone, the Grimms assert, who "still treated [the stories] as children's tales (not so his inferior imitators, Aulnoy, Murat)" (Grimm [1812–14] 1986, 1:xvi; translated in Harries 2001, 22). There is a sense in which the Grimms misread and misrepresented all three of these French writers, whose fashionable literary works were evaluated retrospectively through the lens of a romantic nationalist understanding of the folktale—as naive, childlike, artless, pure, simple, unadorned, transparent, and impossible to simulate or feign.

While nineteenth-century scholars and commentators regarded the genre as inherently childlike, the setting in which the tales of Perrault, d'Aulnoy, and Murat were generated and later published was the *salon*, not the nursery. These writers did contribute to an association between the fairy tale and children—but they did not do so in a straightforward way. For example, in his dedication of *Histoires ou contes du temps passé* to the fashionable and learned Princess Élisabeth Charlotte, the nineteen-year-old niece of Louis XIV, Perrault acknowledges that the tales appear to bear "childish simplicity" but promises that their depth of meaning is limited only by the reader's sophistication and perceptiveness (Jones 2016, 8). As Lewis Seifert argues, adult and specifically aristocratic fascination with this form may be seen as "a fundamental paradox of the 'genre': its readers are presumed to display both the rapture of children and the critical perspective of adults" (1991, 179). D'Aulnoy in particular inscribed the dynamics of salon conversation into her fairy-tale writing, embedding tales into her novels (see, for example, Stedman 2005) or framing and linking individual tales with playful repartee, dialogue, and debate, often between aristocratic women (Harries

1996, 100–115).[1] Perrault offers no such sustained narrative framework, but the paratextual material of his volume invites and guides readers to view the tales as only "superficially simple," as Christine A. Jones has argued. Jones draws attention to the frontispiece image of Perrault's 1697 text, which was reproduced in the English translation of 1729: an older woman sits at fireside, drop spindle in her hands, three diminutive aristocrats in rapt attention, a placard reading *contes de ma mère l'oye* ("tales of my mother goose") hanging on the door behind her (see figure 11). In partnership with the book's dedicatory letter to Princess Élisabeth Charlotte, Perrault's tales are presented as "a set of writings whose subtleties must be teased out and meanings made whole" by a perceptive, knowledgeable, and active reader (Jones 2016, 10).

The superficial simplicity of the (seemingly) self-contained, relatively brief tales is what generated the Grimms' response and has allowed for centuries of decontextualization and anthologizing of Perrault's tales, to the point that they are perceived as timeless, universal, "classic." But in a fundamental way *all* tales of this period retain traces of their origins in dialogic, highly intertextual forms of writing and salon performance, offering perspectives on social, familial, or romantic dilemmas as each writer recasts, reworks, and sometimes recombines tale types and motifs. Recent scholarship on the emergence of the *contes de fées* tradition has drawn attention to the fact that "when Marie-Catherine d'Aulnoy and Charles Perrault were writing their tales, there was no single set of practices that defined the genre and necessarily precluded other practices of plot, structure, or ending" (Jones 2003, 55). D'Aulnoy and Perrault each developed a distinctive set of narrative and stylistic strategies, resulting in distinctive (re)visions of the genre. Seifert

---

1   According to Melvin D. Palmer's bibliographic research, d'Aulnoy's framing narratives—included in the 1721 *Collection of Novels and Tales of the Fairies*—were last printed in English in 1817. Palmer notes that in the nineteenth century d'Aulnoy's tales were generally known to readers through children's editions, simplified versions of isolated tales, or in the form of fairy-tale extravaganzas or pantomime (1975, 250).

(1996) recognizes in the tales of women writers like d'Aulnoy a rethinking of sexual desire and gender, which sometimes threw into question the very possibility of matrimonial bliss[2]—the "happy ending" we have since come to expect from the genre and which has been a convention of pantomime plot structure. Marina Warner points out that Perrault's informal subtitle and title page illustration effectively cross-dressed his own authorship, presenting the tales as the product of a female discursive domain, figured as a genre both of women and for a primarily female audience (1994b, 4). Jack Zipes (1997) finds in Perrault's tales an appropriation of a women's genre and folk style in service of dominant patriarchal ideologies, which would seem to fit more neatly with Victorian constructions of ideal childhood and children's literature than d'Aulnoy's complex and deeply cynical worldview ever could—a perspective that more recent scholarship on Perrault and Victorian children's literature has extended but also modified.

Importantly, the texts of d'Aulnoy, Perrault, and their contemporaries were shaped by a shared stylistic ideal: *négligence*, a discursive register associated with a conversational but sophisticated "naturalness of expression." As Seifert explains, writers of this era refer often to this style as "*naïveté, simplicité*, and *enjouement*, all [of which] reflect the seventeenth-century esthetic ideal of *négligence*—a refinement designed to give the appearance of being innate, effortless, and aristocratic" (1991, 185). Simplicity in narrative style thus indexed a radically different class context in late seventeenth-century texts than it did in nineteenth-century print culture. In the former context, *négligence* was understood as an artistic achievement rather than an innate or natural quality of expression. As Mme Marie-Jeanne Lhéritier

---

2   For a sustained discussion of d'Aulnoy's subversion of romantic convention, see Allison Stedman's analysis of *Histoire d'Hypolite*—d'Aulnoy's 1690 novel in which her first fairy tale, "L'Île de la Félicité," was embedded. The tale focuses on the romance between Russian prince Adolphe and the princess Félicité but ends tragically with the eponymous island of happiness transformed into one of "eternal grief and despair" (2005, 32).

observed, "Il faut être tres-éclairé pour connoitre les differences des stiles & l'usage qu'on en doit faire. La naïveté bien entenduë, n'est pas connuë de tout le monde" (1696, 317). (One must be really bright to know the differences between the styles and the usage we must make use of; naiveté, understandably, isn't familiar to everyone.)[3]

Appreciation of this beautiful and *crafted* "simplicity" required a certain sophistication and could also be construed as a nostalgic reminder of a beautiful fantasy of times past: "Il me paroît," Lhéritier continues, "qu'on fait mieux de retourner au stile des Troubadours, que de s'en tenir à de telles insipiditéz. Ce qui seroit à souhaiter, est qu'en nous ramenant le goût de l'antiquité Gauloise, on nous ramenât aussi cette belle simplicité de mœurs, qu'on prétend avoir été si commune dans ces temps heureux" (1696, 309–10). (It seems to me that we'd be better to return to the style of Troubadors rather than clinging to insipid styles. Hopefully in bringing back the antiquated tastes of the Gauls we would also bring back the beautiful simplicity of morals, which we claim were so common in these happy times.) Alternately, this aesthetic ideal could imply a rejection of didactic poetics and of a dominant literary tradition that demeaned women's writing as frivolous and trivial. French critiques of artifice and excess in *contes de fées* date to the early decades of their literary history. For instance, in a 1699 commentary on the vogue for fairy tales, the abbé de Villiers declares: "La plûpart des femmes n'aiment la lecture, que parce qu'elles aiment l'oisiveté & la bagatelle; ce n'est pas seulement dans la Province, c'est aussi à Paris et à la Cour qu'on trouve parmi elles ce goût pour les Livres frivoles [. . .] elles s'amusent d'un Livre avec la même esprit dont elles s'occupent d'une mouche ou d'un ruban" (1699, 286–87). (Most women enjoy reading only because they enjoy laziness and the trivial; not only in the provinces but also in Paris and at the court one finds among women this taste for frivolous books. [. . .] They amuse themselves with a book in the same way they

---

3   I am indebted to Amanda McCoy for her assistance with the translation of passages from Lhéritier. For further discussion of the passages themselves, see Seifert (1991, 185).

play with a button or a ribbon.) Villiers asserts that literature has been sullied by the presence of women writers and readers, and feminine sensibilities in the literary marketplace: "Qui ne se persuade pas que les Livres sont une marchandise qui change de mode comme les garnitures & les habits?"(1699, 278–79). (Who is not convinced that books are now a modish merchandise like accessories and gowns? [translated in Harries 2001, 25–26].) In the face of such opposition to their literary efforts, women writers of the fairy tale appear "altogether comfortable with the idea that what they write will not be considered significant or edifying in a traditional sense." Instead, they recast those notions of frivolity and triviality evident in the framing of *contes de fées* as trendy merchandise, "reclaiming a charged discourse that had long been used against women tellers and innovative thinkers" (Jones 2003, 58).

D'Aulnoy and Perrault may have shared a general aesthetic ideal, but they offered differing interpretations of it and their work was received in differing ways. Importantly, both of these writers employed formal and narrative devices, often excluded in English editions, which obfuscate meaning and foreground moral ambiguity. D'Aulnoy's approach to the *conte de fées* differs from that later valued by the Grimms and their followers, and her nineteenth-century reputation as a writer suffered for it. Her tales extend from and are framed by representations of a distinctly aristocratic mode of oral storytelling, characterized by a narrative voice that repeatedly breaks frame to comment on both the action within the tale and on the conventions of the genre —what D. J. Adams has called a persistent "self-questioning" (1994, 20) or even "burlesque self-mockery" (21) that serves to foreground the artificiality and the absurdity of the fantastic.[4] These narrational asides,

---

4   Adams points to a few representative examples (see 1994, 20):

Lorsque cette marâtre la vit revenir, elle se jeta sur la fée, qu'elle avait retenue; elle l'égratingna, et l'aurait étranglée, si une fée était étranglable. (When the cruel mother/stepmother saw her returning, she threw herself on the fairy she had retained; she scratched her and would have strangled her, were fairies strangle-able.)

Adams suggests, "hint at a sophisticated complicity expected from at least some readers of [d'Aulnoy's] *Contes*, breaking the consensus on which such stories need to operate if they are to be taken on their own terms" (21). The result of these metadiscursive asides is the amplification of what Richard Bauman would call an "intertextual gap"—in this case, a gap between literary precedents and d'Aulnoy's own "emergent circumstances and agendas" (2004, 7), as *conteuse*. These tales imply a reader ready, willing, and able to find pleasure in the subversion of generic convention, ready, willing, and able to find pleasure in complicity with a subversive narrator.

That the Grimms could cast their retrospective and unsympathetic gaze at such literary efforts is perhaps unsurprising, but could they also have misread Perrault? I posit that the Grimms are indeed part of a long tradition of straight (mis)reading of these tales, overlooking Perrault's indirectness, irony, and even satire—qualities that appear to have no place in the Grimms' own emergent and often implicit definition of the genre. Importantly, the Grimms make no mention of the rhyming morals with which Perrault concluded each tale in the 1697 volume; it is here that the narrator's voice is at its most wry, worldly, and even cynical as he reflects on courtship, desire, power, and matrimony in ways that often run counter to the implied meanings of the narratives themselves.[5] To a late Victorian folklorist like

---

"[. . .] sans vous je serais morte, et vous m'avez sauvée; je vous le revaudrai." Après ce petit compliment, elle s'enfonça dans l'eau, et Avenant demeura bien surpris de l'esprit et de la grande civilité de la carpe. ("[. . .] without you I would be dead, and you saved me; I am indebted to you." After this little compliment, she sank into the water, and Avenant remained surprised with the spirit and great civility of the carp.)

[. . .] il manquait beaucoup à la satisfaction de Lutin, puisqu'il n'osait ni parler, ni se faire voir; et il est rare qu'un invisible se fasse aimer. ([. . .] Lutin missed out on a lot of satisfaction, since he dared neither to speak nor to make himself seen; and it is rare that an invisible [person] makes himself loved.)

5   As examples, Muratore cites the concluding verse morals to Perrault's "La belle au bois dormant" ("The Sleeping Beauty in the Woods"), which "contrasts La

E. S. Hartland, Perrault's morals appeared strained, attached as they were to a genre that Hartland had defined in terms of entertainment value, tales "out of which it would puzzle even the compilers of the *Gesta* to extract a moral" (Hartland 1900, 9). As Mary Jo Muratore has suggested, Perrault's

Belle's patience with the exuberant ardor of the women of his day"; the concluding comparison of the wolf from "Le petit chaperon rouge" ("The Little Red Riding Hood") to "the seventeenth-century dandy's seduction of innocent young maidens"; and the two morals that end "La barbe bleue" ("The Blue Beard")—one "regarding the dangers of curiosity" and the other offering "a more contemporary reading critical of the outmoded characterization of the tale" (1991, 165).

There are additional details in these particular cases worth some attention here. For instance, the second stanza of the moral to "La belle au bois dormant" begins with the narrator shifting the locus of moralizing from his own hands to the story itself: "La fable semble encor vouloir nous faire entendre / Que souvent de l'hymen les agréables nœuds, / Pour être différés, n'en sont pas moins heureux" (Perrault 2002, 130). ("It seems that the story also wants to give us to understand / that frequently, though the pleasant bonds of matrimony / may be deferred, they are no less enjoyable for that.") Here it is the story that has a message to convey, not the teller. It is in the face of women's ardor and impatience that the narrator declares himself unwilling to preach the story's moral: he concludes, "Je n'ai pas la force ni le cœur, / De lui prêcher cette morale" (2002, 130–31). ("I have neither the strength nor the heart / to preach such a moral to them.") Perrault thus acknowledges the implied moral of the story (women's patience reaps great rewards—a conclusion that readers are tempted to draw), while simultaneously modeling an alternative way of reading the story that is resistant to clear moralizing. In the case of the *moralités* offered at the conclusion to "La barbe bleue," it is again worth noting that the last word is given not to a "straight" reading of the story and its implied message but to a counter reading. The *autre moralité* that follows the narrator's reflection on the dangers of indulging female curiosity makes reference to the modern *filer doux*, or mild-mannered husbands, and thus appears to have little bearing on the contents of the tale. In fact, even the conventional reading of the tale as a warning against curiosity emerges as problematic, if pressed. After all, the heroine ultimately profits from her discovery, inheriting Bluebeard's wealth and remarrying a man "qui lui fit oublier le mauvais temps qu'elle avait passé avec la Barbe-Bleue" (2002, 146–47) ("who made her forget the bad days she had spent with Bluebeard").

verse morals "often seem peripheral to the fictions that ostensibly explicate. Less concerned with uncovering the locus of universal meaning than with relating these anonymous, timeless fictions to specific temporal realities, the narrator concludes with morals that hover along the narrative edges rather than bisect the fictional core" (1991, 165). Perrault's concluding morals can thus be seen as modeling a way of taking meaning from the genre that is fundamentally unruly, unpredictable, and open-ended; this may be the reason that the concluding morals are now seldom reproduced in English editions of the tales. Readers of a Perrault tale, Muratore suggests, "are left with the option of either interpreting the moral itself, now more enigmatic than the tale it ostensibly elucidates or re-interpreting (even re-thematizing) the tale from Perrault's exegetical perspective" (1991, 166). If the morals serve primarily to reveal the indeterminacy of the tales' meanings, as both Muratore and Marc Soriano (1968, 341) have argued, then Perrault's prefatory claim that his text was designed as a pedagogical tool to help "civilize" children takes on a distinctly ironical tone.

Some of this irony, evidently, was lost in translation, a fact that Jones has sought to remedy in her recent project of retranslation (2016). As Harries observes, the growing taste for "folk style" among Victorian readers of fairy tales favored the apparent "blunt terseness" of Perrault over the more clearly "digressive, playful, self-referential" style of d'Aulnoy (2001, 17). Emergent conventions for the representation, reception, and analysis of the oral traditional tale in the nineteenth century, post-Grimms, shaped the representation, reception, and analysis of earlier literary tales. English editors' uses of "Mother Goose" and "Mother Bunch" as posthumous noms de plume for Perrault and d'Aulnoy, respectively, has generally been taken as a sign of a trend toward infantilizing or diminishing a sophisticated, imported literary tradition (see, for example, Verdier 1996; Blamires 2008; Jones 2009), but very little consideration has been given to the specific ways in which these names resonated in centuries past. Mother Goose has a French counterpart, Mère l'Oye, and was signaled as an evocative figure, a source of narrative, in the frontispiece illustration of both Perrault's French text (1697) and its first English translation in 1729, which included a version of that same illustration. Mother Bunch, by contrast, is a name imposed on d'Aulnoy's work only after her death and once her *contes* were integrated to English print culture. As we will see, the name of Mother Bunch is situated in a complex intertextual field: by the time the name of Mother Bunch became attached to d'Aulnoy's tales, it had long-standing associations with worldly knowledge and sexual appetite, wit and storytelling, commerce and fortune-telling, and little to do with child care. Like Perrault's corpus of fairy tales, several of D'Aulnoy's *contes* have a significant place in the pantomime tradition, as demonstrated by David Blamires's recent case study of "The White Cat" in both print and theater cultures (2008) as well as my own exploration of "The Yellow Dwarf" in the previous chapter. But as I suggested at the outset, Mother Goose and Mother Bunch also make many curious appearances on the Victorian pantomime stage, where many of those earlier associations continued to echo; and it is to these fascinating figures that we now turn our attention.

Cross-Dressed Authorship: Charles Perrault and Mother Goose

When Perrault's *Histoires ou contes du temps passé* made verbal and visual reference to *ma mère l'oye* in the book's subtitle and frontispiece illustration, this name was already associated with the general category of fairy tale: *contes de ma mère l'oye* was a phrase in general usage and would have been recognizable as such by Perrault's readership, as would have more oblique references to other names for what we might call "fairy tale." The authoritative 1694 *Dictionnaire de l'Académie française* cites the common (*le vulgaire*) usage of *conte de ma mère l'oye* to designate "des fables ridicules telles que sont celles dont les vieilles gens entretiennent et amusent les enfants" ("all those ridiculous fables the likes of which old people tell to entertain and amuse children"; see Warner 1994a, 52; Jones 2016, 6). Alternatives listed by the *Dictionnaire* included such phrases as *conte au vieux loup* (old wolf tale), *conte de peau d'asne* (tale of a donkey's skin), and *conte de la cigogne* (tale of the stork).[6]

Importantly, the Mother Goose depicted in Perrault's book is distinctly human, her "gooseness" a metaphorical overlay that remains unexplained and unexploited. Nevertheless, two of the iconic animals from the "vulgar" lexicon of 1690s terms for fairy tale, the wolf and the donkey, play significant roles in specific Perrault tales. In Perrault's *contes*, the wolf and donkey appear in their animal skins: as villainous, sweet-tongued, devouring threat (in the story we know as "Little Red Riding Hood") and as a source (simultaneously) of excrement, gold, disguise, and protection (in "Donkeyskin"). Given their established usage in common names for the genre, Perrault's characters of *le loup* and *l'âne* also seem to operate metafictively, as embodiments of perspectives on tales and tale-telling, without needing to be imagined as storytellers per se. In other words, the various functions these beasts serve in their respective tales can be read as a form of commentary on the complex functions tales themselves can serve—saccharine but dangerous, profitable yet quietly subversive—all delivered with Perrault's characteristic ironic touch.

While stork characters are absent from Perrault's fairy tales, the association of *contes* with *la cigogne* can help us to get a fuller sense of the fields of metaphoric and cultural reference that inform this 1697 volume. For Jones, the stork is evocative in its cultural links with maternity and care for the young. This is reflected in the illustration history associated with Perrault's *contes de fées* from the nineteenth century to the present day, where the image of an elderly female storyteller was rendered as a good-natured and

6   The contents of the 1694 *Dictionnaire de l'Académie française* have been digitized. The entry "conte" is available at artflsrv02.uchicago.edu/cgi-bin/dicos/pubdico1look.pl?strippedhw=conte. Elsewhere in *Staging Fairyland*, I have adopted the modern convention of treating Mère l'Oye as a proper noun, capitalized (like the English Mother Goose); but in the 1694 dictionary this terms and its alternatives are all written as common nouns.

affectionate grandmother, and her audience was imagined to be progressively infantile (Jones 2016, 75). For Warner, the stork is of interest in its early modern association with sex, gynecology, and midwifery, as well as bawdiness—associations that carried over when "women storytellers were dubbed with the name Mother Stork or Mère Cigogne." As Warner argues, "Innuendoes, connected to bodily functions of various unmentionable kinds, would have also sounded in contemporary ears" when Mère Cigogne was invoked (1994a, 61). Just as the pantomime Mother Goose in England finds herself in the company of other fairy-tale mothers, each with her own distinctive networks of association—histories in print, oral tradition, theater, and in visual art—so may Mère l'Oye circa 1697 be considered in dynamic relationship with this kind of stork mother: knowing and knowledgable, witty and potentially subversive.

As Warner notes, the stork mother could be invoked in reference to female tale-tellers, but she also has a significant place in the history of popular theater: the French word *cigogne* underwent some re-formation or deformation to produce the figure known alternately as Mère Gigogne, Dame Gigogne, or sometimes Madame Gigogne (1994a).[7] This historic figure has been reclaimed in recent decades by the writer, philosopher, and critic Hélène Cixous, who sees Mère Gigogne as a potent embodiment of marvelous monstrosity, magical transformation, and transgressive creativity (2001). Mère Gigogne's most familiar iteration is a character "with the stock feature of a skirt out of which came many children" (Jones 2016, 6)—a woman who would seem to be defined exclusively in terms of maternity. Such a character was known to nineteenth-century British audiences through marionette shows that had adapted the French trick puppet of Mère Gigogne.[8] This was an imported tradition of puppetry that Victorian

---

7   On the etymological deformation of *cigogne*, see Jones (2016, 75n23).

8   A Victorian account of Parisian puppet theater highlights the "traditional Mère Gigogne—a sort of Parisian Old-Woman-who-dwelt-in-a-Shoe, in so far as her multiplicity of children is concerned" and also foregrounds shared roots

commentators understood to be derived from Italian troupes and one that was still echoing in British performance traditions. As one commentator noted, this French-derived comic character is a descendent of "the old Italian *commedia dell'arte* [. . .] from which, as we all know, the English pantomime has descended" ("Parisian Shows" 1886, 84). In that nineteenth-century British context, Mère Gigogne was often conflated with homegrown characters like Mother Shipton and Mother Goose, both of whom were part of the Victorian marionette theater repertoire (see McCormick 2004, 144); she also made regular appearances in pantomime. Contemporary audiences know this figuration of Mère Gigogne from the *grand divertissement* of the *Nutcracker* ballet composed by Pyotr Ilyich Tchaikovsky and choreographed by Marius Petipa, where the part is almost always played by a man—a fact that we should not gloss over: it signals something of Mère Gigogne's complexity as a stock character associated with an outrageous, comically exaggerated capacity for childbearing.

By the debut of that celebrated ballet in 1894, the French theatrical character of Mère or Dame Gigogne was approximately three hundred years old. Varied iterations of this character type preceded her appearance in the Petipa-Tchaikovsky ballet, characterized by forms of bodily and sartorial excess, spectacle and comic possibility, and a tradition of burlesque cross-casting. There are records of a Dame Gigogne as one of several newly introduced stock characters in performances as early as 1599 and 1601(Hawkins 1884, 1:53 and 2:356)—about twenty years after a Venetian troupe had introduced commedia dell'arte and its array of character types to the French court

of puppetry and British pantomime in commedia dell'arte: "the Continental puppet-play is like the old Italian *commedia dell' arte*, from which perhaps it is derived, and from which, as we all know, the English pantomime has descended" ("Parisian Shows" 1886, 84). Like commedia dell'arte, puppetry was part of seventeenth-century Parisian fair entertainment and borrowed material and stock characters from commedia troupes. As Marion Jacobus notes, there is also evidence of "live actors acting simultaneously with puppets" in the early years of the eighteenth century (1966, 115).

of Henri III. As just one of several manifestations of "boisterous performance of old women by male clowns" (Senelick 2000, 230), Dame Gigogne joined the ranks of Italian commedia characters on which varieties of seventeenth-century performance could draw. Importantly, many Dames Gigogne appeared in popular and courtly entertainments of the 1680s, immediately preceding the heyday of the literary *contes de fées*. As Rebecca Harris-Warrick and Carol G. Marsh note, at least two *danses de Gigogne* were staged at the Comédie-Française in 1684. Another "dance for a Dame Gigogne" was performed by Louis XIV's eleven-year-old daughter at a ball in 1685, and court masquerades in subsequent years regularly drew "from the pool of stock comic types that appeared over and over in the theatrical entertainments of the seventeenth century" (Harris-Warrick and Marsh 1994, 41)—including the appearance of two Dames Gigogne in *Le mariage de la grosse Cathos* in 1688 (Marsh and Harris-Warrick 1988, 398). Dame Gigogne thus has deep associations with a tradition of comedic cross-dressing in musical and comedic performance, as well as an association with the portrayal of unruly, libidinous older women in the theater of Perrault's time, both popular and courtly.

The cross-casting of older female characters, ones associated with child-bearing or childcare, was itself a source of comedy in the plot of the 1688 masquerade *Le mariage de la grosse Cathos*. In this performance, Harlequin makes an unsuccessful attempt at exactly this kind of theatrical disguise, trying to join the ranks of the cross-cast actors playing the Dames Gigogne and pass himself off as a nurse. In fact, the category of "nursery tales" and the association of traditional narratives with nursemaids take on a transgressive valence when one takes into account the dominant representations of *la nourrice* in French theater. In sixteenth-century farce, a nurse character "is typically a lively, excessive, rather vulgar (in all senses of the term) figure of dubious morality [. . .] whose bawdiness would have been a reliable source of humour." As developed by the great seventeenth-century dramatist Pierre Corneille, this comic role was "traditionally performed by a cross-dressed male actor wearing a grotesque mask" (Prest 2006, 18). *La nourrice* has her parallels in the theatrical traditions of Italy and Great Britain, most notoriously in the character of Juliet's nurse in Shakespeare's *Romeo and Juliet*. The stage role of *la balia*, or Nurse, is often characterized by an intimate knowledge of matters of sex, love, procreation, whose own desires are frequently presented as comical, an expression of her own "'preposterous' sexuality" (Calabresi 2015, 127).

Even more striking in the present context is the fact that the early modern French theatricals that featured bawdy cross-dressed "dames," "mothers," and "nurses" *include* ones bearing the title of *Contes de ma mère l'Oye*—the subtitle that became attached to Perrault's collection of tales. Recall that this is the phrase that would appear on the placard depicted in the frontispiece illustration to his book, both in French and later in English. For example, Warner (1994a) notes that "the same year [as Perrault's collection, 1697], the *commedia dell'arte* players at the Hôtel de Bourgogne staged a burlesque romance called *Les Fées ou Les Contes de ma Mère l'Oye*." This performance "was set in a 'cave of ogres' and featured Harlequin and Pierrot as well as all the stock figures of fairy tale: a weeping and about-to-be-ravished princess, her beloved prince, the ogre who wakes up to the scent of 'the fresh meat' of the prince and says that the princess can have a haunch if she loves him so. The script throws in seven-league boots, an old wife [a cross-cast part] who tells a tall tale as well as lots of metamorphoses" (54–55). This show may very well have been an effort to capitalize on the instant popularity of Perrault's volume, but the flow of influence does not necessarily move in that expected direction.

Popular entertainments bearing the title *Contes de ma mère l'Oye* were already in fashion when Perrault titled his collection and actually date back to 1695 (see Jones 2016, 167n1)—or possibly earlier. Over a century ago, Charles Deulin identified 1694 as the date for Charles Dufresny's *Les fées ou les contes de ma mère l'Oye*, and this date corresponds with the version of the comedy published recently by Théâtre classique.[9] Whether the date was 1694

---

9 See www.theatre-classique.fr/pages/pdf/BARANTEDUFRESNY_FEES.pdf, accessed August 15, 2017.

or 1695, the fact remains that a theatrical production—rooted in commedia dell'arte, featuring a cross-cast old woman character, and bearing the title of *Contes de ma mère l'Oye* —was staged *before* Perrault's volume had appeared in its published form. It was popular enough to be revived and imitated, generating a production with the same title from Dufresny's competitor, Florent Carton Dancourt, in 1697 (Deulin 1878, 29), that is, within months of the publication of Perrault's *Histoires ou contes du temps passé*.

While Perrault's work has been conventionally understood in relation to the *contes des fées* of other French writers of his day, or in relation to the work of earlier Italian writers like Gianfrancesco Straparola and Giambattista Basile, the context I have sketched here suggests that his work likely would have resonated intertextually with forms of popular theater and courtly performance *as much* as it did with the tales of fellow *salonnières* and those of their Italian literary predecessors. In this multimedial context, a figure like the one illustrated in the 1697 frontispiece can be read both as potentially cross-dressed and as indicative of a satirical discursive register. On the one hand, this figure and the placard that hangs behind the intimate social interaction that she dominates could be interpreted as a nod, perhaps, to Perrault's position as writer of "ridiculous tales" associated with old women[10] of a much lower social standing than his own. It could also be seen as a tongue-in-cheek acknowledgment of his position as a man working in a genre dominated by and associated with fashionable women, members of the nobility. But the reference to Mother Goose and the depiction of the woman in the frontispiece illustration also signal that the book can operate as a kind of comic and socially satirical performance, tinged with

---

10   Warner looks at Mother Goose as Perrault's alter ego, writing that "Perrault himself put on Granny's bonnet, as it were, when he hid behind the figure of an old nurse, telling stories to children of higher social rank than herself." For Warner, this authorial cross-dressing is metaphorical, most likely rooted in memories of actual nursemaid storytellers: "The image might represent a memory of Perrault's own childhood, but even so, it offers an alter ego for Perrault himself which he uses as a cover" (1994a, 182).

magic, wonder, and excess in ways that resonate most deeply with comme-dia dell'arte and related forms of Continental performance.

For North American audiences today, the name Mother Goose is asso-ciated much more closely with a canon of nursery rhymes than it is with nursery tales; but, once again, history points us to the durability of Mother Goose's links to satire and forms of cross-dressing, whether literal or met-aphorical. An eighteenth-century book first connected the name Mother Goose to this form of verse: *Mother Goose's Melody: Or, Sonnets for the Cra-dle*, released in 1780 by successors to the pioneering publisher of works for children, John Newbery.[11] Many famous nursery rhymes made their print debut in this volume, including "Little Tom Tucker," "See Saw, Margery Daw," "Hey Diddle Diddle," "Hush-a-Bye Baby," "Little Jack Horner," and "Bah Bah Black Sheep." The title page announces its pairing of "the most celebrated songs and lullabies of the old British nurses, calculated to amuse children and to excite them to sleep" with select verse from "Master William Shakespeare." *Mother Goose's Melody* thus playfully and explicitly aligns the bard with Mother Goose, casting both as "old British nurses": Shakespeare himself is referred to as "that sweet songster and nurse of wit and humour" (1791, title page). This association between *wit* and the figure of the nurse and/or Mother Goose is sustained in the preface by an author identified only as "a very Great Writer of very Little Books." The author suggests that "sing-ing these songs and lullabies to children" is a practice "of great antiquity"—forming the infant repertoire of both commoners and kings: "*Caractacus*, King of the *Britons*," he postulates, "was rocked in his cradle in the isle of *Mona*, now called *Anglesea*, and tuned to sleep by some of these soporiferous sonnets" (1791, title page).

[handwritten marginal note: tracing "Mother Goose" character thru a wide & disparate scrap of intertextual references]

---

11   Daniel Hahn foregrounds the fact that Newbery's stepson, Thomas Carnan, registered copyright and advertised the book in 1780, but no edition of that date has been preserved. The earliest extant edition bearing a year of publication is the one issued by Newbery's grandson, Francis Power, in 1791 (see Hahn 2015, 401). All references to *Mother Goose's Melody* refer to Power's 1791 edition.

The author of *Mother Goose's Melody* goes on to suggest that nurses' repertoires of rhyme (like Shakespeare's sonnets) became part of a larger shared cultural field of reference, one that can be mined in the speech play of children and adults alike. The writer's chosen example draws on legendry surrounding another English monarch, Henry V. The king's disgruntled troops are said to have used both the form of the nursery rhyme and that genre's patroness saint in their own parodic and subversive verse. Set to a melody that the "great prince" had composed "to lead his troops to battle, well knowing that music had often the power of inspiring courage, especially in the minds of good men" (1791, vi), the troops insulted their king on many levels. As the preface to *Mother Goose's Melody* reports, "Some of the malcontents adopted the following words to the king's own march, in order to ridicule his majesty and to shew the folly and impossibility of his undertaking.

> There was an old woman toss'd in a blanket,
> Seventeen times as high as the moon;
> But where she was going no mortal could tell,
> For under her arm she carried a broom.
> Old woman, old woman, old woman, said I?
> Whither, ah whither, ah whither so high?
> *To sweep the cobwebs from the sky,*
> *And I'll be with you by and by."*

Soldiers are thus reported to have decontextualized a familiar nursery rhyme, casting their king "as an old woman, engaged in a pursuit the most absurd and extravagant imaginable" (*Mother Goose's Melody* 1791, vii). Of course, the "malcontents" themselves are in some sense also aligned with an old lady, namely, Mother Goose, whose "songs and lullabies" they presumably learned in childhood and are now able to adopt and adapt to their own adult purposes.

We are all Mother Goose or her goslings, the author seems to say, tracing the lineage of "nonsense verses" from "this practice among the old

British nurses" to the chants of school children, and then to instances of military insubordination such as that detailed above. As the "very Great Writer of very Little Books" concludes the book's preface, he returns to the topic of old British nurses with a gesture of reverence—somewhat at odds with the derogatory use of "old woman" in the emasculating insult of his earlier example. Of nurses, he writes: "They have, indeed, been always the first preceptors of the youth of this kingdom, and from them the rudiments of taste and learning are naturally derived. Let none therefore speak irreverently of this antient [*sic*] maternity, as they may be considered as the great grandmothers of science and knowledge" (1791, x). To this we might add that old British nurses may likewise be considered as the great-grandmothers of satirical verse and other forms of subversive verbal art.

In the early years of the nineteenth century, references to Mother Goose as an iconic old British nurse or as a representative of old women, in general, started to be upstaged by ones that granted the character a distinctive identity and story of her own, including a house in the woods, a son named Jack, a pet goose that lays a golden egg, and a series of conflicts with authority figures (such as a crooked merchant, often rendered as a "Jew," and a lecherous squire). This story made its way into chapbooks like *Mother Goose and the Golden Egg* (ca. 1820) and *Old Mother Goose*, printed by W. S. Johnson (ca. 1850). Such books were clearly derived—and attempting to profit—from the fame and popularity of a pantomime, with references to the title character's transformation of her son and his lover into Harlequin and Columbine, respectively. As we have seen, that pantomime is one that has earned a place in theater history: the 1806–7 Covent Garden production of *Harlequin and Mother Goose, or the Golden Egg*, which made a star of its clown, Joseph Grimaldi, in the role of Squire, and whose "drollery and feats of agility drew down repeated plaudits" ("Theatre" 1806, n.p.). The part of Mother Goose herself has since come to be "considered one of the best comic characters in the whole pantomime tradition," particularly as it was developed by the comedian Dan Leno into a classic pantomime Dame role at the turn of the twentieth century (Pickering 1993, 137). But in the 1806 pantomime, Mother Goose possessed magical and transformative powers;[12] the role was played by Samuel Simmons and immortalized in engravings like that which adorned Fairburn's sixpence "description" of the production. Like many other pantomime Mothers Goose and Bunch, the seemingly humble character of Mother Goose in this production served as the show's good fairy or benevolent agent, the character who initiates the transformations of character, costume, and scenery, as the show transitioned from its sequence of opening scenes to the much longer sequence of scenes composing the harlequinade. As David Mayer details, the benevolent agent is herself "usually a fairy or supernatural being" whose powers of metamorphosis allow her to direct the actions and appearances of fellow players, the movement of the plot, and the dressing of the stage itself. As someone sympathetic to the desires of the show's young lovers (toward whose ultimate union the plot is driven), the benevolent agent "facilitate[s] their escape from obdurate elders," transforming them into Columbine and Harlequin—and granting the latter his trademark implement of magical and distinctly phallic power: a sword or slapstick (Mayer 1969, 24). Like so many of her predecessors, this cross-dressed and comical Mother Goose was understood to possess powers associated with magic, physical transformation, knowledge of love and sex—and the ability to subvert figures of traditional patriarchal authority.

Narrative Disguise: Madame d'Aulnoy and Mother Bunch

While the names of Charles Perrault and Mother Goose have maintained some currency, those of both Marie-Catherine d'Aulnoy and Mother Bunch have faded into relative obscurity for English-language audiences. But as the pantomime examples from the previous and current chapter suggest, these names were once well known and frequently referenced, each one carrying

---

12   See Ryoji Tsurumi, "The Development of Mother Goose in Britain in the Nineteenth Century" (1990) for comparison of the 1806 pantomime Mother Goose to a witch.

with it a complex and sometimes self-contradictory set of associations likely to be lost on the modern reader. I suggest that narratives about the (perhaps unlikely) figures of d'Aulnoy and Mother Bunch are, in fact, highly relevant to the history of folklore study: analysis of their forays into adjacent traditions—those of the literary fairy tale, popular print culture, and theater, to name but a few—foreground the complexity of the discursive field within which the disciplinary tradition of folklore emerged.

D'Aulnoy's name had become well known in eighteenth-century England, as her novels, her accounts of European travel and court scandal, and especially her intricate, highly self-aware, self-referential and influential fairy tales were translated and adapted for English audiences—resonating in the works of Ann Radcliffe, Maria Edgeworth, Anne Thackeray Ritchie, and many others.[13] In French, d'Aulnoy's writing is characterized by irony and a comic touch, by the use of what Jean Mainil calls "déguisements narratifs," or narrative disguises, which play on various levels ("jouant sur différents niveaux"; 2001, 95). As Jones has demonstrated (2009), early translations of d'Aulnoy's work situated the author as a great wit and bourgeois genius, but by the turn of the twentieth century her name had been all but forgotten in English-language contexts. This occurred not only because adaptations of her fairy tales ceased to be fashionable but also because d'Aulnoy herself had been granted a disguise, and one that was not of her choosing: she had been subsumed by the English "Mother Bunch," to whom translations of her tales were first attributed in the Newbery edition of 1773 and with whom they were repeatedly associated in decades to come. David Blamires cites six Newbery editions of *Mother Bunch's Fairy Tales* extant by 1779 (2008, 69), and Jones has traced the predominance of this attribution in editions from the 1790s through the early decades of the nineteenth century (2009, 253–54).

Who is Mother Bunch, and why should she be chosen posthumously as d'Aulnoy's alter ego? Mother Bunch's varied guises have been undertheorized:

13　On d'Aulnoy's influence on English fiction and English print culture, in general, see Adams (1994) and Palmer (1975).

when meriting any mention at all in the history of the fairy tale, she has been assumed to represent one of several generalized English peasant-woman storytellers. For example, in the *Oxford Companion to Fairy Tales*, Mother Bunch does not earn an entry of her own but is dismissed as one of many "representation[s] of the motherly, lower-class storyteller" (Zipes 2000, 325), considered suitable as a children's author, but a far cry from d'Aulnoy's representations of herself as a sophisticated and fashionable woman writer addressing a "feminine, aristocratic listening audience" (Harries 2001, 56). For Elizabeth Harries, the erasure of the tales' origins in a specifically French, aristocratic, literary context is energized by the association of Mother Bunch with orality, specifically women's storytelling. Marina Warner has offered an extended analysis of Mother Goose, the most durable of these English personae, but dismisses Mother Bunch as just another of the "beldames of folklore," one of "Mother Goose's counterparts" (1990, 13). Similarly, Blamires notes only that Mother Bunch was thought to be a woman who was "knowledgeable in English folklore" and who had presence in English writings from the sixteenth century onwards (2008, 75). Neither Warner nor Blamires give much consideration to Mother Bunch as a distinct figure with a distinct but quite complicated history in print and on stage. This is a history Margaret Spufford mentions in her important study of popular seventeenth-century fiction (1982) and one that has received more recent attention, most notably from Pamela Allen Brown (2003)—but it has not, to date, been extended to the nineteenth century, nor has it been brought into sustained dialogue with fairy-tale studies. As we will see, by the 1770s Mother Bunch had a complex history of her own: although the name already signaled legendary verbal skill, Mother Bunch was *not* associated with the circulation of fairy tales before this point in time. Moreover, the complex set of associations Mother Bunch carried with her in the late eighteenth century was not eclipsed by her new role in the history of the fairy tale, as is especially evident if we return to her many and varied appearances on the English pantomime stage.

Mother Bunch appears as a character in many nineteenth-century pantomime treatments of French fairy tales and takes a variety of forms, but none of these includes her better-known role as d'Aulnoy the writer. As the examples with which this chapter opened suggest, Mother Bunch appears often in pantomime renditions of tales by French writers *other than* d'Aulnoy, including many tales by Charles Perrault. For example, the 1822 Covent Garden production of *Harlequin and the Ogress; or, The Sleeping Beauty of the Wood* features three "mothers" of pantomime fame—Mother Goose, Mother Shipton, and Mother Bunch—as does E. L. Blanchard's *Mother Goose and the Enchanted Beauty*, some sixty-five years later. In some cases, Mother Bunch shares the stage with characters who *are* of d'Aulnoy's creation, recontextualized, in pantomime fashion, to other tales. This is the case in William Walton's 1897 *Sleeping Beauty and the Mystic Yellow Dwarf.* Here, Mother Bunch is not a speaking part but one of five cross-dressed "mothers" who support the malevolent actions of Old Mother Baneful. Alternatively, and as in those earlier examples, Mother Bunch can serve the role of the good fairy or benevolent agent, as she does in Charles Rice's *The Babes in the Wood and the Great Bed of Ware* (1874), and George Conquest and Henry Spry's *Mother Bunch, the Man with the Hunch, the Reeds, the Weeds, the Priest, the Swell, the Gipsy Girl and the Big Dumb Bell* (1881).

In the latter example, Mother Bunch is the most prominent of four witches (Mothers Goose, Shipton, and Hubbard being the others) who embody the spirit and energy of pantomime itself. There is some resonance with the portraits of Bunch as proprietress of a toy shop or bookshop in the midcentury *Beauty and the Beast* pantomimes discussed at the outset: in the Conquest and Spry pantomime, the opening scene is set in an elfin library of "tales [. . .] often told," where Bunch reflects on her responsibility to an audience of "little dears" eager for a yearly treat (1881, 7). As a library rather than a book or toy shop, the magical domain of this pantomime Mother Bunch is less obviously a site of commercial transactions, but she is likewise engaged with the production of cultural forms that target and profit from a child audience. Presented with possible subjects for the Surrey Theatre's 1881 pantomime, this staged Bunch requests something not so familiar and "well worn" as Aladdin, Sindbad, Red Riding Hood, Cinderella, Bluebeard or the Yellow Dwarf, all of which entered the canon through translation from the French and had long been established as pantomime favorites. On this stage, such tales are declared by Mother Bunch herself to be "quite used up, in present form at least," leaving her "in despair about [the Surrey's] Christmas feast" (1881, 8). By 1881, adaptations of the work of Galland, Perrault, and d'Aulnoy had been thoroughly naturalized, domesticated, and embraced by English audiences. The character "Novelty" thus contrasts such tales (now classics of the English pantomime repertoire) with an exciting alternative: "Suppose we boldly trench," suggests the embodiment of all that is new and fresh, "On foreign ground—suppose we say the French?" In unison, and apparently without a hint of irony, the three mothers exclaim "Oh, that's very new and novel!" and Mother Bunch prepares to welcome a new "little stranger," Victor Hugo's *Hunchback of Notre Dame*: "though from *abroad*, pray make yourself *at home*. / You'll be our honoured guest, so happy be you / As long as folks will pay their cash to see you" (1881, 8). In the conventional role of benevolent agent, Mother Bunch is responsible here for supporting the unfolding of the plot as it moves toward its desired and expected conclusion in romantic pairings-off, but she is also responsible to the audience (seeking novelty and diversion) and the theater (generating cash).

By this point in time, Mother Bunch is a multivalenced figure, serving as much more than the generalized representation of the peasant storyteller: she carries with her a wide range of intertextual and cultural associations on which dramatists could draw—still powerfully connected to the genre of the fairy tale and, specifically, to a tradition of French tales in translation. How can one make sense of the transmogrification of the French aristocratic writer Madame d'Aulnoy into the specific form of Mother Bunch, this English folk figure who predates d'Aulnoy by nearly a century? This maneuver does not simply signal the trivialization and infantilization of d'Aulnoy's work by the English reading public. In fact, Mother Bunch would appear to be a highly unstable cultural icon, both before and after her association with d'Aulnoy's fairy tales.

The early modern iterations of Mother Bunch are associated variously with the English alehouse, the marketplace, and open fields, as well as the theater—not the worlds of the French court and salon. Nevertheless, there are points of resonance between d'Aulnoy's persona and those associated with Mother Bunch that render evocative what might otherwise appear to be a very odd pairing indeed. By the time Sir Francis Palgrave wrote a survey of nursery stories and popular fictions—in the guise of a review of Benjamin Tabart's 1818 collection *Fairy Tales, or the Lilliputian Cabinet*—he was compelled to distinguish between *two* ways of conceptualizing Mother Bunch. First, he references and then dismisses "the Mother Bunch whose fairy tales are repeated to the little ones." Next, he invokes the Mother Bunch "whose 'cabinet,' when broken open, reveals so many powerful love spells: it is the Mother Bunch who teaches the blooming damsel to recall the fickle lover, or to fix the wandering gaze of the cautious swain, attracted by her charms, yet scorning the fetters of the parson, and dreading the still more fearful vision of the churchwarden, the constable, the justice, the warrant, and the jail" (1819, 109). A wise woman when it comes to matters of sex and love, with power over the actions and choices of young men and women, this latter Mother Bunch has authority that rivals the more hegemonic representatives of church and state authority, and resonates with many of the "mothers" discussed earlier.

Interestingly, the *Oxford English Dictionary* currently offers its own pair of definitions for Mother Bunch: "strong ale (as proverbially served by Mother Bunch)" and "a stout, untidy, or awkward-looking woman or girl." These lingering associations of Mother Bunch with ale, on the one hand, and a kind of unruly or unkempt female body, on the other, have their roots in her first significant appearance in English book history: *Pasquil's Jests mixed with Mother Bunch's Merriments*. The jest book, an Elizabethan collection of bawdy anecdotes, jokes, and tall tales, was published in 1604, more than 150 years *before* Mother Bunch became associated with d'Aulnoy. In the jest book, Mother Bunch is both an alehouse keeper and a masterful storyteller. Brown notes that in this volume Mother Bunch's own body "sometimes attracts satire" (2003, 77) or is utilized in transgressive ways, producing laughter and flatulence, inspiring both "terrour" and "amazement" as the "wind in her belly, and one blast of her taile [. . .] blew down Charing-Crosse, with Paul's aspiring steeple." All in all, this Mother Bunch is "an excellent companion, and sociable; shee was very pleasant and witty, and would tell a tale, let a fart, drink her draught, scratch her arse [. . .] as well as any Chymist of Ale" (reprinted in Hazlitt 1864, 112–13). Powerful and carnivalesque, this Elizabethan alewife is a far cry from d'Aulnoy's self-representation as an aristocratic woman and sophisticated writer. And yet, like d'Aulnoy, this Mother Bunch is a highly self-aware and skilled orator. Brown argues that although Mother Bunch is "laid open to laughter she is strikingly unscathed by it, flourishing as a seller of ale and teller of tales, both of them saleable and appetizing commodities" (2003, 77). In contrast to Warner's characterization of Mother Bunch as a woman whose "clowning camouflages [her] power" (1990, 13), Brown suggests that Mother Bunch's jests—remembered, recounted, collected, repeatedly consumed—comprise a form of social power.

Mother Bunch's power is infectious, and as producer and dispenser of the strong ale that bears her name, she is rumored to have had the most profound effect on her female patrons. With a masterful hand on the ale tap faucet, Mother Bunch "raised the spirits of her spigot to such a height, that Maids grew proud, and many proved with childe after it, and being asked who got the childe, they answered, they knew not, only they thought Mother Bunches Ale, and another thing had done the deed, but whosoever was the father, Mother Bunches Ale had all the blame" (reprinted in Hazlitt 1864, 10). As Brown comments, the Elizabethan Mother Bunch is striking in her ability to "flout all rules" (2003, 78), including social conventions and restrictions on women's speech, women's economic independence and women's bodies—her own as well as those of her patrons. Her powers are imagined in terms that are powerfully sexual, potently transgressive. Unlike the pantomime Mothers Bunch developed two hundred years later, this character doesn't grant a young lover the magical and phallic bat he lacks: instead, she possesses and raises her own generative spigot.

The cultural "life" of the Elizabethan Mother Bunch overlaps with that of Mother Bunch the fairy-tale narrator, creating an intertextual field that is far more complex than earlier accountings have suggested. Reprinted at least seven times in the seventeenth century, *Pasquil's Jests* remained in print throughout the nineteenth century, revived and reprinted in 1864 by William Hazlitt as one of the jest books on which Shakespeare would have drawn. Hazlitt notes that this alewife's "celebrity was, doubtless, extreme," and that "subsequent book-makers did not scruple to trade upon it." The result, in Hazlitt's view, is the proliferation in popular print culture of "*pseudo-Bunchiana*, to wit: 'Mother Bunch's Golden Fortune-Teller,' 'Mother Bunch's Closet Newly Broken Open,' and the like, the chronology of which publications is rather dubious, from the persistent absence of dates" (1864, 5). In fact, we do have a sense of the publishing history of some of the pseudo-Bunchiana to which Hazlitt refers: *Mother Bunch's Closet, Newly Broke Open* is a collection of stories of romantic and sexual mishaps, about which the thrice-wed and newly widowed Mother Bunch offers practical advice and tips for divining fortunes. This text was printed in numerous cheap editions between 1685 and the mid-nineteenth century and was reprinted both in 1885 by folklorist George Laurence Gomme (as a volume in his Chapbooks and Folk-Lore Tracts series) and then in 1889 by Robert Hays Cunningham (*Amusing Prose Chapbooks, Chiefly of the Last Century*). *Mother Bunch's Closet* begins with the anonymous speaker recounting the "story of an old woman" well known both for her fortune-telling abilities and, along the lines of the classic pantomime Dame, her voracious sexual appetite: readers are introduced to Mother Bunch as an "old woman" who has "newly buried her husband, [and] was taking a walk in the fields, for the benefit of the air, sometimes thinking of the loss of her husbands, for she had had three, yet had a great desire for a fourth" (1685, 1–2). She encounters a series of pretty maids, and a few young men, offering them divination tools and sexual advice (in language "thick with innuendo," as Margaret Spufford notes [1982, 63–64]). Classified retrospectively (by an 1860s commentator) as one of the "useful" variety of chapbooks, *Mother Bunch's Closet* offers stories of advice sought and simultaneously dispenses advice to readers. With its focus on seeking spouses and sexual fulfillment, *Mother Bunch's Closet* is defined—like d'Aulnoy's corpus of tales—by a largely if not exclusively homosocial communicative frame (see Spufford 1982, 61) in which closets are burst open, secrets are revealed, and the private is made public.

As both the jesting alewife and the sexually experienced fortune-teller, Mother Bunch entertains and profits from her verbal skills. It is worth noting that d'Aulnoy, like her fellow *conteuses*, was publishing fairy tales in France at a time when the social status of the professional writer was increasing and gaining "acceptance and a certain respectability" (Hannon 1998, 165). Nevertheless, the presence of professional women writers like d'Aulnoy in the world of letters was controversial and perceived to be potentially transgressive (see 164–78). It is precisely the act of inscription, of speaking to and writing for a predominantly female public that is emphasized in d'Aulnoy's paratextual materials (prefaces, frontispiece illustrations, etc.). This is symbolized visually by the open inkpot and especially by the poised pen: in one early frontispiece to d'Aulnoy's *Contes nouveaux*, a woman "in the flowing robes and turban usually associated with a sybil" is pictured in the act of inscribing the title of one of d'Aulnoy's tales in a book; in another, a woman wearing a winged helmet writes with a quill as a predominantly female audience sits rapt at her feet (see Harries 2001, 52–56). This iconography seems to have no bearing on the English Mother Bunch: despite her shape-shifting capacity, Mother Bunch was never associated with the act of writing. Rather, Mother Bunch's associations with the genre of the fairy tale, in print and on stage, are generally described in fanciful and corporeal terms: she is seen as both the transmitter and the embodiment of fairy-tale magic. For example, in an 1822 *London Magazine* review of the season's pantomimes, the periodical's adult readership is instructed to recall childhood debts and thus to "cherish Mother Bunch, Mother Goose, and all those old enchanting mothers, who suckled us with fairy milk" ("The Pantomime" 1822, 134). Although Mother Bunch is not connected to potential transgression via ink, she is, as we have seen, associated nevertheless with a number of other densely symbolic fluids that threaten (or promise) to obfuscate boundaries; that intoxicate, impregnate, and nourish; that defy efforts to contain them: ale, semen, and now breast milk.

The universalizing and allochronic dimensions of such discursive constructions is striking: d'Aulnoy's specificity as a talented, influential, innovative woman writer is erased in this fantasy of Mother Bunch's body as a wellspring of liquid enchantment. These fantasies take a slightly more solid form in an 1831 article from the *Edinburgh Literary Journal*, in which Mother Bunch represents a source of nourishment and rejuvenation for grown men, more powerful than time itself: "In the Christmas week we think of nothing [but pantomime]. We dream of the pantomime; we breakfast, dine, and sup on the pantomime; we give up all our ordinary pursuits, and do not care one farthing for the state of Europe [. . .]. [F]or five blessed hours, what looks of rapture! What peels of merriment! What thrillings of delicious emotions! 'Time! Time! Time!' how thou dost change all these things!—but, thank Heaven! 'Mother Bunch' is greater than thou, and when she comes to our aid, we defy thee, wrinkled cynic!" ("The Edinburgh Drama" 1831, 17). Here pantomime is said to satisfy hunger, the longings of the body, the desire for diversion, the thirst for the extraordinary; it defies temporality; and it is represented by the figure of Mother Bunch. To the catalog of cultural functions Mother Bunch has served, we can add one more: she has served as the embodiment of apolitical, ahistorical, romantically nostalgic fantasies in which complicated histories of literary and theatrical production—censorship, translation, adaptation—matter not at all. And yet, if one resists the "rapture" promised by such invocations of Mother Bunch's name, if her varied and competing appearances in popular cultural forms from the seventeenth through the nineteenth centuries are brought into view, then such references emerge as far more complicated than they might otherwise appear to be.

The points of resonance between Mother Bunch's various personae and those of d'Aulnoy suggest that the history of the *contes de fées* in England is anything but an uncomplicated trajectory toward simplistic fantasy and then obscurity. Likewise, consideration of the performative traditions that resonate in the figures of both Mère l'Oye and Mother Goose highlights the satirical and provocative dimensions of a genre so frequently dismissed as simplistic and moralizing. Neither "Mother Goose" nor "Mother Bunch" can be adequately contained by current conceptions of the benevolent grandmother/storyteller as source and personification of innocuous fairy tales. Long characterized by appetites, desires, and sexual knowledge, distinguished by forms of bodily excess and transgression, these fairy mothers may indeed embody the spirit of the genre—a spirit that is worldly, playful, challenging, and often marginalized.

5 Cross-Dressed Tales
The Performative Possibilities of Artifice and Excess

IN AN 1871 article in *The Contemporary Review* titled "The Burlesque and the Beautiful," the sixty-nine-year-old poet, critic, and writer Richard Henry Horne reflected fondly on the pantomimes of his early nineteenth-century childhood. Horne offers a nostalgic perspective that contrasts with more conventional historical accounts of the fairy-tale genre: he recalls "beautiful" fairy tales, as they had flourished onstage—and as he had experienced them when he was a young boy. Further, he argues that that beauty could be recaptured in the English theater with a return to "real" fairy tales as the basis for these Christmas entertainments. From our current vantage point, it is noteworthy that the corpus of story lines on which fairy-tale pantomime had been drawing in the interceding decades had not changed significantly: Horne's childhood coincided with a period in which the varieties of fairy-tale plots and characters, discussed in earlier chapters, was gaining traction in British pantomime. In other words, Horne's reflections seem to have little to do with the specific tales that were being staged; instead, his comments join a chorus of voices that invoked the notion of the "real" fairy tale and, by implication, its shadow binary opposite. Horne objects to what he sees as the English taste for "ugliness"—the "burlesque" of his title, which he sees epitomized in the theatrical productions of his adulthood: pantomimes that foreground costly props and costumes above all else, that grant "over-attention to material actualities and minute details, ignoring the 'so potent' art of stage illusion" (1871, 398). The unabashed materiality and costliness of Victorian pantomime seem to be at the core of Horne's complaint, and what renders fairy-tale pantomime ugly rather than "real" and beautiful. Despite Horne's lament about perceived change, the emphasis on novelty is something that had remained constant, and compelling forms of stage illusion had been central to pantomime's financial success for decades.

By the late nineteenth century, pantomime seems to be caught in a kind of double bind, attracting sharp criticism while also remaining an object of nostalgic affection. For instance, a pair of 1876 engravings by Fred Barnard turned the collective gaze to pantomime audiences, past and present, depicting an awestruck boy at his first pantomime in the early years of the century (figure 17) juxtaposed against his elderly (and apparently well-heeled) self, now snoozing through his last pantomime (figure 18). In Horne's era, English theater managers ran pantomimes "as a matter of policy" during the Christmas season, usually opening on Boxing Day and often running for as long as four months; whether individual audience members were rapt or asleep, tickets were sold and profits made. As Michael Booth has documented, the yields from Christmas pantomime were "absolutely crucial to the financial health" of theaters in both London and the provinces, "a vital instrument of managerial policy." If "going to the pantomime had not become a family tradition," Booth reflects, "provincial theatre in the Victorian period could hardly have existed" (1991, 36). The financial centrality of pantomime was evident to the late Victorian observer. For example, in an 1896 article for *The Theatre*, Charles Dickens referred to the well-known "fact that the Christmas pantomime is still the backbone of Drury Lane . . . and that the prosperity of scores of country managers depends entirely on the success or failure of their pantomimes" (1896, 22). Horne may turn a wistful and nostalgic eye toward the performances of his childhood—a period in which yet another generation of adult theatergoers had been bemoaning the degradation of pantomime—but there is no question that, in his adult years, costly and

— this is Char. Dickens Jr.
?

Figure 17. "My First Pantomime—When My Grandfather Took Us Children to Sadler's Wells," by Fred Barnard. *The Illustrated London News*, December 23, 1876, 612. Collection of the author.

Figure 18. "My Last Pantomime—When I Took My Grandchildren to Covent Garden," by Fred Barnard. *The Illustrated London News*, December 23, 1876, 613. Collection of the author.

elaborate pantomimes certainly were thriving as a popular form for a broad audience.

Comic grotesqueries and what Horne calls "costly balderdash" (1871, 400)—enormous processions, tableaux vivants, and complex scenery—were closely associated with the genre. To a large degree, the "goods" of pantomime performance, past and present, draw attention to their own artificiality: individual audience members may suspend disbelief at will, but they are offered access to the winking knowledge that each horse is, in fact, composed of two awkward bodies beneath a fabric costume; that our humble hero (the "finest lad in England") is a comely actress in tights and tunic; that lusty Granny Hubbard or Mother Goose or Widow Twankey is a cross-dressed man; that the riches of Diablo's cavern are only paste and colored glass. Exaggeration and artifice might be considered pantomime's ruling aesthetic principles, contributing to the success of a performance rather than detracting from it, as examples in previous chapters suggest. The materiality of pantomime also has had the capacity to offer a self-reflexive commentary on the dynamics of performance, the performance of social and national identities, economies of desire, and the economics of theatrical production—the very processes in which performers and audience alike are engaged. These are topics I examine in greater depth here, using two case studies to do so. First, I consider a range of late Victorian pantomimes of "Little Red Riding Hood" to examine the ways in which the economics and erotics of pantomime shape that tale's stage representation. Next, I turn to a Boer-war era production based on "Jack and the Beanstalk," which used a cross-dressed figure to crystallize anxieties around imperialism and industrial capitalism. The pantomimes on which I draw here all feature potent examples of pantomime cross-dressing, in the most literal sense, but the term can also be approached metaphorically. As I suggested at the beginning of this book, there is a sense in which all fairy tales, familiar and obscure, are "cross-dressed": they may obfuscate or playfully disguise their own histories; they can employ style, stylishness, or stylization in a variety of meaningful and frequently humorous ways; and they certainly are always more than they appear to be.

Artifice and Identity

I began this study with some discussion of a relatively obscure book: John Thackray Bunce's 1878 survey of Victorian theories of folklore. As we have seen, many of Bunce's rhetorical strategies typify discursive patterns and ideological assumptions that extend far beyond his work—ones that have proven to be remarkably durable. These include his representation of a child audience as travelers in need of adult guidance and protection and his use of pantomime as a significant frame of reference for both popular and learned conceptions of the "fairy tale"—including his anxious response to the worldly humor and potentially transgressive modes of embodiment associated with pantomime. The productions I address in this chapter offer yet another opportunity to circle back to Bunce: they center on two of the four "popular tales" that he had assumed children would know best during the golden age of Victorian folklore research. In his "Conclusion: Some Popular Tales Explained," he writes: "There are four stories which we know best—Cinderella, and Little Red Riding Hood, and Jack the Giant Killer, and Jack and the Bean Stalk—and the last two of these belong especially to English fairy lore" (1878, 185). It is interesting to note that despite the advent of field-based tale collection nearly sixty years earlier, and the relative commercial success of translations of the Grimms' German tales (by Edgar Taylor and Margaret Hunt), or the translation of Asbjørnsen and Moe's Norwegian tales (by George Webbe Dasent), none of the stories from these volumes are presumed to be known well by Bunce's child readership. Instead, Bunce's conclusion highlights the continued currency of tales that had been prominent in eighteenth- and early nineteenth-century chapbooks and also on pantomime stages: two tales derived from Perrault and two from English popular tradition.

The emergence of a new fairy-tale aesthetic in the early to mid-nineteenth century was strongly associated with translation of the Grimms' tales into English, framed as authentic, ancient, natural, pure, and some-times as "manly"—despite the fact that real or imagined icons of oral storytelling were almost invariably old women. As we have seen, that emer-gent aesthetic cast the well-established popularity of certain fairy tales in a new light. Two key ideas concerning the circulation of imported tale tradi-tions have underpinned a dominant master narrative of the genre's history in Britain. First, there is the notion that fairy tales were generally scorned in early nineteenth-century England, when a tradition of imported French tales dominated the market, alongside home-grown stories like "Jack and the Beanstalk." Second, there is the belief that fairy tales gained a degree of middle-class respectability only by midcentury, with the introduction of alternative aesthetic and ideological frameworks offered by the field-based tale collections of the Grimms and their many followers.

In previous chapters I have suggested that this understanding of fairy tales in nineteenth-century British popular culture is complicated when theatrical renditions of fairy tales and the performative registers of various forms of print tradition are integrated into that history. I began with the example of an early nineteenth-century pantomime, the first to be based on Perrault's "Cendrillon": the 1804 Drury Lane production of *Cinderella*, which generated a remarkable variety of print ephemera. My second exam-ple challenged the distinction between literary tales and field-based ones: the pantomime *Harlequin and the Eagle: Or, The Man in the Moon and His Wife* (1826), based on the "Daniel O'Rourke" story from Thomas Crofton Croker's landmark collection *Fairy Legends and Traditions of the South of Ire-land*. The pantomime examples that have followed these introductory case studies typify points of intersection among folklore, children's literature, and theater, and they also represent the changing shape of "pantomime" over the course of the century. By the fin de siècle, discussions of folklore and fairy tale almost always contained at least one offhand and usually disparaging remark about the French literary fairy-tale tradition, but at the same time several French fairy-tale plotlines and characters continued to feature prominently in popular Christmas pantomimes. In fact, the same critical discourse used against the French tradition was mobilized in critiques of pantomime, and writings about folklore contain oblique references to pantomime—easy to overlook but dense with meaning and preoccupied with matters of artifice and commerce, anxieties about purity and contamination.

The fit between French tales of the late seventeenth and early eighteenth centuries and English pantomime of the nineteenth century makes sense on a certain level: many of the tales imported, translated, and repeatedly printed and performed in Great Britain explore forms of power and desire, as they are linked to and negotiated through material goods, physical appearances, and gender performance. Such thematic preoccupations translate well to forms of spectacular theater and would seem to have a kind of inherent theatricality—whether that term is used metaphorically, to emphasize performative dimensions of social life and the presentation of self, or in terms of "the exhibitory actions, the encoded actions, and the embodied actions" that Willmar Sauter isolates as key components of theater as a cultural phenomenon (2000, 50–72; see discussion in T. C. Davis and Postlewait 2003, 23). As we have seen, French literary tales can be considered in dynamic interrelationship with the forms of popular and courtly theater (spectacular, farcical, fanciful) that flourished alongside this literary movement; the history of British pantomime is certainly deeply indebted to both. While some of the subtleties of the French *contes de fées* were undoubtedly altered or lost in the process, the tales in their various English forms were still rife with fanciful imagery and evocative material detail, from d'Aulnoy's descriptions of lush palaces and bejeweled chariots to Perrault's delight in gustatory and sartorial descriptions.

By the end of the nineteenth century, some critics dismissed the French *conte de fées* as overwrought and artificial, as a perversion of a form that, they believed, should be pure, simple, and direct. An anonymous writer for the *Edinburgh Review* in 1898 argued that the *conte de fées* was no more than a "*jeu d'esprit* . . . full of side thrusts, of double entendre. Serving for the play of the keen-edged wit of its authors," the French tradition "wholly lacks the serener grace, the tranquil sincerity and simplicity which constitute the supreme charm of elder fairy narratives" ("Fairy Tales as Literature" 1898, 41), epitomized by the tales of Jacob and Wilhelm Grimm. The *Volksmärchen* collected, edited, analyzed, and published by the Grimms made important claims at antiquity, at timelessness, but their print entextualization and circulation can certainly be historicized: they have a history in the print forms that brought them to the attention of English audiences—and it was one that was considerably shorter than that of the *contes de fées* to which the German märchen were often compared. First written in manuscript form in 1810, first published in German in 1812, first translated into English in 1823, the tales that constitute the *Kinder- und Hausmärchen* have a publishing history that is at odds with their characterization by English commentators as "elder fairy narratives": that claim is predicated on a conception of oral traditions as static, singular, and unchanging, the belief that the Grimms' various written sources and oral informants offer a window onto those traditions and that English readers could access these ancient, sincere, simple, and charming narrative artifacts in book form. If we approach those books as material artifacts that have their own complex histories and ideological underpinnings, then we have to account for the fact that the French tales of d'Aulnoy and company had been circulating in England, both in print and onstage, for over a century before Jacob and Wilhelm Grimm set out to collect stories and to commit them to paper. Nevertheless, for many observers circa 1898, the vision of oral tradition as both nationally distinctive and as unchanging, eternal, and timeless, eclipses chronologies of performance, specific storytelling events, and print publication.

The French tale, the writer for the *Edinburgh Review* continues, "has always about it the atmosphere of the extravaganza; and it is—according to the custom of its country—artificial to the core" ("Fairy Tales as Literature" 1898, 41). As a statement that highlights the theatricality of French fairy tales and the intimate relationship between those tales and contemporaneous forms of popular performance, this claim would actually seem to be highly perceptive. But it is also clearly francophobic and dripping with disdain for certain forms of popular theater: this writer casts artificiality as a defining quality of both the local extravaganza and French culture as a whole. The statement is also characterized by a strange but not uncommon manipulation of chronology and causality, evident in the comparison of seventeenth-century French tales to the distinctly nineteenth-century category of theatrical "extravaganza." Word choice matters here: the term *extravaganza* only entered the English popular lexicon at the close of the eighteenth century and was applied primarily to British performances. By the time this piece in the *Edinburgh Review* was published a century later, extravaganzas were understood in Britain to be fanciful, spectacular forms that had reached the height of popularity with an earlier generation of theatergoers, around midcentury. The English extravaganza undoubtedly drew on Continental models, but the form is most powerfully associated with the work of Planché, an Englishman of French descent. As noted earlier, Planché's fairy extravaganzas are sometimes considered in conjunction with Victorian pantomimes (see, for example, Richards 2015, 65–123; Buczkowski 2001) but are frequently cast as a related but more genteel form of musical, spectacular, holiday entertainment. Like many nineteenth-century pantomimes, Planché's extravaganzas drew heavily on the *contes de fées* of Old Regime France for plotlines and dramatis personae, including not only pantomime favorites "The Yellow Dwarf," "Beauty and the Beast," "Blue Beard," and "Puss in Boots" but also tales that had not previously been staged in England, such as "The Discreet Princess" and "Riquet with the Tuft." In short, from the vantage point of 1898, fairy-tale extravaganzas were of relatively recent and distinctly local provenance. Nevertheless, the topical humor, spectacular extravagance and delight in artifice associated with the fairy tale on various Victorian stages could be cast, retrospectively, as qualities *inherent* to the French fairy-tale tradition on which so many productions drew.

The reviewer continues, establishing a critique of the French tales themselves in pointedly antitheatrical terms:

> The fairies of the *conte* were born neither of the shadows nor of the sunshine, neither of the mist or the gold or the purple of hill side or mountain summit. In them there is no blurring of the demarcation between the natural and the supernatural. They have no part or lot in the mysteries of sunset dreams. They are, in truth, little more than pieces of stage property—the purely mechanical inventions of a popular literary fashion. [. . .] It is a pantomime of flashing tinsel, mock gems, and artificial flowers. (*Edinburgh Review* 1898, 45)

Somewhat ironically, it is in Britain that the fairy extravaganza and conventions of modern fairy-tale pantomime were developed, where the side thrusts, risqué double entendres, and unabashed delight in artificiality were (and continue to be) played out yearly for large crowds of adults and children. In English theatrical form, traces of French literary tales enjoyed tremendous and sustained popularity, and yet in a print culture that now included field-based tale collections and a new breed of literary fairy tale, forms like pantomime also provided a vocabulary through which that foreign literary tradition could be criticized. The oral traditional tales introduced to the English reading public in translation from the German, and absent from pantomime's history at that point in time, carried with them their own discursive baggage—that of romantic nationalism, being framed as pure, serene, natural, and ancient. In contrast to the oral traditional tale's "sunset dreams," pantomime generated dreams of its own: materialist and sensual fantasies seldom considered in connection with the Victorian fairy tale but which contain echoes of earlier associations between "fairy tale" and indulgence. An 1897 illustration titled "A Dream of Pantomime" (figure 19) depicts a grown man engrossed in a fantasy in which a full chorus of miniaturized fairy attendants have stepped off the stage to provide him with

A DREAM OF PANTOMIME.

Figure 19. "A Dream of Pantomime." *The Sketch: Journal of Art and Actuality*, December 27, 1893, 485.

champagne, physical delight, and relief from financial burdens. This illustration was published in tandem with one called "Boxing Night at the Theatre, From Various Points of View" (figure 2), underscoring the fact that late Victorian fairy-tale pantomime drew a broad and diverse audience but also carried strong associations with sex and money, desire for bodily pleasure and for wealth. These associations provided fuel for some critics, but they must also be seen as an integral part of the general public's experience of the genre.

As we will see, there are a number of ways in which pantomime's costliness as well as its profitability are made explicit in pantomimes of this period rather than being obfuscated by discourses of cultural value. These include periodical articles about the cost and mechanics of props, sets, and costumes, which emphasize the pantomime as spectacle. Victorian productions also feature a form of metacommentary, moments when performers "break frame" (the fourth wall dissolves), the complicity between audience and performers (especially those in the conventionalized roles of Clown and cross-dressed Dame) is foregrounded, or the potential tension between pleasure and money, theatrical artistry and filthy lucre, is addressed directly. "Little Red Riding Hood"—one of the four stories isolated by Bunce in his own concluding chapter—is often acknowledged to be a story with sexual overtones but is rarely approached as a tale that has had anything to do with money; nevertheless, it is to late nineteenth-century pantomimes of this well-known tale that we now turn our attention.

Sex, Money, and "Red Riding Hood"

The tale known in English as "Little Red Riding Hood" was first adapted for the pantomime stage in 1803, seventy-four years after Charles Perrault's "Le petit chaperon rouge" entered English-language print culture through Robert Samber's translation (1729). To put this in further book historical context, the 1803 pantomime debut of "Red Riding Hood" occurred twenty years before an English-language version of the Grimms' "Rotkäppchen" was published and nearly a decade before that (now pervasive) version of the story—in which a heroic huntsman cuts the title character and her grandmother from the sleeping wolf's belly—was published in German. When we jump ahead to 1878, "Red Riding Hood" had been part of English print culture for nearly 150 years and part of English theater culture for 75 years. In other words, English book buyers in Bunce's day would have had many choices: they could have found the tale as it had been collected and published in German or chosen one of several English translations of the German story. Nevertheless, Bunce assumes his readers will be familiar with English-language versions derived from Perrault's story, which ends with the wolf devouring the title character. In fact, Bunce refers to the plotline derived from the French tale as "the English version of the story," so thoroughly had it been naturalized and incorporated into British culture and consciousness by this point in time.

Bunce sought to educate his young readers about current folklore scholarship and theories, and about the origins and meanings of "fairy tales," in particular; such knowledge, he seems to suggest, will set those readers apart from the masses of young fairy-tale consumers. When it comes to discussion of the tale of "Little Red Riding Hood," Bunce alerts his readership to the existence of the Grimms' *Kinder- und Hausmärchen*: this work was already a foundational text in folklore's historiography, but it is not one he assumes his readers will have in their repertoire. It is in the *Kinder- und Hausmärchen*, however, that readers can find an alternative to the "English version of the story":

> In the German story there is another ending to it. After the wolf has eaten up Little Red Riding Hood he lies down in bed again, and begins to snore very loudly. A huntsman, who is going by, thinks it is the old grandmother snoring, and he says, "How loudly the old woman snores; I must see if she wants anything." So he stepped into the cottage, and when he came to the bed he found the wolf lying in it. "What! do I find you here, you old sinner?" cried the huntsman; and then, taking aim with his gun, he shot the wolf quite dead. (1878, 187)

To elucidate the "full meaning of the story," Bunce focuses attention on the tale as it was documented in Germany, by the Grimms, a version of the story not yet considered canonical in the world of children's literature. It is,

however, framed as superior to the version known in English (by way of Perrault); for Bunce, the Grimms' "Little Red Cap" provides a key to the story's
"full" and true meaning.

Popular conceptions of the fairy-tale genre tend to assume simplicity
of style and clarity of meaning, but Bunce apparently sees the interpretive
process as something that requires guidance and instruction. The meaning
of such a story is not something that children would be able to discern
on their own, or so Bunce's writing implies. He turns to ideas associated
with the comparative mythology and solar theories of Max Müller (ones
surveyed in the body of his book), and within this analytical framework he
explains that the tale represents the vestigial remains of a sun-god myth,
with the title character representing "the evening sun, which is always
described as red or golden; the old Grandmother is the earth, to whom
the rays of the sun bring warmth and comfort," the wolf substitutes for
a dragon character, representing "the clouds and blackness of night," his
snoring is "the night-thunder and the storm winds," while the huntsman is
"the morning sun [. . .] in all his strength and majesty," who "chases away
the night-clouds," and so on (1878, 188). Whether a solar-mythological
reading of "Little Red Riding Hood" could or ever did capture the imag-
inations of Bunce's target audience is difficult to ascertain. Twenty years
later the playwright and theater historian T. Edgar Pemberton would take
"some delightful dips" into this "charming volume," quoting at length from
Bunce's fanciful and rhapsodic rhetoric concerning pantomime fairies
(1896, 26), but Pemberton displays little interest in a solar-mythological
interpretive model.

In fact, a general audience, including Bunce's intended child readers, would have already been quite familiar with versions of the story in
which Little Red Riding Hood did triumph, in one way or another, over the
wolf—whether figured as animal or human. In British theaters, the pantomime version of the story (which would seem extremely resistant to a solar-
mythological interpretation) rarely ended with the title character's death. By

1878, Red Riding Hood was firmly entrenched as a stock pantomime character, and the story with which she was associated was a stock pantomime
plot—one that necessarily incorporated and was shaped by the plot conventions of that theatrical form. Onstage, our red-hooded heroine was usually
an orphaned village beauty who inevitably had a love interest (often Boy
Blue of nursery-rhyme fame); an inheritance about which she was unaware
and which rendered her the target of a scheming older man (often an uncle
or distant relative, who may be represented as wolfish or who may employ
the assistance of evil and wolfish immortals); and a grandmother with a
large personality and hefty libido (jealous of Red's beauty and the attention
she garnered from male admirers). The narrative almost always resolved
happily: with the intervention of a good fairy, the wolf and other representatives of the forces of greed and evil would be reformed and forgiven, and
marital and sexual union is indicated for as many characters as possible,
Granny included. This kind of "Red Riding Hood" could well be considered
another "English version of the story"—very well known and widespread by
1878, but clearly it is not one that would have served Bunce's agenda. Bunce
dances between mobilization of his readership's theatrical literacy and will-
ful blindness to specific tales in pantomime form. It is as if such theatrical
Red Riding Hoods did not exist.

Following in the footsteps of many folklore scholars, John Thackray
Bunce stands as an example of a Victorian commentator who both acknowledged pantomime as part of the fairy tale's multimedial landscape but also
privileged specific iterations of tales and specific modes of interpretation,
painting a highly selective portrait of a genre, one in which certain fairyland dwellers are acknowledged but then relegated to the shadows. This can
be countered by reclaiming live performance, both as a significant mode
of transmission of fairy tales and as a master trope for understanding the
dynamic, multivalent, and unpredictable nature of the genre.

Jack Zipes has provided an important overview of print and select theatrical renditions of the tale in the nineteenth century (1993, 37–39), emphasizing

the frequent infusion of bourgeois morality and a prudish sensibility to Victorian versions of a story that, he argues persuasively, can be considered a misogynist tale about rape rooted in male "fear of women's sexuality" and designed to caution young girls against the dire consequences of being "disobedient and careless" (1993, 81, 17). Such ideological currents are not wholly absent from the pantomime Red Riding Hoods that flourished in tandem with Victorian print traditions, despite radical transformation of the plotline onstage, which rarely features any significant acts of disobedience on the part of the heroine but frequently maintains the eroticization of the wolf's appetite. For example, Charles Rice's 1873 Covent Garden pantomime *Red-Riding Hood and Her Sister Little Bo-Peep* is one of the few pantomime versions of the tale that ends with the girl's death. In this pantomime, the wolf declares that his "wish to eat that child's grown quite a passion," as he anticipates devouring "the little one with all her tender charms," who will "unsuspecting, fall into my arms" (25). But the fairy tale in pantomime form has been shaped by a distinct set of aesthetic principles and a pervasive sense of self-parody that complicates histories of the tale. Self-aware, playful, localized, and addressed to an all-ages audience of adults and children, late nineteenth-century pantomime Red Riding Hoods do not conform to the general vision of the tale offered by Zipes. In many ways, they anticipate the varied and creative twentieth- and twenty-first-century retellings of the tale, with the "self-reflexivity characteristic of later postmodern texts" (Beckett 2002, 71). Despite its relative invisibility in recent fairy-tale scholarship, the Christmas pantomime (as a form of popular performance) had been thoroughly naturalized to English popular culture by the fin de siècle—as "Red Riding Hood" had been, both in print and onstage—familiar enough to be subject to self-mockery and parody. Examples from several pantomime "Red Riding Hood"s of that era can help us to navigate this terrain, both in terms of generic and performative norms, and their self-reflexive dimensions.

To satisfy audience demands for novelty in pantomime, the stock of story lines and characters featured in eighteenth-century performances had expanded to include those from fairy tales, nursery rhymes, and popular literature—any source that seemed to offer the possibility of adventure, romance, fantasy, and spectacle. As we have seen, a remarkable number of these were French imports. As one cynical observer, George Augustus Sala, commented in 1875, the modern English pantomime consisted of two consecutive but not necessarily "coherent" parts: the "opening" and the "comic business." The opening, Sala notes, may be "founded on a fairy tale from the *Arabian Nights* or from the Countess d'Alnois, or upon the briefest of nursery rhymes" (347). By the turn of the twentieth century, the harlequinade had largely been replaced by two or three scenes of physical humor—the "comic business" decried by Sala. The harlequinade now represented a charming option for pantomime productions rather than a central feature of their structure. The kind of harlequinade Richard Henry Horne had recalled from childhood had indeed become a rarity, but Victorian pantomime would be expected to include its own "succession of conventional moments, without which the audience would feel cheated," as Peter Holland details: these include the opening chorus of peasants or townspeople; the honest, humble setting from which our romantic leads emerge; "an introductory scene for a comedian telling jokes and throwing sweets to the children in the audience"; at least one of several conventionalized routines of slapstick comedy, including the mirror sketch (featured in the Marx Brothers' *Duck Soup* but dating back to the mid-nineteenth century), the kitchen or "slop" scene, the balloon dance, and the undressing scene (1997, 195), to which I return below.

If the names Harlequin and Columbine had come to be associated with the faded glories of theatrical history, the romance plot itself was anything but a relic—and it has remained central to fairy-tale pantomime, as it has the fairy tale across media. Victorian pantomime's hero and heroine were not those stock characters adapted from the Italian commedia dell'arte, but their homegrown progeny: the roles known in pantomime as principal boy and principal girl. In addition, the erotic dynamics and sexual tensions of the pantomime stage shifted with the introduction of two cross-dressed parts, those of both the principal boy and the Dame, the latter of which is arguably the single most popular role on the modern pantomime stage. The use of cross-dressed players lends itself particularly well to the performance of tales that feature disguise, masquerade, and iconic items of dress, including d'Aulnoy's "Yellow Dwarf," Perrault's "Cinderella," and "Little Red Riding Hood"—with the latter containing what Marjorie Garber calls "the primal scene of narrativized cross-dressing" (1992, 389). On the other hand, the romantic pairing of a principal girl and a cross-dressed principal boy required some radical revision of a tale like "Little Red Riding Hood," which lacks a male romantic counterpart to the title character.

The part of the principal boy was a staple and beloved role in Victorian and Edwardian pantomime performance, casting a woman in the role of hero and male romantic lead. Dressed in a costume that typically accentuated her waistline and most especially her legs, striding confidently across the stage and invoking what Peter Holland calls a "set of gestural devices" that parody "manly postures," the actress playing the principal boy was—along with the man playing the Dame—generally one of the performance's headline players. While Holland deems the relationship between principal boy and principal girl "asexual" (1997, 199), close reading of nineteenth-century scripts and commentaries can challenge that characterization of the dynamic between the two romantic leads. Principal and secondary boys and girls flirt, embrace, kiss, and engage in banter heavy with double entendre, and commentators appear to be well aware of this flirtation between players and between players and the audience. Although many twentieth-century commentators have read the romance between such figures as pantomime's Red Riding Hood and Boy Blue as chaste or even "asexual" (Holland 1997, 199), this retrospective evaluation simply does not seem to fit with the documentary evidence. Certainly, the casting of these two parts was seen as extremely important to the box office success of a pantomime production.

Gender and sexuality on the pantomime stages of past centuries have been the subject of popular interest and critical inquiry, most notably in the work of David Mayer (1974), Peter Holland (1997), Caroline Radcliffe (2010), and Jim Davis (2014). The focus of such studies has generally been placed on the cross-dressed roles of Dame and principal boy—but the female lead, the principal girl, has received far less critical attention. The physical merits of these actresses were paraded on stage, in reviews, and in the promotional photographs that appeared in periodicals such as *The Sketch*, *The Theatre*, and *The Stage* and as cabinet, cigarette, and post cards.[1] Periodicals did sometimes publish pages of theatrical photographs that juxtaposed shots of actresses appearing as principal boys alongside those featured as principal girls. Much more often, however, the December numbers of image-heavy periodicals such as *The Sketch* would run pages of photos of one or the other, and the representational conventions of each are readily apparent. For example, little emphasis was placed on the stage costumes of late Victorian and early Edwardian principal girls or on the set design of the productions in which they appeared. The heroine is frequently depicted as dreamy, with her gaze focused away from that of the viewer; she is draped in light, gauzy fabric and is unfettered by corset, hairpins, or petticoats, as in the portrait of principal girl Hettie Montefiore (figure 20); this is also the mode of photographic representation satirized by Dan Leno in a comic photo shoot from 1900 (figure 21). Onstage, the principal girl was expected to represent feminine virtue, but she was also expected to be somewhat provocative, as Victorian commentators noted:

> What makes a Principal Girl a good one, in the judgment of special connoisseurs of pantomime, is a mystery hidden from mere common playgoers. When and where Principal Girls should be pert and when and where they refrain from pertness; how close they should come to being what the uninstructed might call minxes and yet how they should differentiate themselves from minxes in the eyes of the experts;

---

1   On the subject of Victorian theatrical photographs in periodicals, see David Mayer (2002, esp. 243).

Figure 20. Portrait of Miss Hettie Montefiore. *The Sketch: Journal of Art and Actuality*, January 1, 1896, 501.

THE INIMITABLE DAN LENO, LONDON'S LAUGHTER-MAKER.

From Photographs by Langfier, Old Bond Street, W.

AS A LADY, HE IS AESTHETIC.   AND DISPLAYS HIS BACK.

Figure 21. "The Inimitable Dan Leno, London's Laughter-Maker" (impersonation of a principal girl). *The Sketch: Journal of Art and Actuality,* November 14, 1900, 145.

to how many affairs of the heart they should make lyric reference while adhering like gum, in their prose passages, to their respective Sind-bads, Princes Charming, Little Boys Blue [etc.].[2]

The fairy-tale pantomime's nymphet heroine was thus imagined to balance an air of innocence with keen awareness of her attractiveness; she is subjected to the evaluative gaze of audience members "expert" in varieties of female charm; and she is the object of our hero's desires, our villain's designs, and the Dame's envy.

In the 1881 pantomime *Little Red Riding Hood, or Harlequin the Demon Wolf and the Good Fairies of the Enchanted Wood,* our heroine is neither

----

2 The quote is from a clipping in the Victoria and Albert Theatre Museum's "miscel-laneous pantomime" file; unfortunately, the source and exact date are unknown.

disobedient (as she appears to be in the Grimms' tale) nor unversed in the ways of the world (specifically, those of courtly and sweet-tongued men, as she is in Perrault's text). In this pantomime, Red Riding Hood is inadvertently made a target by her father, who intended to leave his money and property to her and thus incurred the jealousy of his own brother, Baron Badlot. The demon king (a character called Chimaera) serves as an intermediary between the greedy Baron Badlot and the character of the Wolf—a kind of villain for hire whose encounters with Red Riding Hood are financially motivated and masterminded by others. "So bad he finds the times," explains Chimaera, that the Wolf "is game for any quality of crimes." Newly returned from London, Badlot is determined to eliminate the rightful heir to his brother's fortune, his niece Red Riding Hood, as he explains to his new co-conspirators:

> **Baron:** Her father was my brother; when he died
> His house, his lands, his gold, and all beside,
> Which should have gone to *her*, were seized by *me*,
> She blocks my path.
> **Chimaera:** We now begin to see!
> **Baron:** Waylay and kill her—in the deed be bold—
> And I'll reward you with this bag of gold!
> [Gives bag of gold to Wolf]
> **Wolf:** You've fee'd me well!
> **Baron:** Fee'd you to *get* a feed.
> **Wolf:** Her doom is sealed—I'll have the maiden's "bleed"!
>
> (Jones 1881, 4)

Forces of greed are conflated here with the devouring lechery that is often associated with the tale of "Little Red Riding Hood": later in this pantomime, Boy Blue does indeed refer to the Wolf's "*devouring* passion" or what Red Riding Hood calls his "love [of] our sex." These destructive appetites are to be combated and, we may rest assured, ultimately defeated by a combination of female fairy magic and British bravery: the good queen Dryada and her fairy followers declare their ability and intent to shift shape and gender, if necessary, to embody all the might of St. George, St. Andrew, St. David, and St. Patrick. Our heroine is inevitably granted her rightful inheritance, forgives the baddies, and all turns out well. This happy conclusion is reached whether she is saved directly by feminine magic, as she is here, or by a mortal hero in the form of a principal boy, supported by the invisible forces of fairy benevolence.

The conventions for highlighting the attributes of the heroic principal boy stand in stark contrast to those of the principal girls, both in terms of the invocation of elements of set design, re-created or roughly replicated in the photographer's studio (Mayer 2002, 227), and in terms of the focus on the body of the actress: her stance, her costuming, her corsetry and makeup, and most especially her legs, thighs, and bum. Fin de siècle portraits of principal boys Ethel Earl and Nellie Bowman (figures 22 and 23) provide examples of the range of conventional gender markers actresses could utilize, from Earl's confident stance and unsmiling expression, one hand on the hip and the other holding a cigarette, arm resting casually at mantel level, to Bowman's seated posture and demure smile, ankles crossed modestly, head tilted toward her exposed shoulder. If one were in any doubt regarding the eroticization of the principal boy's physique as a commonplace and expected feature of late Victorian and Edwardian pantomimes, then consider the cover illustration of the December 1912 edition of *The Sketch*, which featured an angular, gawky, knobby-kneed woman dressed in the typical principal boy garb of three-cornered hat, tunic, corset, tights, and boots. The caption for the picture reads "Guaranteed not to be a portrait: The only excuse for abolishing the *Girl Principal Boy*" (figure 24). The dynamic between the two romantic leads, both played by comely women, was sometimes foregrounded, as on the cover of an early twentieth-century playbill from the pantomime *Sleeping Beauty* at the Lyceum Theatre, London, where

MISS ETHEL EARL, PRINCIPAL BOY AT THE PRINCE OF WALES'S THEATRE, BIRMINGHAM

Figure 22. Portrait of principal boy Ethel Earl. *The Sketch: Journal of Art and Actuality*, January 8, 1896, 561.

the two players are depicted in the moment just before they kiss. But more to the point here is how this played out onstage.

The effect of same-sex, cross-dressed flirtation is magnified in Walter Summers's 1897 pantomime *Little Red Riding Hood* from Newcastle-upon-Tyne. The principal boy, Boy Blue, was played by Miss Amy Augarde, but

MISS NELLIE BOWMAN, WHO PLAYS TOM IN "MATCH-BABIES" AT THE GARRICK.

Figure 23. Portrait of principal boy Nellie Bowman. *The Sketch: Journal of Art and Actuality*, December 24, 1902, 374.

Figure 24. "Guaranteed not to be a portrait: The only excuse for abolishing the girl principal boy." Cover of *The Sketch Supplement*, December 25, 1912.

the cast also included a cross-dressed Jack, Tommy Tucker, a host of "village lads," and a chorus of cross-dressed "village sportsmen" (including tradesmen, woodcutters, morris dancers, and Canadians)—a production choice reminiscent of the parade of cross-dressed suitors presented to Princess All-Fair in H. J. Byron's 1869 *Yellow Dwarf;, or, Harlequin Cupid and the King of the Gold Mines*, discussed in chapter 3. The 1897 *Little Red Riding Hood* pantomime was somewhat unusual in that the title character, Red Riding Hood herself, does not ultimately have a romantic match: her story line is resolved once she has been saved from the wolf through the magical but invisible intervention of the Fairy Glow Worm, forgives the wolf, and then learns of and claims her inheritance. The primary romantic pairing in this pantomime is that of Boy Blue (Augarde) and Miss Muffet (played by Marie Montrose). The flirtation begins in scene 1, after Muffet leads a chorus of fairly naughty schoolgirls in an enthusiastic rejection of books and an equally enthusiastic spending spree: "That's it, girls," Muffet declares. "No more work and lots of play, those are the sentiments of Little Miss Muffet. So here goes reading [throws book], writing [throws book], and arithmetic [throws book]. Now, girls, I have a shilling, so we will have some ice cream, some ginger pop, some peppermint drops, some rice pudding, some stick jaw, and a packet of cigarettes, then I shall just have a penny left" (Summers 1897, 17). Although Boy Blue later denies Dame Hubbard's insinuation that he is an amateur when it comes to matters of the heart—he declares that he is "quite a Don Juan among girls"—in his first encounter with Miss Muffet he waxes romantic, while Muffet exhibits cool detachment:

Boy Blue: From the leafy bower of the old oak that overlooks the playground of Dame Hubbard's seminary I have watched you for hours. I have seen you play kiss-in-the-ring and oh! how I have wanted to be there. I have seen you play leap frog, and I have wished mine was the back over which you leaped. I have seen you play marbles, and oh! the horror, one day I saw you swallow one. I have seen you laugh; I have seen you cry; and one day you were having a slide, and I saw you fall. Shall

I forget that fall—never! You have been in my thoughts, sleeping and waking, for
months. Do you know what that means?

Miss Muffet: That I am a woman with a past.

Boy Blue: No; you are a girl, and the girl I love.

Miss Muffet: Love! Don't be silly.

Boy Blue: Love is fatal to us all. You will be my sweetheart?

Miss Muffet: H'm! Yes; until Sunday.

Boy Blue: Only until Sunday?

Miss Muffet: I'm of rather a practical turn of mind, so we will see how we have pro-
gressed by then.

(19)

Both "practical" and clearly experienced when it comes to matters of courtship, Muffet represents a dominant type of pantomime girl: slightly street-
wise, sharp tongued, and unlikely to fall prey to unwelcome male advances.

In Victor Stevens's *Little Red Riding Hood, or The Saucy Squire of Sunnydale*, produced for the Christmas season of 1900 at the Fulham Grand
Theatre, Red Riding Hood's youth and generally acknowledged beauty make
her a focal point of her Granny Hubbard's envy, as well as that of other young
female characters or secondary girls, such as Miss Muffet and Jill (of Jack
and Jill, played by sisters in this production). The opening scene introduces
the audience to Jack (played by one of the Guest sisters), the saucy character of Tommy Tucker (played by Eva Sandford), and a chorus of secondary
cross-dressed "boys":

Tommy Tucker: Oh, don't think for a moment that I am blind to the fact that Sunnydale is famous for its feminine beauty, and I am sure I feel proud to think that I am
surrounded by so many bewitching little sirens. It is also very gratifying to receive
so many tokens of your incessant adoration. I won't say that I am unworthy of it,
that would be unkind to myself. I can only say that I feel sorry for you all girls—my
heart is another's—Don't give way—try and bear up—someday, perhaps, you will

forget the pangs of unrequited love, and forgive one, whose only fault was, that he

was in a position to satisfy the demands of so many dainty little ducklets!

[Walks away with an air of mock-conceit]

Omnes [girls]: Isn't that lovely?

Omnes [boys]: Let's bow to my Lord conceit!

[They do so]

Tommy Tucker: Thank you! [Aside] I suppose they're making game of me.

[Aloud] Alright boys, chaff away—but you wouldn't mind slipping into my shoes.

(15)

The "boys" of Stevens's pantomime engage in flirtatious banter with the "girls" with whom they share the stage, with many opportunities to squeeze and kiss their romantic counterparts. All the while, they seem to be nodding to members of the audience who are invited to project themselves into their subject positions—as "boys," who may be defined as such in either the pantomime sense or the more conventional understanding of the gender marker; as cheeky, confident suitors; as both objects and agents of physical desire.

Winking asides such as these were certainly not appreciated by all members of the English theatergoing public: pantomime of this era did have its detractors, and one of the most frequently cited faults of this theatrical form was its supposed indecency. In an 1881 article titled "Puerile Pantomime," Jeremiah Wiencke questioned the apparent relaxation of standards of theatrical propriety during the Christmas season: "Does it not seem strange, to use no stronger word, that during the portion of the year when more juveniles—say, from six to sixteen—go to theatre than at any other, when it is emphatically 'the children's season,' the performance presented for their delectation should be far more vulgar and debasing than the very worst productions during the regular season?" Wiencke complains of the "parades of scantily-apparelled damsels, slangy and suggestive dialogue, and dances [. . .] by music-hall 'artistes.'" And yet, "at heart we all—old fogies or otherwise—have a sneaking affection for the fairy tales of our boyhood, and would one and all support a good representation of them" (1881, 204). Even in the context of such criticism, Wiencke is mindful of the significance of pantomime's profits to the theatrical world in general, noting that his criticism does not necessarily indicate a need for the abolishment of pantomime. Instead, Wiencke suggests that the "purification" of pantomime could be achieved and viable, that it "would not be a financial mistake" (1881, 206).

Writing one year later, Davenport Adams focused his critique on the sexuality of the pantomime stage, with a focus squarely on bodies and costuming rather than suggestive dialogue and gesture. Adams focuses his complain on the choruses of "girls" and cross-dressed "boys," "the rows of infinitesimally-clothed damsels who [. . .] are not the sort of spectacle to which it is judicious to introduce the 'young idea,' especially when it is at that age at which curiosity concerning the forbidden is beginning to display itself. Over and over again must mothers have blushed (if they were able to do so) at the exhibition of female anatomy to which the 'highly respectable' pantomime has introduced their children" (quoted in Holland 1997, 203). While cross-dressed principal and secondary boys were objects of fascination because their wardrobes erred on the side of scantiness, cross-dressed Dames were and continue to be distinguished by wardrobe excess.

The making of the Dame, those backstage processes of transformation, seems to be a topic of enduring fascination. For instance, in a 1938 photo essay from *Weekly Illustrated* Nelson Keys is followed into his "dressing room at Covent Garden Opera House, where he will appear as 'The Dame' in pantomime Red-Riding Hood" and is watched performing the "metamorphosis of debonair man-about-town into one of the season's funniest characters" ("Pantomime Dame" 1938, 22). Despite such exposés of the Dame-in-the-making, the great quantity of promotional photographs of principal boys and girls does not find a counterpart when it comes to the Dame, unless a production featured a popular performer such as Dan Leno (figure 25) or Harry Randall (figure 26), both of whom had successful careers in music halls as well as seasonal pantomimes. In such photos it is notable that the

Figure 25. Portrait of Dan Leno. *The Sketch: Journal of Art and Actuality,*
January 22, 1896, 663.

Figure 26. Portrait of Harry Randall. *The Sketch: Journal of Art and Actuality*, November 18, 1903, 149.

viewer's gaze is directed primarily to the actors' comic expression or, in some cases, a comically dainty stance rather than the contours of their costumed bodies; onstage, however, pantomime scripts and the "comic business" of physical comedy have the Dame working double time to draw attention to her physical attributes, desire for wealth, and sexual appetite—all of which are as excessive as her wardrobe. Dames then and now seem to steal every scene in which they appear.

In *Little Red Riding Hood, or the Saucy Squire of Sunnydale*, Granny Hubbard is played by Victor Stevens himself, and she is the one character who stands in the way of marriage between Red Riding Hood and Boy Blue. Red Riding Hood's sexual and romantic maturity is seen as a direct threat to Granny's comfort and security, as is made clear in this early scene, as the young lovers ask Granny for her blessing:

Red Riding Hood: There Granny, don't be too hard on Boy Blue, you know, he has
   always loved me—and—I've always loved him.

Granny: Ah, no one ever says anything like that about me.

[Deep sigh.]

Boy Blue: Ah, Granny, everything comes to those who wait!

Granny: Indeed. I've still a chance; for I've waited long enough, goodness knows.

Boy Blue: Look here. To cut a long story short, we make bold to ask your consent to our marriage.

Red Riding Hood: Yes do!

Granny [severely]: Well, I never. Now if someone had asked me to marry, there'd be some sense in it. But you! The preposterousness of the ridiculousness is too absurdless for wordlets.

[…]

Well you shall be married—

Boy Blue & Red Riding Hood: Yes. [Eagerly]

Granny: The same day that I am.

Boy Blue: Oh, that may be never.

Granny: Oh dear no. [Rather conceitedly] I have a presentiment that I shall go off this season.

Red Riding Hood: Oh, would it were to-morrow.

Boy Blue: To-day, you mean. [Artfully]

Granny: Ah, sooner than that—now! [Jumps about excitedly]

Boy Blue: Are you mad?

Granny: Yes, mad with joy, at the thought of it! Ah didn't I jump the day my second proposed to me. And after we were married—He kept one jumping, I can tell you!

(Stevens 1900, 28–29)

Hungry for a new husband and with a preposterously inflated ego, this grandmother is a force to be reckoned with, not an ailing, feeble, elderly woman. While this represents a significant departure from twenty-first-century understandings of "Little Red Riding Hood," and even from the sense of the story that a Victorian writer like Bunce wished to highlight, it is perfectly sensible within the conventions of fairy-tale pantomime. What, then, are we to make of this?

First, this characterization of both of the cross-dressed pantomime characters (principal boy and Dame) as libidinal, desirous, and fully sexed is not unique to *The Saucy Squire of Sunnydale* but is, in fact, quite typical of late Victorian pantomime. If we are to accept the challenge to see gender as performative—not as inherent and biological, nor as a fixed or stable social construction, but instead, as Judith Butler proposes, as "an identity instituted through a stylized repetition of acts [. . .] a continual and incessant *materializing* of possibilities" (1997, 402, 404; emphasis in original)—then pantomime's two cross-dressed parts serve not (or not only) "as a means of coming to terms with women" or "men's assumptions about women" (Mayer 1974, 60). These stock characters can also be seen as situated in a potentially destabilizing metapraxis of desire, all the more powerful because these sexually ambiguous, intentionally unsettling figures are not intended to fool the spectator (to "pass"). Each offers the promise and possibility of safe psychic retreat into essentialism, but in the development of a unique set of performative conventions each also stands as a distinct type, as an alternative to the performances of gender and sexuality in everyday life. Cyril Fletcher, a veteran of the mid-twentieth-century pantomime stage, said in an interview: "The trick is this. The audience must always see the trousers under the skirt—metaphorically speaking" (Grand 1974, 75). Fletcher recognizes the delight and reassurance that audiences seem to derive from the knowledge that the "trousers," functioning here metonymically, are still there under the skirt, that nothing has gone awry in the dominant system of binary gendering. This was as true in the Victorian era as it was in Fletcher's day: a review of an 1880s production of *Jack and the Beanstalk* at the Crystal Palace noted parenthetically that "Jack's mother is a low comedian imperfectly disguised in petticoats," the head of "a most eccentric and peculiar household" ("Two Pantomimes" 1885, 50). If generations of theatergoers have been fascinated by the making of the Dame, they have been equally fascinated and amused by the spectacle of the Dame unmaking or undressing herself.

Given that "Red Riding Hood" is a story preoccupied with clothing and disguise, acts of dressing and undressing, the comic routine of the undressing scene seems a perfect fit, linking established and ongoing thematic concerns in the tale with the performance conventions of pantomime; but the inclusion of this comic routine in specific productions is lost to obscurity, folded into the "comic business" to which scripts and reviews refer but rarely detail. Introduced in the 1880s and generally credited to the comic inventiveness of the legendary Dan Leno —who played Dame Trot in the 1899 *Jack and the Beanstalk* to which I will turn shortly—the undressing scene is one of several comic sketches introduced to audiences in the nineteenth century that persists into the twenty-first (see Senelick 2000, 244). In Elaine Grand's 1974 interview with Fletcher and another veteran Dame, Arthur Askey, the latter proclaimed decisively:

> "You can't have a pantomime without the Dame undressing. [. . .] It takes you about a quarter of an hour just to load up," he explains. "You come in wearing a dressing gown and a big sleeping cap, and under the dressing gown you have a bodice with your false boobies, and you have 12 petticoats, you must have 12 and each one a different colour, and you start stripping them all off so you end up in your drawers and they have a big pair of black hands printed on the seat, and you turn to the audience, and you say—Oh by the way we had the sweep around this morning."
>
> "You get roars with that," agrees Fletcher. "And then you have layers and layers of drawers which you take off, and each pair has simply dreadful messages printed on them. Things like 'No Parking Here,' things like that."

"And the corsets, old whalebone corsets. Don't forget those," Askey adds.

"With a padlock in front. . . . A padlock!"

And the two men dissolve in laughter.

(76–77)

If the ruling aesthetic principle of pantomime is unabashed delight in artifice and excess, then the undressing scene could be taken as a performative emblem of that principle, and it is fitting that it be associated with the character of the Dame.

As Millie Taylor details, the Dame repeatedly draws attention to the frame of performance itself through "comic interaction and asides [. . .] reflexive references to pantomime traditions, the rehearsal period, stage management and technicians, the band and the audience [. . .] and the presence of cross-dressed actors" (14), both establishing a rapport with the audience and celebrating their heightened awareness of the performance form in which they are annual participants. The promise of Granny Hubbard's petticoats is that they will seem to go on forever, a virtual cornucopia of linen, whalebone, and finally a padlock. The treasure that they hide is relatively insignificant; the delight of this routine is in the tease, the surprises revealed layer after layer, and the knowledge that the body underneath will never be exposed. Members of a pantomime audience know where this routine is headed, just as generations of pantomime audiences have known that renditions of "Red Riding Hood" will recast the abrupt and violent conclusion of Perrault's tale so that all will be resolved by the end of the show, as the characters are quickly and unproblematically paired off, only to appear one last time in their fanciest dress, to sing one last rousing chorus before the curtain falls.

Anxieties about the competing ideals of artistry and profit have often played themselves out on the stage—not only indirectly, as characters battle their own desires and ambitions, but also in encounters between these ideals, in personified form. For instance, in Harry McClelland's *Little Red Riding Hood* pantomime from Christmas 1903, the usual opening chorus of townsfolk is preceded by a metapantomimic scene: a chorus of immortals, "fairies and fays" who sing of pleasure and the theater. Prominent among these characters is the Spirit of Pleasure, who declares her disregard for matters of wealth and social class. In typical pantomime fashion, the otherworldly characters can be representative of magical forces of both good and evil, and they speak in rhyming couplets. "Yet in the poor man's cot I'm often seen," sings the Spirit of Pleasure. "Smoothing the path where wealth has never been, / For gold cannot my presence conjure up." The figure named Good Luck quickly switches modes, with the assistance of her sidekick Happy Thought, to remind the Spirit of Pleasure of the necessity of material wealth to their combined venture, which happens to be putting on a show:

> **Good Luck:** But now to business, which is most dramatic.
>
> Being re Pantomime, it's also operatic,
>
> The Demon Millionaire will soon be here,—
>
> **Happy Thought:** He's seeking you!—
>
> **Spirit of Pleasure:** Don't let him find me, dear!
>
> **Good Luck:** Oh, yes, I must, he'll run our pantomime,
>
> So we must pander to him for a time.
>
> We'll play upon him, get him in the mood,
>
> He'll soon produce for us, "Red Riding Hood."
>
> Then for his sins in grinding down the poor,
>
> We'll change him to the Wolf, a sort of bore.
>
> **Spirit of Pleasure:** A "kaffir circus" he's appeared in oft before!
>
> At the "Bear market" he's always at the door!
>
> [Noise heard.]
>
> **Good Luck:** But hush! tis he! the devouring one draws near!

[Enter the Demon Millionaire]

Millionaire: What an enchanting spot? I'm so glad I took
The advice I found in "Dagonet's" guide book!

(McClelland 1903, 6–8)

While the Spirit of Pleasure seeks to avoid the powers of wealth, her exchange with other immortals implies that would-be performers (or the theater world, in general) are necessarily slaves to, or in bed with, "the wolves"—patrons, theatrical producers, the moneyed class—and that the turn-of-the-century audience is well aware of this fact. The Demon Millionaire is a necessary ally of Pleasure, Happy Thought, and Good Luck, although this trio takes on the project of reforming him. Furthermore, he is both an immortal and an embodiment of a recognizable social type, enmeshed in an economic system familiar to any member of the Peckham audience. The Demon Millionaire's wealth is associated with the London Stock Exchange, and he is recognized as part of the "kaffir circus," which at the turn of the century represented any of the jobbers who dealt in South African gold shares (and one usage of the derogatory term for a South African), but a decade earlier the phrase was associated with a market crash, when more than £1 million of inflated gold valuation was wiped out in the span of seven months. This character has sought out an "enchanting spot"—the theater's stage, doubling as fairy bower—and he also seems to be slumming in the world of pantomime and the world of the theater, as some members of the Peckham audience may have been. The fairy bower is not, after all, his usual domain: he requires a guidebook to reach it.[3]

As this 1903 pantomime suggests, a seasonal pantomime is big business, a key component of British theatrical management then as it continues

---

3   The reference to "Dagonet" seems a likely allusion to the journalistic writings of George Robert Sims, who wrote of conditions in the London slums. These include a popular 1870s ballad, "Christmas Day in the Workhouse," from *Dagonet Ballads* (1881) and works like *Dagonet Abroad* (1895). Sims was well connected in the world of theater and was the author of many successful plays (melodramas, burlesques, and several Drury Lane pantomimes).

to be. Writing in 1997, Peter Holland echoes Charles Dickens's words—from almost exactly a century earlier—noting that pantomime stands as "the single most popular form of British theatre, the cornerstone of the British theatrical economy—its takings subsidizing many theatres' work for the rest of the year" (Holland 1997, 195). In addition to professional productions, pantomime has proven a great favorite with amateur troupes, school groups, charity groups, and so on. Popular internet vendor the Pantomime Store can promise to provide both professional and amateur companies with "all your Pantomime Requirements," from scripts and musical scores to rentals of a confetti cannon (£35), a bubble machine (£25), a battery-operated Wee Willie Winkie Candlestick (a mere £4), a medium-size Cinderella coach (£100) or the coveted deluxe coach, and a Large Motorised Beanstalk (£250) ("Pantomime Special Props"). The radical decontextualization and commodification of fairy-tale icons as pantomime prop rentals is humorous but also attests to the ongoing popularity of this seasonal tradition (the fact that there is a market for such things) and the intrinsic appeal of pantomime materials (the "goods" involved in these theatrical productions). A preoccupation with pantomime as spectacle, with the challenges and delights of its props and scenery, and with the costumed, exaggerated, patently artificial bodies of the cross-dressed players, characterizes reception of pantomime (as entertainment and as a vehicle for social commentary) from the nineteenth century to the present day.

Britannia in tights: "Jack and the Beanstalk"

Seasonal pantomimes have maintained a prominent place in the larger theatrical economies in which they are situated, and in the nineteenth century we can see that pantomime and the book trade also had a dynamic relationship—sometimes working in tandem to generate profit and cultivate an audience for both fairy-tale-themed performances and fairy-tale-themed reading material. The field-based tale collections that were gaining popularity at that time—imported, translated, framed as reflections of foreign national character—may seem to be situated outside that economic network of mutually supportive commodities, but there are some interesting continuities between such folklore books and the fairy-tale pantomimes they often referenced, obliquely or dismissively. Like the field-based collections I explored in *National Dreams* (2003), pantomime served constructions of Englishness in complicated ways, both drawing from "foreign" theatrical and narrative traditions and finding in these moves opportunities for reflection on English national character. The potential of a pantomime, based on an English tale and featuring characters in British military uniform, lent itself particularly well to various forms of social and political commentary at the turn of the century. Once again, matters of gender, sexuality, profit, and power intersect and overlap.

On Boxing Day 1899, a pantomime version of *Jack and the Beanstalk* opened at the Drury Lane theater. This production is renowned for explicit references to the Boer War that had begun only a few months earlier; it would seem to represent a stage counterpart to a phenomenon Brian Szumsky has observed in a century of print versions of the story, from Benjamin Tabart's edition of 1807 through Edith Nesbit's version of 1908. Szumsky argues that such "Jack and the Beanstalk" texts reverberate with nationalist and colonialist discourse—thematic preoccupations with poverty and class struggle, commodities rendered magical, the conquest of new lands as a source of transformative wealth, and so on. He suggests that a critical history of the tale's "versions and variants [. . .] can be read as the history of literary response to sociopolitical circumstances," most especially those shaped by "colonial practice and ideology" (1999, 12), and he provides insightful close readings of many print texts to explore this argument. Nevertheless, there is one thread of Jack's textual history that doesn't figure prominently in Szumsky's account, nor in his approach to textual analysis: comedy. As Iona Opie and Peter Opie document, the story of Jack's ultimate defeat of a wealthy giant has a long history as burlesque, including the "tragicomic farce" based on the related story of "Jack the Giant Killer," staged at

Haymarket Theatre in 1730 (1980, 60–61).[4] As a pantomime, this history dates to 1819, when *Jack and the Beanstalk; or, Harlequin and the Ogre* was first staged at Drury Lane (Pickering 1993, 113). The brand of buffoonery associated with early nineteenth-century harlequinades had transformed by the end of the century, as a music-hall sensibility (and music-hall performers) came to dominate pantomime. But both traditions—"Jack and the Beanstalk" as politically inflected fairy tale and the story as burlesque comedy—resonate in the 1899 pantomime I would like to consider here, a production that Jim Davis recently discussed in his examination of Drury Lane's annual pantomimes under the management of Sir Augustus Harris and his successors (2010, 101–5). The perspectives on war and empire offered by this pantomime *Jack* are both more complicated and more ambivalent than they may initially appear.

As we have seen, English pantomime has both an international history and the status of national institution: it emerged from the adaptation and extension of Italian commedia dell'arte and French performance forms, and by the nineteenth century was considered to be both uniquely and characteristically *English*. Mark Connelly has traced the ways in which nineteenth-century pantomime served as outlets for social critique, reflections on national history and national character, and satirical representations of political allies and foes—all set in a "jolly and festive atmosphere" that encouraged conviviality rather than fractiousness, at least among the audience members (1999, 47). As Connelly observes, the topical allusions that characterize pantomime dialogue and song from at least the mid-eighteenth century also celebrate imperial ambitions and achievements, from the battle of Quebec to the Crimean war and beyond. In his landmark study of early nineteenth-century pantomime, David Mayer considered a range of military references—celebration of British naval strength, lampooning of the

---

4   William J. Burling's *Checklist of New Plays and Entertainments on the London Stage, 1700–1737* lists several early *Jack* comedies in the 1720s and 1730s, based on the related story of "Jack the Giant Killer" (1993, 112, 136).

less impressive army, and, during the final decade of the war with Napoleon, satirical treatment of a conflict that was, in Mayer's words, "unpopular, alarming, and distant" (1969, 270).

In the decades that separated the end of the conflicts with Napoleon and the end of the century, Britain's imperial and military strength reached new heights: as Steve Attridge argues, despite the army's continued inferiority, as compared to the navy, Britons were able to "wage war [in Africa and India] on a shoestring, bullets against spears, soldiers against mostly disunited African and Indian tribesmen" (2003, 1). But the conflict in southern Africa between the British and two independent Boer republics did not follow the model of earlier imperial campaigns. The Boer War would be a much lengthier, messier, costlier, and bloodier conflict than expected when it began in October 1899. The war generated extensive and unprecedented written and pictorial coverage in the British press; this press coverage offered examples both of the expected "bluster of imperialist language" but also increasing "anxiety and introspection" (3).

As the pantomime season began in 1899, the British forces in southern Africa had already encountered some unexpected setbacks: they were facing off against civilian militia—farmers and hunters who drew on superlative riding skills, their experiences in previous conflicts with the British, and what would prove to be superior weaponry. These conditions posed challenges to assumptions about the scale, duration, and difficulty of this new war. When Arthur Collins's production of *Jack and the Beanstalk* opened on Boxing Day 1899, the devastating losses of what was known as Black Week were very fresh in public consciousness: during the week of December 10–17, British forces suffered three successive staggering defeats, and nearly three thousand men had been killed, wounded, or captured. Press coverage of Black Week occurred exactly when newspapers and periodicals normally would have been featuring articles, photographs, and advertisements related to the season's upcoming pantomimes. In fact, when my own research on British pantomime led me to chronological perusal of *The Sketch: Journal of*

Art and Actuality, I discovered that in 1899—as military conflict loomed in South Africa—the usually abundant coverage of Christmas pantomimes experienced a precipitous decline.[5] In addition to a Christmas supplement, *The Sketch*'s December and January issues typically included copious pantomime-related images: photographs of pantomime players, pantomime-related cartoons and caricatures, engravings depicting pantomime set designs, costumes and audiences, and so on. In some sense, the English seasonal obsession with cross-dressed fairy-tale heroes, spectacular processions of nursery rhyme characters, elaborate stage mechanics, and the like must have felt distasteful to a readership anxious about the prospect of a second Boer War; but while periodicals like *The Sketch* may have temporarily diluted their coverage of the pantomime season, the war did in fact became part of the fabric of this performance tradition. British pantomime already had a long tradition of topical references and localized humor, and in the 1899–1900 holiday season, fairy-tale pantomime served as a remarkably rich medium for reflection on Britain's military and imperial positioning. Situated at the intersection of fairy tale and war we find a cross-dressed figure standing boldly with hand on hip: in this case, one of the most important roles in any late Victorian pantomime, the principal boy.

Nearly forty years ago, David Mayer argued that principal boys offered late nineteenth-century audiences opportunities to both explore and contain cultural anxieties about female sexuality (Mayer 1974). More recently, Caroline Radcliffe has underscored the capacity of the principal boy, as object of male gaze, to "reinforce interpolated gender roles" (2010, 122). As Peter Holland argues, the role is something more than an excuse to reveal a woman's

5   Established in 1893, *The Sketch: Journal of Art and Actuality* was one of three popular pictorial periodicals operated by the Illustrated London News Company. Editor C. K. Shorter sought to differentiate *The Sketch* from its parent publication by defining its audience as both youthful (in spirit if nothing else) and interested in news and the latest trends in the arts, fashion, and high society (Law 2009, 577). The matters of perceived interest to *The Sketch*'s readership included pantomime, which received copious coverage (both written and photographic).

legs, thighs, and bum onstage: conventions of performance—including the principal's boy typical posture (the wide stance, hand on hip, continual thigh slapping)—imbue her with "a remarkable complex of gender markers" (1997, 197). Eroticized and regarded as potentially titillating, at least by a good portion of the audience, the late Victorian principal boy possessed an appeal that was not necessarily limited to heterosexual male viewers. The boy is at once fully in charge of the stage and infinitely desirable in a cultural milieux that did not typically seem to associate ideal femininity with mastery and assertiveness; the principal boy could be seen as existing *outside* of established gender categories, even as s/he performed in exaggerated fashion some of the markers of both normative femininity and masculinity. For Holland, this role serves to highlight some of the "paradoxes of gender": "in performing maleness, the Principal Boy both defines herself as not male, and in addition defines male behavior as not male" (Holland 1997, 195). Whether defeating villains, introducing a parade of national "types," or leading the audience in song, the cross-dressed principal boy *also* could serve as a focal point for fantasies of Englishness. Extending Holland's logic, one might posit that this pantomime role had the potential to highlight the performative nature of national identities as well as gendered ones. More specifically, I would like to suggest that the principal boy's ambiguous relation to gender categories positions her as an apt embodiment of the ambitions, desires, and anxieties of the Empire at the fin-de-siècle.

The 1899 Drury Lane pantomime featured an Australian woman, the popular operetta singer and Drury Lane regular Nellie Stewart, cast as England's beloved Jack during this time of political crisis. Despite the fact that Stewart was ill on opening night, when understudy Mollie Lowell took the part of Jack, she was depicted on posters and playbills, reportedly resuming the part later in the run and remaining strongly associated with it. Following the December 26 premiere, *The Times* of London praised this production of *Jack and the Beanstalk* first and foremost for its Jack and the understudy who "played and sang and looked her part." The pantomime was then praised for its "distinctly commendable beanstalk, a cleverly-contrived and imposing piece of stage machinery"; and then for its "giant, rejoicing in the appropriate name of Blunderboer, who is nominally Mr. T. Hendon, but for the most part [. . .] pasteboard and buckram. He has the features of the conventional Boer of caricature; he wears in his bandolier cartridges carrying a bullet of about half a pound of avoirdupois, and his mighty chest heaves up and down several feet when he breathes" ("Boxing Day" 1899, 9). A good principal boy and impressive props were of such central importance to late nineteenth-century pantomime conventions that they were frequently foregrounded in reviews, but the most memorable point in the performance, for *The Times'* reviewer and others, was unquestionably the military scene, which drew on *both* these assets, featuring both the principal boy and spectacular stagecraft.

As *The Times'* review details and a playbill for the production highlighted (figure 27), "Blunderboer lies prostrate on the stage, [and] miniature British troops, some in the scarlet of infantry, some in khaki, some gunners, some bluejackets with a machine-gun, some mounted infants in the strict sense of the word, and some Australian Lancers throng the stage and walk over the body of the Giant. [. . .] On other nights, as last night, there will be enthusiasm when the childish soldiers [Jack by their side] raise their helmets on their rifles and 'Rule, Britannia' is raised" ("Boxing Day" 1899, 9). Likewise, on December 27 *The Sketch* also ran a review that lauded the theatrical spectacle of "a mighty army of British and Colonial troops, each one realistically uniformed and wonderfully trained" ("Old Drury's" 1899, 382). It is this moment, this comic and rousing enactment of a fantasy of British conquest, that has given the 1899 *Jack and the Beanstalk* a place in pantomime history.[6] And this is the scene to which we will return in a moment.

---

6   Interestingly, it is another moment from the production that has entered the annals of cinema history: music-hall comedian and pantomime clown Herbert Campbell, who was featured as Jack's younger brother in the 1899 pantomime, made a short film for the British Biograph and Mutoscope Company, also in

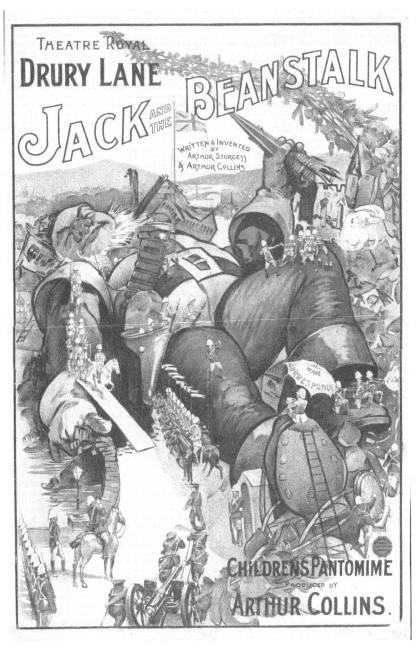

Figure 27. Poster advertising *Jack and the Beanstalk* at the Theatre Royal, Drury Lane, 1899. © Victoria and Albert Museum, London.

The events of the early months of the Boer War and of Black Week, specifically, resonate in the Drury Lane *Jack and the Beanstalk*, resulting in what Jim Davis has characterized as theatrical expressions of "patriotic frenzy" and "anti-Boer propaganda" (2010, 103). But in the midst of patriotic flourish one can also detect ambivalence and uncertainty, concerning affairs both domestic and military. The script of the Drury Lane production, which was sold during the run of the show, offers an important but incomplete document of words and movements on the stage.[7] Also of interest here is the detailed account of a performance published almost fifty years later by the theater historian Walter MacQueen-Pope. In his nostalgic account of the late Victorian and Edwardian theater culture of his own childhood, *Carriages at Eleven* (1947), MacQueen-Pope devotes a chapter to the Drury Lane theater. That chapter includes a detailed account of this very production, told from the perspective of a child audience member and narrated, rather curiously, in second person—"you go," "you see," "you think," "you want," and so on—positioning it less as personal memoir than as a kind of shared experiential history. MacQueen-Pope's description of the Boer War–era *Jack and the Beanstalk* may not stand as hard-and-fast evidence of what "actually" occurred onstage and in the minds of audience members in late December 1899, but it offers an accounting of that specific performance *and* of a way of receiving pantomime that presumably made sense to

----

1899, titled *Herbert Campbell as Little Bobbie*. In this early example of a film comedy "facial"—presenting "the spectacle of a facial close-up, projected to a monstrous size on the screen" (Popple and Kember 2004, 91)—Campbell (re)enacts a pantomime feast, gorging himself on food and drink. See the discussion of this film by Simon Popple and Joe Kember (2004, 90–93).

7   It is worth noting that in addition to the souvenir script this production is associated with another print artifact (and yet another example of early cross-marketing in the history of the fairy tale): an illustrated storybook titled *The True Story of Jack and the Beanstalk, A Gift from the Drury Lane Theatre, Christmas 1899*—digitized by the University of Florida Library and accessible at ufdc .ufl.edu/UF00088951/00001.

a mid-twentieth-century adult readership who shared memories of the period and possibly of that production. In other words, MacQueen-Pope is himself constructing a fantasy about an earlier era and about this popular theatrical form, but it is one that is positioned as collective, as shared, rather than idiosyncratic. Close reading of dialogue and examination of the adaptation of two standard parts of pantomime performance in this production can help to highlight the intersection of erotic ambiguity and political uncertainty.

The first aspect of the production worth considering in this regard is the opening chorus, the part of a pantomime that conventionally serves two functions: it begins a performance with the spectacle of large numbers of players onstage, often set in a marketplace or town square, and it conveys "happiness, equilibrium and a sense of community" (M. Taylor 2007, 177). In short, the opening chorus can establish the overriding tone of the performance, no matter what trials the protagonists may face midway. The 1899 *Jack* includes a seemingly conventional chorus scene of this kind: set at Dame Trot's dairy, this scene introduces a jolly chorus of washerwomen, singing about work to be done, and another chorus of chimney sweeps, lamenting the coldness of their suitors. As MacQueen-Pope recalls, "Never were there such gaily dressed or more beautiful customers as the village lads and lasses who trip in to buy milk" (1947, 95). But, importantly, the dairy scene is *not* the scene with which the performance began: instead, this production—like the 1804 *Cinderella* discussed in chapter 2—has a "prologue" set in the magical realm. What is unusual in this case is that the prologue also includes a chorus of players, and it is one that stands in sharp contrast to the washerwomen and chimney sweeps who would fill the stage minutes later. The opening scene is one of labor and lamentation, far less happy than that situated at Trot's Dairy.

Scene 1 is set at "The Roots of the Magic Beanstalk," a busy construction site for Gnome and Co., Contractors. A chorus of gnome workers is first encountered singing the praises of their pork-and-beans lunch, but their respite from their labors is short lived. A gong signals the return to work and their sinister overseer, the Demon Worm, demands a progress report. The collectivity staged here is not that of the typical jovial villagers but of alienated workers: the gnome laborers (who literally work "for beans") are reported to be "very discontented" for "they want to know" what the beanstalk they are building "is for; and where it is to go; / Who ordered such a monstrous plant; and why." The Demon Worm evades their questions, and tries to mollify the crowd by talking about their upcoming payday (Sturgess and Collins 1899–1900, 16). Nevertheless, the Demon Worm also lets it slip that the project is being financed by (literal) giants; upon hearing this news, the gnome foreman wants to resign immediately. Adding insult to injury, the Demon Worm explains that not only are they laboring on behalf of giants, but that there has been a kind of corporate takeover: the firm is now to be known as "Giant Blunderbore [*sic*] and Worm." This newly minted business partnership is associated with a lamentable deterioration of business ethics: they "sell bad actions—merely for a song," and even "tried to sell an Army from our shore" (16). Alienation of common workers and corruption at the corporate level are established as the underpinning to the pantomime's plot and also as forces to be reckoned with at the level of national defense: they are threats to home and country.

Given the thematic concerns established in the opening scenes of this *Jack and the Beanstalk*, it is perhaps unsurprising to find that another classic pantomime performance convention—that of the procession—also takes on a military tone. Elaborately costumed, visually impressive processions that call out to audience members' repertoires of historical, cultural, and theatrical knowledge are characteristic of Victorian pantomime, as mentioned in chapter 3. Noteworthy processions were also one of many trademark forms of spectacle developed by Augustus Harris, manager of Drury Lane from 1879 to his death in 1896; the tradition was carried forward by his successor, Arthur Collins, the producer of this pantomime (see J. Davis 2010, 100–1). The unifying themes of processions were wide ranging; for example, an 1885 pantomime of this tale featured an "inevitable procession" of well-known pantomime characters: "Crusoe and Friday, Ali Baba and his Ass, Dick Whittington and his Milestone, Bluebeard, Cinderella, and all the rest of them" ("Two Pantomimes" 1885, 50). Michael Booth cites the 106 Shakespearean characters who marched across the stage in an 1889 *Jack and the Beanstalk*; twenty-nine nursery-rhyme and fairy-tale characters and twenty-one popular sports made up the two processions of the pantomime *Little Bo-Peep, Little Red Riding Hood, and Hop o' My Thumb*; a procession of all the kings and queens of England from William I onward was featured in an 1893 *Robinson Crusoe*; and so on (1991, 34–45). As I mentioned in my initial description of this pantomime, the spectacular defeat of the giant Blunderboer is the scene most often detailed in contemporaneous reviews and the scene that has earned this particular production some retrospective notoriety, and it includes a notorious and remarkable procession.

In this climactic scene, Jack has rescued family and friends, leading them back down the beanstalk to the garden of the home he shares with his mother, Dame Trot. He fells the beanstalk with his magic sword and the giant tumbles to the ground. MacQueen-Pope recounts:

> The lights go up again. For the first time you see the whole Giant. He lies there, dead and helpless, occupying the entire stage, big as it is. Everyone cheers and by now your hands are sore with clapping.
>
> Everyone climbs over him. Jack delivers an oration from his chest, clasping the Princess to his ample bosom. The King bestows a blessing and even you realize that there is every likelihood of his marrying into the family by wedding Dame Trot.
>
> Then a thoughtful soul opens the pockets of the Giants tunic, and out of them, oh, crowning glory, comes the entire British Army, in khaki (a novel sight then)—horse, foot and artillery—even nurses, whilst Jack waves a Union Jack and the whole crowded theatre goes mad with delight. You are quite speechless.
>
> (1947, 98–99)

The pantomime moves toward closure, with the satisfying defeat of the giant but also the romantic pairings-off of cross-cast characters to their predictable counterparts. But the enthusiasm of the audience is roused specifically by the sight of the procession of child players, dressed as "the entire British Army" and emerging from the pockets of the fallen giant. This is interesting in several ways, not least of which is the grounding of this climactic moment in a military frame of reference, one that occupied the minds of many Britons and was fundamental to the production as a whole. The fact that the procession associated with this scene has remained prominent in pantomime history suggests that it was especially resonant: in this case, it literalized and mocked South African president Paul Kruger's infamous boast that he could fit the little British army in his pocket. The spectacle of a slain Boer giant and a triumphant British military (in miniature), all located in an English cottage garden, speaks to anxieties about the war, seen through the comic lens of pantomime. It inspires "mad delight" in the audience.

It is also notable that this scene of triumph is the first one in which the foe, the giant, is seen in his entirety by the audience. Like the gnome workers from the opening scene, the audience has not been privy to the big picture, so to speak. Part of the satisfaction in this scene, as MacQueen-Pope suggests, is precisely this revelation, the exposure and defeat of shadowy forces of corruption against which the pantomime's hero has been struggling. The felling of beanstalk and giant alike is a triumph for the mortal characters in the pantomime, one shared by the audience, but it also represents a kind of victory for the magical realm featured in the prologue—the gnome laborers who reluctantly did the bidding of the threatening but unseen giants. The implied link between these two scenes is strengthened by the presence in each one of a "little" chorus: the child players cast as the British army *here* and who also played the gnomes in the very first scene of the pantomime. Seen in this light, the giant represents not only the Boers (or Kruger, specifically), he also embodies the larger project of imperialism toward which common Britons were asked to labor and for which they were losing their lives.

The agent of the chorus's liberation and the audience's mad delight is none other than Jack, our principal boy. MacQueen-Pope's account of the reception of this cross-dressed figure highlights both her potential erotic appeal to heterosexual male viewers and also a range of alternative perspectives, ones associated with adult female and child audience members, who have generally been overlooked in analyses of pantomime's cross-dressed players. And so we return to scene 2, the point at which the audience was introduced to Dame Trot and Jack's brother Bobbie (played by popular comic duo Dan Leno and Herbert Campbell), as well as the two mortal choruses (played by adults). It is at this point that the principal boy's entrance was eagerly anticipated, as described rhapsodically by MacQueen-Pope:

> But where is Jack, the hero? He is what you want to see. A fanfare from the band, a dashing in of the villagers so that the vast stage is crowded with hundreds of people, a quick, brisk, triumphant march—and Jack is here. He is a likely lad with a remarkably well developed chest and legs. He is not like any lad of your acquaintance, with his majestic stride, his masses of golden hair, his gleaming eyes, his silken legs. You hear one of the men behind you say, "Nellie Stewart is stunning as a boy," and you are conscious of a weight upon you. It is caused by your Daddy and your Uncle James leaning forward to see better, with their opera glasses glued to their eyes. You catch a glimpse of your mother glancing with raised eyebrows at your aunt. Nellie Stewart—Jack? Not to you. This is no man, no woman, no girl, no boy. This is indeed Jack the Giant Killer, the very personification of the hero of the fairy tale—having no sex and no earthly counterpart. [. . .] You accept Nellie Stewart as your ideal Jack. And that is that. (1947, 96)

Seen in terms of a heterosexual male gaze, the one so often assumed in theater history scholarship—and represented here, more or less, by Daddy and Uncle James—the figure commanding the stage is identified *as* Nellie

Stewart and not as Jack, and she or he or they or ze is "stunning," an erotic delight. Yet for the implied speaker and, by extension, the implied reader of this account, the principal boy is both different from other boys—*neither*, in fact, a boy nor a girl, a man nor a woman—but otherworldly and "ideal" within the frame of pantomime performance. Importantly, there is a third perspective wrapped into this evocative account of audience response: that of adult women. Mother's raised eyebrows and her moment of tacit understanding with her sister are open to interpretation: a knowing glance can suggest their shared understanding of Nellie Stewart's mesmeric effect on children and most especially their husbands, but it need not be limited to this kind of androcentric reading. It may also indicate their own shared interest in that compelling and powerful cross-dressed figure on the stage, for whom the audience (women included) is cheering. So what, then, does such a cheer signify? MacQueen-Pope's imaginative re-creation of this moment suggests the extent to which the collective delight of a pantomime audience can signal multiple forms of pleasure, inspired by a single sight perceived variously.

Striding boldly across the stage and across the lines of conventional gender performance, Jack is at that moment an emblem of this most English of performance forms, consolidating a sense of national identity even as she transgresses boundaries. In this sense she *is* Britannia, in both her aspirations to imperial prominence and her attempt to resolve the threats to stable identity associated with those global ambitions. The principal boy personifies a fantasy that "has no earthly counterpart," which is therefore unattainable but is no less magnetic, desirable, and rousing for that. Who better to wield the magic sword and the Union Jack, which seem to promise, at least within the confines of the theater and at least on one level, to bring order, confidence, and sense back to a troubled world? On the other hand, it strikes me as important to read this iconic scene in the context of the larger pantomime performance, which is one that has been framed by a cynical portrait of power structures, a not-so-subtle critique of the marriage of military, imperialist, and industrial capitalist forces. We might then read Jack's defeat of the giant and release of the British military not as simple patriotic flourish but in terms of the principal boy's status as both embodiment and agent of magical transformation. Jack is capable of inspiring multiple forms of desire and admiration, turning bloody conflict into festive spectacle, beleaguered troops into cheerful children, the imposing specter of a military foe or of the imperial project itself into an impressive bit of stage property—a slain giant from which all can be freed.

Seen from the broader perspective of fairy-tale history, not just from the narrow confines of the late Victorian era, or the received narrative about the Victorians' moralizing impulse in fairy tale and children's entertainment, the complexity of this moment is neither aberrant nor surprising. Instead, it may suggest that the centuries-long tradition of ironic, self-aware, double-voiced, and potentially or subtly transgressive uses of the genre was alive and well in Victorian England. It may have been treated as invisible by recent generations of scholars, but it was far from marginalized in its day.

Afterpiece

Dreams of Pantomime

NINETEENTH-CENTURY WRITING ABOUT pantomime, like nineteenth-century writing about folktales, is peppered with references to dreams and dreaming. Folklore enthusiasts of the period often experimented with the problematic notion that oral traditional tales represent a kind of collective imagining, a form of "national dream" (to borrow George Webbe Dasent's evocative phrase; see Schacker 2003, 117–37). Alternatively, they invoked images of "sunset dreams" ("Fairy Tales as Literature" 1898, 45), a domain both natural and elusive. Those who used the trope in relation to pantomime tended to alternate between invocation of shared experiences of stage magic and the realm of individual memories and longings. For example, the lead essay in the periodical *The Theatre* for New Year's Day 1881, offers recollections of a festive theater season just passed, the highlights of which would have been familiar to the periodical's readership. The essay is titled "A Dream of Christmas," with that reference to dreaming left unexplained, reminiscent of earlier representations of the Christmas season as one that was dominated by thoughts or "dreams" of pantomime ("Edinburgh Drama" 1831, 7). In this case, a review of the past month's theatrical offerings leads the writer considerably further back in time, into what would seem to be a very individual frame of reference: tender memories of his own child self, "bewildered with delight at the contemplation of my first pantomime, a child of eight years old" ("Dream of Christmas" 1881, 3). These reflections on the pleasures of fairy-tale pantomime in one writer's childhood suggest that the form was indeed widely known and memorable: part of that individual's own personal "dream" of Christmas but one that simultaneously was assumed to play a part in every English adult's dream-like recollection of wintery childhood evenings at the theater. Importantly, in cases like this one, such youthful experiences are given voice only by adults, for whom the magic and transience of theatrical performance, like childhood, seems to inspire both awe and a bittersweet sense of nostalgia. The dream of Christmas is a dream of pantomime and also a dream of childhood, both personal and collective.

David Mayer and other historians of eighteenth- and early nineteenth-century theater have demonstrated that pantomime of that earlier period was a significant form of performance for adult audiences. But despite the fact that most of the audience for pantomime in the early nineteenth century would have been well beyond childhood, reviews from that period often seem to assume that their (adult) readership would in fact associate the genre with children. For instance, Covent Garden's 1821 *Harlequin and Mother Bunch; or, The Yellow Dwarf* was praised for its ability to afford "no less amusement to the young personages for whose gratification it was principally intended, than to the more aged part of the audience, who, as a holiday indulgence, had brought their juniors to witness it." The reviewer suggests that adult enjoyment would have been rooted in memories of youth, triggered by a story line and theatrical form known since infancy. A performance like the 1821 *Harlequin and Mother Bunch*

> is founded on one of those tales which, though they have neither incidents, language, nor even probability to recommend them, always incite in us a vivid interest from their association with the pursuits and pleasures of our days of childhood. Indeed, it is owing to the recollections so excited in our minds, aided as they are by the delight which we derive from seeing the image of our own feelings at those early

years reflected back to us from the happy countenances of the smiling children around us. ("Covent-Garden Theatre" 1821, 2)

While many adults may have rationalized their attendance of the pantomime in terms of seasonal indulgence of children's desires, the experience afforded them particular forms of pleasure—and reinforced a vision of these entertainments that served constructions of childhood and Englishness itself.

In the course of the century, pantomime came to epitomize—at least imaginatively—the ideal of a truly democratized form of popular entertainment and one that bridged the divide between age groups and between theatrical experiences, past and present. A pair of illustrations from the December 27, 1893, edition of *The Sketch*, referenced earlier in this study, indicate popular awareness of the form's multigenerational audience; they also highlight pantomime's appeal to specifically adult sensibilities and fantasies and suggest that the notion of the pantomime "dream" can signal something other than nostalgia or fond memories of childhood. The first illustration depicts observers observed, "Boxing Night at the Theatre, from Various Points of View" (see figure 2), and here readers of the periodical *The Sketch* are invited to consider strata of the pantomime audience: working-class theatergoers lolling in the gallery; the bourgeois family, dominated by a white-bearded paterfamilias, in the boxes; and the world-weary ladies and gentlemen of the stalls. If one wonders what might be on the minds of the latter audience members, the facing-page illustration offers some clarification. As we have seen, the featured gentleman's "Dream of Pantomime" (see figure 19) does not transport him back to childhood wonder or to a Ruskinian utopia of simple and wholesome town life. Instead, the dream features a virtual orgy of fairy attendants, as they pour his champagne, loosen his clothes (note the suspenders and tie removed), whisper in his ears, and offer him coins and banknotes. This decadent, materialistic, hedonistic dream vision is a far cry from the image of pantomime as portal to sentimental visions of childhood pleasure and is strikingly different from current conceptions of the fairy tale's imaginative potential. While such pantomime dreams may seem more closely aligned with the experiences that John Ruskin described as nightmarish, they were framed neither as unusual nor, in this particular case, as problematic. In the reception of the fairy tale as pantomime, the boundaries of class, age, and propriety have often been remarkably permeable.

It is has become something of a cliché to observe that forms of children's entertainment signify differently to adults than they do to the children at whom they are ostensibly directed. Following that logic, one might be tempted to conclude that fairy-tale pantomime simply triggered quite distinct forms of fantasy for distinct sectors of the audience, that the references to sex and money were there solely for the amusement or titillation of adults. But it is important to note that pantomime's grounding in worldly matters and desires, including economic ones, was not limited to representations of an adult experience of pantomime. For instance, the title character of Ellis Davis's fantasy novel for children, *Annie's Pantomime Dream* (1877), finds herself in a topsy-turvy world populated by pantomime characters, ruled by King Gold and a court of sentient coins. The novel's narrator offers little to no description of the Drury Lane production that inspired Annie's flight of fancy, noting only that "the pantomime was like most others, based upon a fairy tale, and it had the usual amount of grotesque absurdity, sportive fancy, and beautiful scenery in it" (14). In a striking example of narrative interpellation, the focus shifts to the book's child audience and suggests that the fantasy world in which money reigns supreme is one to which every child deserves entry: "You, dear little readers," the narrator continues, "have, we hope, seen many such, and if not, be very good, and mamma and papa will take you next Christmas" (1877, 15). In terms of the Victorian fairy tale, one must account for pantomime—grotesque, absurd, fanciful, beautiful, risqué, tremendously and unabashedly profitable, source of sensory, sensual, and monetary fantasy—as a powerful and nearly ubiquitous means of transmission, for adults as well as children. Pantomime provides a complex intermedial backdrop for the fairy-tale texts with which contemporary readers are so much more familiar.

The tradition of associating pantomime and the genre of the fairy tale, more generally, with children and childhood (real and imagined) is powerful, sometimes obfuscating abundant evidence of adult interest in the form, but it is neither "natural" nor inevitable. In the field of children's literature, one can detect a retrospective attempt to radically differentiate audiences and forms. Take, for example, Peter Hollindale's description of pantomime in the entry "Drama" in the *International Companion Encyclopedia of Children's Literature* (1996). Hollindale traces a now-familiar history of modern British pantomime structure from its eighteenth-century roots to its nineteenth-century focus on "fairy stories." He highlights the moment that has been considered a watershed in historical accounts of pantomime, from David Mayer's landmark 1969 study, *Harlequin in His Element: The English Pantomime, 1806–1836*, onward: the relaxation of the theater licensing laws in 1843. Hollindale relates this development in the regulation of entertainment directly to the emergence of pantomime as both "complex" and characterized by unspecified "ambiguities." He writes: "On the one hand, pantomimes became specifically associated with Christmas, and closely rooted in local communities for whom they were specially written. As Christmas entertainments they naturally became established as performances for children. On the other hand, the parallel and similar form of the 'burlesque' was emphatically *not* for children, but unavoidably affected pantomime conventions." The notion that Christmas entertainment was "naturally" geared toward children overlooks far lengthier historical associations between the disorderly conduct of adults and Yule, a season of sanctioned indulgence and general misrule. Hollindale also seems to echo Charlotte Yonge's complaints about a burlesque sensibility infecting both fairyland and childhood. Indeed, he goes on to cite Victorian complaints about music-hall influences and vulgarity, critiques of the kind that I have discussed in earlier chapters, bemoaning the fact that "over a hundred years later, pantomime is still for many children the main or only family experience of theatre, but it habitually displays the same uncomfortable blend of fairy tale, burlesque, and risqué music hall turns" (212). For whom, exactly, is this blend is "uncomfortable," and why? Music-hall performance styles and stage tricks play a significant part in the "dream factory" of early British cinema (Chanan 1996, 127–55), and they also influenced early French films like those of Georges Méliès, based on fairy tales and approached with a comic sensibility (see Zipes 2011, esp. 31–48). Nevertheless, pantomime seems to continue to challenge dominant conceptions of the fairy tale as well as those of childhood itself.

My work in the field of fairy-tale studies has been motivated in large part by a sense that no matter how prominently the genre and ideas about it now figure in popular consciousness, there are compelling chapters in the history of the fairy tale generally ignored, forgotten, or repressed. For instance, the "traditional fairy tale" (an amorphous category in itself) is often imagined to be socially and sexually prescriptive, sober in tone and intent, and moralistic in function—a baseline against which modern and postmodern tales can play with humor, transgression, self-referentiality and even self-parody. My work on the histories of folklore and the fairy tale and my own fascination with fairy-tale pantomime—the latter critically neglected by both folklorists and fairy-tale scholars but central to this study—reflect and have served to reinforce my conviction that these apparently postmodern characteristics actually have been part of fairy-tale history for centuries.

A legacy of folklore fieldwork likewise demonstrates that oral tellers of tales are neither finger-wagging didacts nor passive, unreflective bearers of tradition and hegemonic values. In sustained studies of talented tellers, folklorists such as Linda Dégh and Henry Glassie have shown that their informants' artistry is both interwoven with community traditions and values and also the product of individual creative vision, ethos, and style.[1]

---

1   See Dégh's *Folktales and Society: Storytelling in a Hungarian Peasant Community* (1969) and *Hungarian Folktales: The Art of Zsuzsanna Palkó* (1996); Glassie's

On the other hand, wide-ranging and comparative studies, such as that of the Louisiana Storytelling Project coordinated by Maida Owens, or Hasan El-Shamy's work with Arab women tale-tellers, have highlighted subtle and sometimes striking differences in storytelling styles, narrative strategies, and social perspectives. Such studies have also foregrounded the gaps and blind spots in earlier collections, ones that have tended to homogenize narrative traditions to produce coherent visions of particular nations, regions, or folk groups.[2]

Passing the Time in Ballymenone: Culture and History of an Ulster Community (1982) and *The Stars of Ballymenone* (2006). On reflexivity in oral tradition and other forms of performance, see Berger and Del Negro (2002).

2   See *Swapping Stories: Folktales from Louisiana*, ed. Carl Lindahl, Maida Owens, and C. Renée Harvison (1997) and Hasan El-Shamy's *Tales Arab Women Tell* (1999). El-Shamy offers a powerful critique of "the seemingly flawless texts that fill hundreds of published tale 'collections'" but which are actually "more indicative of their writers' re-creative abilities than of the characteristics of the hypothetical folk narrators of these literary texts" (3). This is no small matter, as he points out: these collections have served as the basis for extensive theorizing about both the genre of the wonder tale and about specific culture groups. In the case of Louisiana folktales, this has resulted in collections that fail to represent the cultural diversity of the region. In the case of tales from the Arab world, El-Shamy argues that "development of social scientific theories based on Arab folktales as they are lived in real life has been hampered by (among other things) the scarcity of available texts, especially ones collected from females; and the prevalence of alterations, 'improvements,' and blatant forgeries and fabrications in published anthologies" (3). In this case, the absence of female voices from the written record entailed an "absence of *Märchen* from early folklore studies and tale indexes." As El-Shamy demonstrates, this "was a result of inadequate collecting and careless surveying of the available literature"—and it had (and continues to have) tangible implications for global theories of folk narrative. El-Shamy reminds us of one of these, C. W. Von Sydow's theories "on the origin of the *Märchen* as a genre and its presumed absence among certain unimaginative peoples" (13)—a claim that may have appeared valid when the points of reference were available written records, but which rings false in the light of El-Shamy's vast and diverse field-based collection of Arab-Islamic women's narrative performances.

For more than two centuries, discourses around the fairy tale have been preoccupied with the narration of origin stories and tales of authorship. Although related, these two forms of critical "storytelling" are distinct from each other: the first involves conjecture about the origins of oral traditions and of specific tales; the other fixates on the individual genius and his or her creative process. Scholars have thus established narrative traditions of their own, what Elizabeth Harries has referred to as "fairy tales about fairy tales" (see 2001, 19–45): each draws selectively (as would any skilled storyteller) to delineate boundaries around the "usable past," by necessity marginalizing, obfuscating, or overlooking some details in favor of others (see Glassie 1995, 395). The history of the fairy tale in England is fascinating in its complexity, its resistance to easy narration; it is a history that is characterized by the repeated blurring of the borders of languages, national and local traditions, genres, disciplines, audiences, and communicative forms. Nevertheless, many variants of the genre's historical metanarrative have privileged metaphysical and transcendental rhetoric, framing the fairy tale as "timeless" and "universal," with the unfortunate consequence of generating mystified and often oversimplified reworkings of that history. Many of the writers who have played with the form we generally call fairy tale have tended to be experimental, both drawing on contemporaneous literary styles and also challenging aesthetic and social norms. Retranslations and critical reassessments of important works in fairy-tale history have been expanding and reorienting critical conversations.[3] In short, the more one explores the multimedial history of the fairy tale—complex, self-aware, and playful—

3   Prime examples include Nancy Canepa's critical edition of Giambattiste Basile's *The Tale of Tales* (2007), Christine A. Jones's retranslation of Charles Perrault's *Tales of Times Past* (2016), Suzanne Magnanini's *Fairy-Tale Science: Monstrous Generation in the Tales of Straparola and Basile* (2008), Caroline Sumpter's attention to the place of fairy tale in avant-garde debates and an emergent gay subculture at the fin de siècle (2008), and the collection of essays on the transgressive dimensions of the Grimms' fairy tales, edited by Kay Turner and Pauline Greenhill (2012).

the more baffling current assumptions about this elusive beast referred to as "the traditional fairy tale" seem to be.

Characterized by various kinds of border crossings not only in its performance and casting conventions but also in its history, influences, and relationship to other art forms, English pantomime has generally been neglected in critical histories of the fairy tale. As a form of mainstream entertainment that has drawn heavily on fairy-tale plotlines and characters since the early nineteenth century—considered a "near to obligatory" seasonal event for British families (Miller 1993, 28)—pantomime has played an important role in popular conceptions of the fairy-tale genre, at least in Great Britain where it *remains* extremely popular and highly lucrative.

Pantomime and forms with which it shares historical roots, like ballet and commedia dell'arte, are evolving traditions, with fairy-tale themes, characters, and plot elements remaining essential to the fabric of each. Since the turn of the twentieth century, several other significant forms of fairy-tale theater have emerged, including the Broadway musical—which is certainly thriving in 2018. For example, Maya Cantu observes that the figure of Cinderella is pervasive in Broadway productions of the 2010s (from the "revisal" of Rodgers and Hammerstein's *Cinderella* to the planned musical renditions of the films *Ever After* and *Pretty Woman*; Cantu 2015, 1) but can also be considered iconic in the history of the form. As Cantu writes, "The Broadway musical, throughout its history, has celebrated the rags-to-riches narratives of the American dream," and "its creators have persistently gravitated toward Cinderella stories"—both those few that explicitly retell the Cinderella story and those that index "the Cinderella Paradigm, relying on strategies of adaptation that resonate with modern American myths and narratives of assimilation and upward mobility" (3). Cantu suggests that a critical study of the Cinderellas of Broadway musicals reveals that they "have a long history of complicating and defying the stereotypes of feminine passivity that have long been associated with Perrault's (and later Disney's) heroine" (7–8). Seen in this light, fairy-tale paradigms in Broadway musicals resonate with many of the examples of fairy-tale theater discussed in *Staging Fairyland*, having the potential to both affirm and subvert dominant ideologies.

The vast majority of fairy-tale-themed Broadway shows are currently marketed to audiences of both adults and children, and in this they revive a well-established tradition: children made up part of the audience for fairy plays, pantomimes, and puppet theater in earlier centuries, and private performances of fairy-tale plays figured in the education and entertainment of the elite's children in the eighteenth century (Jarvis 2000, 139). In early twentieth-century America, Winthrop Ames's 1912 musical *Snow White and the Seven Dwarfs* was explicitly framed as a "play for the children" when it debuted at New York City's Little Theatre, a production that was likely to "appeal to them as few productions ever have" ("Play for Children" 1912, 13). Although Ames anticipated that he would produce "more fairy plays for children" ("Fairyland Busy Making Little Words of Big Ones" 1912, 6), this production arguably has a more significant place in film history than it does in theater history: the "perfectly child-like" Marguerite Clark played the title character, a role she reprised in the 1916 silent film, which in turn inspired Walt Disney's animated feature film. Ames's successful Broadway production for children joined a range of American popular performance forms—vaudeville, Wild West shows, musical theater—whose advertising strategies targeted youngsters in the early decades of the twentieth century. Nevertheless, the "fairy play" had all but vanished from Broadway by the 1920s (van de Water 2012, 150n5).

During the same period, fairy tales became (and have remained) "staples" in another form of theater for children: the movement known as Theatre for Young Audiences, or TYA (Thompson 2000, 114). TYA has its origins in philanthropic and often state-supported initiatives, with early examples including New York City's Children's Educational Theatre, established in 1903 by settlement worker Alice Minnie Herts, and the Moscow Central Children's Theatre, first championed by Nadezhda Krupskaya (wife to Vladimir Lenin) and run by fifteen-year-old Natalya Sats (see van de Water 2012, 20–25)—at whose request and for whose theater Sergei Prokofiev composed *Peter and the Wolf* (1936). The work of organizations like the Children's Educational Theatre made a concerted effort to distinguish their uses of drama from those of the world of professional/"adult" theater; in this context, fairy tales were seen as useful tools in children's moral education and cultural assimilation (see Tuite 1998 and van de Water 2012, 9–40). Reflecting in 1939 on the work of settlement workers like Herts, Winifred Ward wrote of "the picturesque beauty of the folk tale play" that served "children who live amid the ugliness of factory and slum districts" and filled "a far greater need than do the [. . .] plays for more fortunate children" (quoted in van de Water 2012, 13). By the late 1930s, folktales and fairy tales were thus embraced by practitioners of children's theater not because they promised spectacle, stage magic, topical comedy, and social critique, but because they were increasingly associated with escapism, transformation, moral elevation, and psychological self-expression. Against such a backdrop, fairy-tale pantomime may indeed appear an uncomfortable approach to the staging of fairyland.

English playwright Mark Ravenhill has declared, provocatively, that one "would be hard pressed to find anything in children's literature or entertainment that is anywhere near as radical as panto" (2006, 328). For Ravenhill, this radical potential resides in play with gender ambiguities and erotic possibilities—a fantasy space that for over two hundred years has been populated by fairy-tale characters and one in which the boundaries and absurdities of class, gender, and sexuality are explored. Ravenhill's observations about contemporary pantomime certainly challenge the commonly held notion that the fairy-tale genre serves an overwhelmingly heteronormative worldview. He argues that the "message of panto is clear: we need hapless fathers, fat men in dresses and women in tunics in love with other women if the world is to be set to rights. [. . .] As every boy or girl knows, the cross-dressed shall inherit the earth" (328). As Ravenhill's words suggest, matters of power, desire, and identity are intimately linked to the *material* aspects of pantomime production, such as costuming and set design, and these links are as evident in nineteenth-century pantomime as they are in pantomime of recent years.

Theater historian Julia Prest has argued that "the cross-cast actor brings into relief the crucial question of reality and falsehood in performance—and in this way he is a quintessentially theatrical figure" (2006, 1). We might extend this observation and approach the cross-dressed figure as one that may also be quintessentially folkloristic, at least in terms of nineteenth-century paradigms and practices. The cross-dressed figure—particularly the type examined by Prest, that of an actor cross-cast as an unruly older woman—could serve as an apt emblem of the complexities and ambiguities of field encounter, potently figured by the Grimms and many of their followers as an encounter between male scholar/collector and an old, low-born female folk narrator, in which the authority of the former relies on his ability to capture and convey the voice of the latter. As Susan Ritchie suggests, there is a long tradition in folklore research of "ventriloquist" representational strategies in which the scholar "presumes to speak on behalf of some voiceless group or individual" (1993, 366). But this is not only a matter of voice: whether one looks at representations of specific storytellers, like the Grimms' iconic informant Dorothea Viehmann or fictionalized ones like Gammer Grethel, Mother Goose, or Mother Bunch, such figures seem to have authenticity written on their bodies, indexed by their gender, social standing, and age. Those bodies become significant to scholars' own constructions of authority and authenticity, and in such contexts those bodies have tended to be stripped of certain signifying potentialities, namely, their association with varieties of female entrepreneurship and sexual knowledge, as well as traditions of satire, jest, and bawdy humor.

"Nursery tales" are rarely considered in relation to the representational history in which nurses are figured as raunchy and subversive. Similarly, when burlesque fairy tales are considered at all, they are often assumed to be beyond the purview of children—ignoring the fact that that sensibility and the term *burlesque* itself had a strong presence in nineteenth-century print and other forms that were marketed quite explicitly as "for children." For instance, in the 1840s the publisher William S. Orr issued the Comic Nursery Tales series for children, written in satirical verse by Frederick Bayley, Albert Smith, and others and accompanied by absurdist illustrations. The specific stories that were parodied in that series were all current pantomime standards: the fairy tales known as "Blue Beard," "Beauty and the Beast," "Red Riding Hood," "Hop o' My Thumb," "Puss in Boots," "Sleeping Beauty," "Jack the Giant Killer," "Cinderella," and "Tom Thumb," and pantomime favorite, "Robinson Crusoe." As theater historian Jim Davis has noted, "Childhood experience of theatre in the nineteenth century, whether as spectator or performer, tended to be through Shakespeare or pantomime" (2006, 191)—and it is no accident that Shakespeare's work and a canon of fairy tales were among the most common objects of burlesque and parody. These are forms of satire that a multiage audience could enjoy, with varying degrees of sophistication.

Importantly, comic elements and references to popular theater were not limited to works for children that were explicitly framed as parody or burlesque. Andrea Immel's work on children's literature of the eighteenth century, particularly didactic tales, demonstrates that the seminal work of the publisher John Newbery and his coterie of (generally anonymous) writers "were famous for lacing moral instruction with humor to make it delightful for the reader" (2009, 148). It is perhaps no coincidence that one of Newbery's most prolific authors was Christopher Smart, who led parallel careers as a poet, essayist, satirist, and comic stage performer, appearing at the Haymarket Theatre as the "witty, provocative" character he called "Mary Midnight" (D. Ennis 2013, 169). Developed by Smart as both a literary and stage persona, Mary Midnight resonates with the traditions of satire and male-to-female theatrical cross-dressing discussed earlier. Immel traces a network of (perhaps surprising) forms of cultural and specifically theatrical reference in Newbery's *Pretty Play-thing* (ca. 1759), aimed at very young children and believed to have been written by Smart: these include references to a popular opera singer and an infamous dancing master, as well as citation of the refrain from a drinking song known by printers' apprentices (2009, 155). The domains of adult sociability, popular performance, and social satire are fundamental to these early examples of English print culture marketed as literature for children.

Nevertheless, the notion that an appetite for parody was a nineteenth-century development in the history of children's literature seems to underpin the arguments of some recent critics, even when the polarities of Victorian critiques have been reversed. For example, Jason Marc Harris's examination of nineteenth-century fairy tales maps the "progression" of the form through successive decades, as writers turned increasingly toward "parody and satire" (2008, 37). He writes: "Many Victorian fairy tales treat the very mechanics that define the märchen as a narrative of magical events and active heroism with levity and skepticism" (60). Similarly, U. C. Knoepflmacher recognizes that "irreverence" characterizes much of the Victorian writing inspired by the fairy-tale tradition (2008, 728). But Knoepflmacher is one critic who also acknowledges that this impulse toward playful invocation of fairy-tale antecedents spans the full history of literary fairy tales, evident in the work the seventeenth-century Neapolitan writer Giambattista Basile, in the tales of Charles Perrault and his contemporaries, and in fairy-tale-inspired fiction that continues to the present day.

Nineteenth-century British writers like George MacDonald and William Makepeace Thackeray engaged in "comic refashioning" of well-known plots, characters, and motifs, particularly ones associated with the work of Perrault (Knoepflmacher 2008, 728), and they also wrote in a cultural milieu in which French fairy tales had often been recognized as already *inherently* "burlesque." Mary Louise Ennis has highlighted the prevalence of fairy-tale parody in both fair theater and salon tales during the reign of Louis XIV: Alain-René Lesage's plays and Antoine Hamilton's stories offered exaggerated parodies of the already playful contemporary *contes de fées* of writers like Perrault and d'Aulnoy (1997). In the context of an 1808 review of M. G. Lewis's *Romantic Tales*, the reviewer refers with assumed familiarity and disdain to "those burlesque fairy tales which abounded in some Parisian coteries during the time of Louis the fourteenth, which must have furnished very pleasant pastime to the particular societies for whose amusement they were immediately composed, but are very little worth the honours of publication" (357). At the turn of the nineteenth century, Britons appear to have been well aware of the satirical dimension of French fairy tales; this is evident even in chauvinistic appraisals of "Parisian" forms of amusement.

In the German tradition, one can point to Ludwig Tieck's ironic 1796 play, known in English as *Knight Bluebeard: A Nursery Tale in Four Acts*, and to the highly self-referential and parodic narration of his 1797 story the "Seven Wives of Bluebeard." These are two works that foreground the self-reflexive, tongue-in-cheek aspects of the Perrault tale on which they are based while playing with received understandings of the genre (see Menninghaus 1999). The Grimms' tales stood as prime examples of purity and authenticity for many Victorian commentators and folklorists, but there are elements of self-parody to be found in that corpus, too. For example, the Grimms' tale known to English audiences as "The Story of the Boy Who Went Forth to Learn Fear" is humorously horrific, absurdist in its mockery of fairy-tale rewards and happy matrimonial endings. Maria Tatar thus refers to the "burlesque effect" of the hero's adventures as he seeks experiences that teach him to shudder (1987, 96). As Knoepflmacher suggests, "Parody is a logical outgrowth of the intertextuality that characterizes fairy-tale tradition" (2008, 727).

It is tempting to view pantomime itself as a "logical outgrowth" of a multifaceted multimedial tradition—but such a conclusion is in danger of reanimating the genealogical model of fairy-tale "adaptation" that *Staging Fairyland* has sought to challenge. This study has explored overlapping domains of sociability and play, scholarship and entertainment, orality and mediated communication, theatrical performance and print culture; doing so requires a willingness to question received paradigms, methodologies, and master narratives that previously have shaped and *limited* the historical study of folklore and the fairy tale. Further research along these lines can only serve to enrich our understanding of (self-)parody and theatricality as significant affordances of the wonder tale, ones that have been explored and exploited in a variety of media, for centuries.

References

Abrahams, Roger D. 1993. "After New Perspectives: Folklore Study in the Late Twentieth Century." *Western Folklore* 52, no. 2/4: 379–400.

An Accurate Description of the Grand Allegorical Pantomimic Spectacle of Cinderella, as Performed at the Theatre-Royal, Drury Lane: to Which Is Added, a Critique on the Performance and Performers, by a Lover of the Drama. Together with the Story of Cinderella. 1804. London: John Fairburn.

Adams, D. J. 1994. "The 'Conte des Fées' of Madame d'Aulnoy: Reputation and Re-evaluation." *Bulletin of the John Rylands University Library of Manchester* 76, no. 3: 5–22.

"Adeline Duchess of Bedford: A Character Study." 1920. *The Spectator*, May 1, 1920, 8–9.

"Adelphi Theatre." 1826. *The Times* (London), December 27, 1826, 3.

Ali, Muhsin Jassim. *Scheherazade in England: A Study of Nineteenth-Century English Criticism of the Arabian Nights*. Three Continents Press, 1981.

Allen, Ralph G. 1981. "Irrational Entertainment in the Age of Reason." In *The Stage and the Page: London's "Whole Show" in the Eighteenth-Century Theatre*, edited by George Winchester Stone Jr., 90–114. Berkeley: University of California Press.

Anonymous. 1745. *The Agreeable Companion; or, An Universal Medley of Wit and Good-Humour, Consisting of a Curious Collection of the Most Humourous Essays, Smart Repartees, Prudential Maxims, Familiar Dialogues, Epigrams and Epitaphs, Tales and Fables, Emblems and Riddles, Shining Epistles, and Beautiful Characters Both Fabulous and Real*. London: W. Bickerton.

Anseaume, Louis. 1759. *Cendrillon, opéra-comique*. Paris: N. B. Duchesne. gallica.bnf.fr/ark:/12148/bpt6k11638653. Accessed May 15, 2017.

Attridge, Steve. 2003. *Nationalism, Imperialism and Identity in Late Victorian Culture: Civil and Military Worlds*. London: Palgrave Macmillan.

Babcock, Barbara A. 1977. "The Story in the Story: Metanarration in Folk Narrative." In *Verbal Art as Performance*, edited by Richard Bauman, 61–79. Rowley, MA: Newbury House.

Bacchilega, Cristina. 2012. "Folklore and Literature." In *A Companion to Folklore*, edited by Regina F. Bendix and Galit Hasan-Rokem, 447–63. Chichester, UK: Wiley-Blackwell.

———. 2013. *Fairy Tales Transformed? Twenty-First-Century Adaptations and the Politics of Wonder.* Detroit: Wayne State University Press.

Balina, Marina, Helena Goscilo, and Mark Lipovetsky, eds. 2005. *Politicizing Magic: An Anthology of Russian and Soviet Fairy Tales.* Evanston: Northwestern University Press.

"Ball at Marlborough House." 1874. *The Englishman*, August 1, 1874, 262–63.

Barnes, Clive. 1970. "The Stage: 'Story Theater' Opens at Ambassador." *New York Times*, October 27, 1970.

Bauman, Richard. 2004. *A World of Others' Words: Cross-Cultural Perspectives on Intertextuality.* Malden, MA: Blackwell.

———. 2011. "The 'Talking Machine Story Teller': Cal Stewart and the Remediation of Storytelling." In *The Individual and Tradition: Folkloristic Perspectives*, edited by Ray Cashman, Tom Mould, and Pravina Shukla, 70–91. Bloomington: Indiana University Press.

Bauman, Richard, and Charles L. Briggs. 1990. "Poetics and Performance as Critical Perspectives on Language and Social Life." *Annual Review of Anthropology*, 19: 59–88.

———. 2003. *Voices of Modernity: Language Ideologies and the Politics of Inequality.* Cambridge: Cambridge University Press.

Beckett, Sandra. 2002. *Recycling Red Riding Hood.* New York: Routledge.

Beebee, Thomas. 1994. *The Ideology of Genre: A Comparative Study of Generic Instability.* University Park: Pennsylvania State University Press.

Beresford, Edwin. 1920. *The XVIII Century in London: An Account of Its Social Life and Arts.* London: B. T. Batsford.

Berg, Albert Ellery. 1884. *The Drama, Painting, Poetry, and Song, Embracing a Complete History of the Stage; an Exhaustive Treatise on Pictorial Art; a Choice Collection of Favourite Poems, and the Popular Songs of All Nations.* New York: P. F. Collier.

Berger, Harris M., and Giovanna Del Negro. 2002. "Bauman's *Verbal Art* and the Social Organization of Attention: The Role of Reflexivity in the Aesthetics of Performance." *Journal of American Folklore* 115:62–91.

Birch, Dinah, and Francis O'Gorman, eds. 2002. *Ruskin and Gender.* London: Palgrave Macmillan.

Blamires, David. 1989. "The Early Reception of the Grimms' *Kinder- und Hausmärchen* in England." *Bulletin of the John Rylands University Library of Manchester* 71, no. 3: 63–76.

———. 2008. "From Madame d'Aulnoy to Mother Bunch: Popularity and the Fairy Tale." In *Popular Children's Literature in Britain*, edited by Julia Briggs, Dennis Butts, and M. O. Grenby, 69–86. Aldershot, UK: Ashgate.

Blanchard, E. L. 1880. *Mother Goose and the Enchanted Beauty* (souvenir script). Theatre Royal, Drury Lane. Pettingell Collection, University of Kent, Canterbury.

Blom, J. M. 1989. "The Life and Works of Robert Samber." *English Studies* 6: 507–50.

Bolter, David, and Richard Grusin. 2009. *Remediation: Understanding New Media.* Cambridge, MA: MIT Press.

Bolton, H. Philip. 2000. *Women Writers Dramatized: A Calendar of Performances from Narrative Works Published in English to 1900.* London: Mansell.

Booth, Michael R., ed. 1976. *English Nineteenth-Century Plays.* Vol. 5. Oxford: Clarendon.

———. 1980. *Prefaces to English Nineteenth-Century Theatre.* Manchester: Manchester University Press.

———. 1991. *Theatre in the Victorian Age.* Cambridge: Cambridge University Press.

Bottigheimer, Ruth B. 2002. "Misperceived Perceptions: Perrault's Fairy Tales and English Children's Literature." *Children's Literature* 30, no. 1: 1–18.

———. 2009. *Fairy Tales: A New History.* Albany: State University of New York Press.

Bottoms, Janet. 2006. "The Battle of the (Children's) Books." *Romanticism* 12, no. 3: 212–22.

"Boxing Day." 1899. *The Times* (London), December 27, 1899, 8–9.

Braid, Donald. 2002. *Scottish Traveller Tales: Lives Shaped through Stories.* Jackson: Mississippi University Press.

Brandreth, Gyles. 1974. *I Scream for Ice Cream: Pearls from the Pantomime.* London: Eyre Metheun.

Briggs, Charles L., and Richard Bauman. 1992. "Genre, Intertextuality, and Social Power." *Journal of Linguistic Anthropology* 2, no. 2: 131–72.

Brown, Pamela Allen. 2003. *Better a Shrew than a Sheep: Women, Drama, and the Culture of Jest in Early Modern England.* Ithaca, NY: Cornell University Press.

Buch, David J. 2008. *Magic Flutes and Enchanted Forests: The Supernatural in Eighteenth-Century Musical Theater.* Chicago: University of Chicago Press.

Buczkowski, Paul. 2001. "J. R. Planché, Frederick Robinson, and the Fairy Extravaganza." *Marvels & Tales: Journal of Fairy Tale Studies* 15, no. 1: 42–65.

Bunce, John Thackray. 1878. *Fairy Tales, Their Origin and Meaning; with Some Account of Dwellers in Fairyland.* London: Macmillan.

Burling, William J. 1993. *A Checklist of New Plays and Entertainments on the London Stage, 1700–1737.* London: Associated University Presses.

———. 2000. *Summer Theatre in London, 1661–1820, and the Rise of the Haymarket Theatre.* London: Associated University Presses.

Butler, Judith. 1997. "Performative Acts and Gender Constitution: An Essay in Phenomenology and Feminist Theory." In *Writing on the Body: Female Embodiment and Feminist Theory*, edited by Katie Conboy, Nadia Medina, and Sarah Stanbury, 401–18. New York: Columbia University Press.

Byron, Henry J. 1869. *The Yellow Dwarf; or, Harlequin Cupid and the King of the Gold Mines: A Pantomime* (souvenir script). Pettingell Collection, University of Kent, Canterbury.

Calabresi, Bianca Finzi-Contini. 2015. "Angelica and Franceschina: The Italiante Characters of Juliet's Nurse." In *Historical Affects and Early Modern Theater*, edited by Ronda Arab, Michelle M. Dowd, and Adam Zucker, 124–36. New York: Routledge.

Canepa, Nancy L., ed. 1997. *Out of the Woods: The Origins of the Literary Fairy Tale in Italy and France.* Detroit: Wayne State University Press.

———. 1999. *From Court to Forest: Giambattista Basile's "Lo cunto de li cunti" and the Birth of the Literary Fairy Tale.* Detroit: Wayne State University Press.

———, trans. 2007. *Giambattista Basile's The Tale of Tales, or Entertainment for Little Ones.* Detroit: Wayne State University Press.

Cantu, Maya. 2015. *American Cinderellas on the Broadway Musical Stage: Imagining the Working Girl from Irene to Gypsy.* London: Palgrave Macmillan.

Chanan, Michael. 1996. *The Dream that Kicks: The Prehistory and Early Years of Cinema in Britain.* 2nd ed. London: Routledge.

Charlton, David. 1992. "On Redefinitions of 'Rescue Opera.'" In *Music and the French Revolution*, edited by Malcolm Boyd, 169–90. Cambridge: Cambridge University Press.

"The Christmas Entertainments." 1869. *The Times* (London), December 28, 1869, 3.

"The Christmas Pantomimes and Burlesques." 1851. *The Times* (London), December 27, 1851, 3.

"The Christmas Pantomimes and Entertainments." 1857. *The Times* (London), December 28, 1857, 9.

"Cinderella." 1804. *Morning Chronicle* (London), January 14, 1804, 1.

Cinderella, or, The Little Glass Slipper; as Performed at the Theatre-Royal Drury Lane, with Universal Applause. 1804. London: T. Hughes.

Cixous, Hélène. 2001. "With a Blow of the Wand," translated by Brian Mallet. *Parallax* 7, no. 2: 85–94.

Clark, Walter H., Jr. 1990. "Literature, Education, and Cultural Literacy." *Journal of Aesthetic Education* 24, no. 1: 49–56.

Clarke, Henry Green. 1851. *London in All Its Glory.* London: H. G. Clarke.

Clouston, W. A. 1887. *Popular Tales and Fictions; Their Migrations and Transformations.* Edinburgh: William Blackwood.

Colley, Linda. 1992. *Britons: Forging the Nation, 1707–1837.* New Haven, CT: Yale University Press.

Connelly, Mark. 1999. *Christmas: A Social History.* London: I. B. Tauris.

Conquest, George, and Henry Spry. 1881. *Mother Bunch, the Man with the Hunch, the Reeds, the Needs, the Priest, the Swell, the Gipsy Girl and the Big Dumb Bell* (souvenir script). Surrey Theatre. Pettingell Collection, University of Kent, Canterbury.

"Covent Garden Pantomime." 1870. *The Graphic*, January 15, 1870, 148.

"Covent-Garden Theatre." 1821. *The Times* (London), December 27, 1821, 2.

Croker, T. Crofton. 1824. *Researches in the South of Ireland, Illustrative of the Scenery, Architectural Remains, and Manners and Superstitions of the Peasantry with an*

Appendix, Containing a Private Narrative of the Rebellion of 1798. London: John Murray.

———. 1825. *Fairy Legends and Traditions of the South of Ireland.* London: John Murray.

———. 1826. *Harlequin and the Eagle: Or The Man in the Moon and His Wife. As Acted at the Adelphi Theatre.* London: C. Smith.

———. 1828. *Daniel O'Rourke; or, Rhymes of a Pantomime.* London: Ainsworth.

———. 1859. *Fairy Legends and Traditions of the South of Ireland, A New Edition with a Short Memoir of the Author by His Son, T. F. Dillon Croker, Esq.* London: William Tegg.

Croker, T. F. Dillon. 1859. "Memoir." In *Fairy Legends and Traditions of the South of Ireland, by Thomas Crofton Croker, with a Short Memoir of the Author by His Son, T. F. Dillon Croker, Esq.* v–xiii. London: William Tegg.

Cromek, Robert Hartley. 1810. *Memoirs of Nithsdale and Galloway Songs, with Historical and Traditional Notices Relative to the Manners and Customs of the Peasantry.* London: Cadell and Davies.

Cunningham, Peter. 1871. *Handbook to London, as It Is.* New ed., revised. London: John Murray.

Cunningham, Robert Hays, ed. 1889. *Amusing Prose Chapbooks, Chiefly of the Last Century.* London: Hamilton, Adams.

"Daniel O'Rourke; or, Rhymes of a Pantomime" (review). 1828. *Literary Gazette, Journal of the Belles Lettres,* February 23, 1828, 115–16.

Davis, Ellis. 1877. *Annie's Pantomime Dream.* London: Arthur Moxon.

Davis, Jim. 2006. "Freaks, Prodigies, and Marvellous Mimicry: Child Actors of Shakespeare on the Nineteenth-Century Stage." *Shakespeare* 2, no. 2 (December): 179–93.

———. 2007. "Boxing Day." In *The Performing Century: Nineteenth-Century Theatre's History,* edited by Tracy C. Davis and Peter Holland, 13–31. London: Palgrave Macmillan.

———. 2010. "'Only an Undisciplined [Nation] Would Have Done It': Drury Lane Pantomime in the Late Nineteenth Century." In *Victorian Pantomime: A Collection of Critical Essays,* edited by Jim Davis, 100–117. London: Palgrave Macmillan.

———. 2014. "'Slap On! Slap Ever! Victorian Pantomime, Gender Variance, and Cross-Dressing.'" *New Theatre Quarterly* 30, no. 3 (August): 218–30.

Davis, Lennard. 1983. *Factual Fictions: The Origins of the English Novel.* New York: Columbia University Press.

Davis, Tracy C. 2005. "'Do You Believe in Fairies?' The Hiss of Dramatic License." *Theatre Journal* 57, no. 1: 57–81.

Davis, Tracy C., and Peter Holland. 2007. "Introduction: The Performing Society." In *The Performing Century: Nineteenth-Century Theatre's History,* edited by Tracy C. Davis and Peter Holland, 1–10. London: Palgrave Macmillan.

Davis, Tracy C., and Thomas Postlewait. 2003. "Theatricality: An introduction." In *Theatricality,* edited by Tracy C. Davis and Thomas Postlewait, 1–39. Cambridge: Cambridge University Press.

Dégh, Linda. 1969. *Folktales and Society: Storytelling in a Hungarian Peasant Community.* Translated by E. M. Schlossberger. Bloomington: Indiana University Press.

———. 1996. *Hungarian Folktales: The Art of Zsuzsanna Palkó.* Translated by Vera Kalm. Jackson: University Press of Mississippi.

Dentith, Simon. 2000. *Parody.* London: Routledge.

Deulin, Charles. 1878. *Les contes de ma mère l'Oye avant Perrault.* Paris: E. Dentu.

Diano, Francesca, ed. 1998. *Fairy Legends and Traditions of the South of Ireland.* By T. Crofton Croker and with a new introduction by Francesca Diano. Cork, Ireland: Collins Press.

Dickens, Charles. 1896. "On the Decadence of Pantomime." *The Theatre,* January 1, 1896, 21–25.

Dorson, Richard, ed. 1968a. *The British Folklorists.* Chicago: University of Chicago Press.

———. 1968b. *Peasant Customs and Savage Myths: Selections from the British Folklorists.* 2 vols. Chicago: University of Chicago Press.

"The Drama." 1821. *The Literary Chronicle and Weekly Review* 137 (December 27): 824–25.

"A Dream of Christmas." 1881. *The Theatre,* January 1, 1881, 1–10.

"Drury Lane." 1883. *London and Provincial Entr'acte,* December 29, 1883, 11.

Dundes, Alan. 1965. *The Study of Folklore.* Englewood, NJ: Prentice Hall.

"The Edinburgh Drama." 1831. *Edinburgh Literary Journal* 112:17.

"The Editor's Album." 1828. *The Mirror of Literature, Amusement, and Instruction* 301 (March 1): 149–50.

El-Shamy, Hasan. 1999. *Tales Arab Women Tell, and the Behavioral Patterns They Portray.* Bloomington: Indiana University Press.

Emery, Ted. 1997. "The Reactionary Imagination: Ideology and the Form of the Fairy Tale in Gozzi's *Il re servo* [the king stag]." In *Out of the Woods: The Origins of the Literary Fairy Tale in Italy and France,* edited by Nancy L. Canepa, 247–77. Detroit: Wayne State University Press.

"An Encomium on Nastiness, Addressed to Young Lady remarkable for dirty Hair, dirty Teeth, and dirty Nails." 1757. *Schofield's Middlewich Journal or Cheshire Advertiser,* no. 29, January 18, 1757.

Ennis, Daniel. 2013. "Christopher Smart, Mary Midnight, and the Haymarket, 1755." In *Reading Christopher Smart in the Twenty-First Century: "By Succession of Delight,"* edited by Min Wild and Noel Chevalier, 165–79. Lanham, MD: Bucknell University Press.

Ennis, Mary Louise. 1997. "Fractured Fairy Tales: Parodies for the Salon and Foire." In *Out of the Woods: The Origins of the Literary Fairy Tale in Italy and France,* edited by Nancy L. Canepa, 221–46. Detroit: Wayne State University Press.

Faden, Eric. 2007. "Movables, Movies, Mobility: Nineteenth-Century Looking and Reading." *Early Popular Visual Culture* 5, no. 1 (April): 71–89.

"Fairy Legends and Traditions of the South of Ireland" (review). 1825. *Quarterly Review* 32:198.

"Fairy Tales as Literature." 1898. *Edinburgh Review* 188 (July): 37—59.

"Fairyland." 1876. *The Times* (London), January 8, 1876: 4.

"Fairyland Busy Making Little Words of Big Ones: What a Visitor Behind the Scenes Discovered When He Called on Snow White and the Seven Dwarfs." 1912. *New York Times*, November 10, 1912, 6.

Felski, Rita. 2011. "Context Stinks!" *New Literary History* 42, no. 4: 573–91.

Findlater, Richard. 1978. *Joe Grimaldi: His Life and Theatre*. Cambridge: Cambridge University Press.

Fitzsimmons, Eileen. 1978. "Jacob and Wilhelm Grimm's *Irische Elfenmärchen*, a Comparison of the Translation with the English Original: Fairy Legends and Traditions of the South of Ireland." PhD diss., University of Chicago.

Fletcher, Kathy. 1987. "Planché, Vestris, and the Transvestite Role: Sexuality and Gender in Victorian Popular Theatre." *Nineteenth Century Theatre* 15, no. 1: 63–70.

Friedman-Romell, Beth H. 1995. "Breaking the Code: Toward a Reception Theory of Theatrical Cross Dressing in 18th-Century London." *Theatre Journal* 47, no. 4: 459–80.

Fullerton, Lady Georgiana. 1846. *Ellen Middleton: A Tale*. Leipzig, Germany: Bernhard Tauchnitz.

Garber, Marjorie. 1992. *Vested Interests: Cross-Dressing and Cultural Anxiety*. New York: Routledge.

Gaskell, Elizabeth. 1855. *North and South*. 2 vols. London: Chapman Hall.

General Stud-Book; Containing (with Few Exceptions) the Pedigree of Every Horse, Mare, &c of Note, That Has Appeared on the Turf, for the Last Fifty Years, with Many of an Earlier Date; Together with Some Account of the Foreign Horses and Mares from Whence is Derived the Present Breed of Racers in Great Britain and Ireland. 1793. London: J. Weatherby Jr.

Glassie, Henry. 1982. *Passing the Time in Ballymenone: Culture and History of an Ulster Community*. Bloomington: Indiana University Press.

———. 1985. *Irish Folk Tales*. New York: Pantheon.

———. 1995. "Tradition." *Journal of American Folklore* 108:395–412.

———. 2006. *The Stars of Ballymenone*. Bloomington: Indiana University Press.

Goldsmith, Elizabeth C. 2015. "Writing for the Elite: Molière, Marivaux, and Beaumarchais." In *The Routledge Companion to Commedia dell'Arte*, edited by Judith Chaffee and Olly Crick, 321–28. London: Routledge.

Gomme, George Laurence. 1885. *Mother Bunch's Closet Newly Broke Open, and the History of Mother Bunch of the West*. London: Villon Society.

Grand, Elaine. 1974. "Good Time Dames." *Nova*, December 1974, 75–77.

Grantham, Barry. 2015. "Classical Ballet and the Commedia dell'Arte." In *The Routledge Companion to Commedia dell'Arte*, edited by Judith Chaffee and Olly Crick, 276–83. London: Routledge.

Green, Roger Lancelyn. 1962. "The Golden Age of Children's Books." *Essays and Studies* 15:59–73.

Greenhill, Pauline, and Sidney Eve Matrix, eds. 2010. *Fairy Tale Films: Visions of Ambiguity*. Logan: Utah State University Press.

Greenhill, Pauline, and Jill Terry Rudy, eds. 2014. *Channeling Wonder: Fairy Tales on Television*. Detroit: Wayne State University Press.

Grenby, M. O. 2006. "Tame Fairies Make Good Teachers: The Popularity of Early British Fairy Tales." *The Lion and the Unicorn* 30, no. 1: 1–24.

———. 2007. "Chapbooks, Children, and Children's Literature." *The Library: The Transactions of the Bibliographic Society* 8, no. 3: 277–303.

———. 2011. *The Child Reader, 1700–1840*. New York: Cambridge University Press.

Grierson, Sir Herbert. 1932–37. *The Letters of Sir Walter Scott*. 12 vols. London: Constable.

Griffel, Margaret Ross. 2013. *Operas in English: A Dictionary*. Rev. ed. Lanham, MD: Scarecrow Press.

Griffin, Mike. 2015. "Goldoni and Gozzi: Reformers with Separate Agendas." In *The Routledge Companion to Commedia dell'Arte*, edited by Judith Chaffee and Olly Crick, 329–37. London: Routledge.

Grimm, Jacob and Wilhelm. (1812–14). 1986. *Kinder- und Hausmärchen gesammelt durch die Brüder Grimm*. 2 vols. Edited by Heinz Rölleke and Ulrike Marquardt. Göttingen, Germany: Vardenhoeck and Rupprecht.

Gubar, Marah. 2009. *Artful Dodgers: Reconceiving the Golden Age of Children's Literature*. New York: Oxford University Press.

A Guide to the Pantomimes of 1869, The History of Pantomime, and a Full Account of All the Pantomimes. London: H. Vickers, 1869.

Hahn, Daniel. 2015. "Mother Goose's Melody." In *The Oxford Companion to Children's Literature*, 2nd ed., 400–401. New York: Oxford University Press.

Hannon, Patricia. 1998. *Fabulous Identities: Women's Fairy Tales in Seventeenth-Century France*. Amsterdam: Rodopi.

Harries, Elizabeth Wanning. 1996. "Simulating Oralities: French Fairy Tales of the 1690s." *College Literature* 23, no. 2: 100–15.

———. 2001. *Twice upon a Time: Women Writers and the History of the Fairy Tale*. Princeton, NJ: Princeton University Press.

Harris, Jason Marc. 2008. *Folklore and the Fantastic in Nineteenth-Century British Fiction*. Aldershot, UK: Ashgate.

Harris-Warrick, Rebecca, and Carol G. Marsh. 1994. *Musical Theatre at the Court of Louis XIV: "Le mariage de la grosse Cathos."* Cambridge: Cambridge University Press.

Hartland, E. S. 1891. *The Science of Fairy Tales: An Inquiry into Fairy Mythology*. London: Walter Scott.

———. 1900. *Mythology and Folktales: Their Relation and Interpretation*. London: David Nutt.

Hawkins, Frederick. 1884. *Annals of the French Stage, from Its Origins to the Death of Racine.* 2 vols. London: Chapman and Hall.

Hazlitt, William Carew. 1864. *Shakespeare's Jest-Books.* London: Willis and Sotheran.

Herbert, Christopher. 2002. "Filthy Lucre: Victorian Ideas of Money." *Victorian Studies* 44, no. 2: 185–213.

Hillard, Molly Clark. 2014. *Spellbound: The Fairy Tale and the Victorians.* Columbus: Ohio State University Press.

Hindson, Catherine. 2016. *London's West-End Actresses and the Origins of Celebrity Charity, 1880–1920.* Iowa City: University of Iowa Press.

Hirsch, E. D. 1988. *Cultural Literacy: What Every American Needs to Know.* New York: Vintage.

Hollindale, Peter. 1996. "Drama." In *The International Companion Encyclopedia of Children's Literature,* edited by Peter Hunt, 203–16. London: Routledge.

———. 1997. "The Play of Eros: Paradoxes of Gender in English Pantomime." *New Theatre Quarterly* 13:195–204.

Holt, Ardern. 1887. *Fancy Dresses Described; Or, What to Wear at Fancy Balls.* 5th ed. London: Debenham and Freebody.

Horne, R. H. 1871. "The Burlesque and the Beautiful." *Contemporary Review* 18:390–406.

Hultin, Neil C. 1986. "Anglo-Irish Folklore from Clonmel: T. C. Croker and British Library Add. 20099." *Fabula* 27, no. 3–4: 288–307.

Hultin, Neil C., and Warren U. Ober, eds. 1983. *Fairy Legends and Traditions of the South of Ireland.* By T. Crofton Croker. Delmar, NY: Scholars' Facsimiles and Reprints.

Immel, Andrea. 2009. "The Didacticism that Laughs: John Newbery's Entertaining Little Books and William Hogarth's Pictured Morals." *Lion and the Unicorn* 33, no. 2: 146–66.

Jacobus, Marion. 1966. "Puppets at Parisian Fairs, 1649 to 1742." *Educational Theatre Journal* 18, no. 2: 110–21.

Jarvis, Shawn. 2000. "Drama and Fairy Tales." In *The Oxford Companion to Fairy Tales: The Western Fairy Tale Tradition from Medieval to Modern,* edited by Jack Zipes, 137–41. New York: Oxford University Press.

Jarvis, Anthea, and Patricia Raine. 1985. *Fancy Dress.* London: Shire.

Jauss, Hans Robert. 1982. "Literary History as a Challenge to Literary Theory." In *Toward an Aesthetic of Reception,* translated by Timothy Bahti, 3–45. Minneapolis: University of Minnesota Press.

Jennings, Louis J., ed. 1885. *The Croker Papers: The Correspondence and Diaries of the Late Honourable John Wilson Croker, LL.D., F.R.S., Secretary to the Admiralty from 1809 to 1830.* 3 vols. London: John Murray.

Jones, Christine A. 2003. "The Poetics of Enchantment (1690–1715)." *Marvels & Tales: Journal of Fairy-Tale Studies* 17, no. 1: 55–74.

———. 2009. "Madame d'Aulnoy Charms the British." *Romanic Review* 99, no. 3/4: 239–56.

———. 2016. *Mother Goose Refigured: A Critical Translation of Charles Perrault's Fairy Tales*. Detroit: Wayne State University Press.

Jones, J. Wilton. 1881. *Little Red Riding Hood or, Harlequin the Demon Wolf and the Good Fairies of the Enchanted Wood* (souvenir script). Grand Theatre and Opera House, Leeds, December 22. Pettingell Collection, University of Kent, Canterbury.

Kaufman, J. B. 2012. *The Fairest One of All: The Making of Disney's "Snow White and the Seven Dwarfs."* San Francisco: Walt Disney Family Foundation Press.

Keene, Melanie. 2015. *Science in Wonderland: The Scientific Fairy Tales of Victorian Britain*. New York: Oxford University Press.

Knoepflmacher, U. C. 2008. "Parody." In *The Greenwood Encyclopedia of Folktales and Fairy Tales*, edited by Donald Haase, 727–29. Westport, CT: Greenwood Press.

Krueger, Misty. 2017. "Vengeance, Vows, and 'Heroick Vertue': Reforming the Revenger in Delarivier Manley's *Almyna: or, The Arabian Vow.*" In *New Perspectives on Delarivier Manley and Eighteenth-Century Literature: Power, Sex, Text*, edited by Aleksondra Hultquist and Elizabeth J. Mathews, 43–56. New York: Routledge.

Kuti, Elizabeth. 2013. "Scheherazade, *Bluebeard*, and Theatrical Curiosity." In *Scheherazade's Children: Global Encounters with the Arabian Nights*, edited by Philip F. Kennedy and Marina Warner, 322–46. New York: New York University Press.

Lancaster, George. 1883. "Notes on the Pantomimes." *The Theatre*, January 1, 1883, 12–20.

Lang, Andrew, ed. (1888). 1977. *Perrault's Popular Tales*. New York: Arno.

"The Last Week of the Present Entertainments." 1794. *The Times* (London), August 13, 1794, 1.

Law, Graham. 2009. "Sketch (1893–1959)." *Dictionary of Nineteenth-Century Journalism*, edited by Laurel Brake and Marysa Demoor, 577. Gent: Academia Press.

Lewcock, Dawn. 2003. "Once upon a Time: The Story of the Pantomime Audience." In *Audience Participation: Essays on Inclusion in Performance*, edited by Susan Kattwinkel, 133–48. Westport, CT: Praeger.

Levine, Caroline. 2015. *Forms: Whole, Rhythm, Hierarchy, Network*. Princeton, NJ: Princeton University Press.

Lhéritier de Villandon, Marie-Jeanne. 1696. *Œuvres meslées, contenant l'innocent tromperie, l'avar puni, les enchantements de l'éloquence, les aventures de finette, nouvelles, et autres ouvrages, en vers et en prose*. Paris: Guignard.

Loveman, Kate. 2008. *Reading Fictions, 1660–1740: Deception in English Literary and Political Culture*. Aldershot, UK: Ashgate.

Lynch, Andrew. 2014. "'Simply to amuse the reader': The humour of Walter Scott's *Reformation*." *Postmedieval: A Journal of Medieval Cultural Studies* 5:169–83.

MacAllister, Marvin. 2011. *Whiting Up: Whiteface Minstrels and Stage Europeans in African American Performance*. Chapel Hill: University of North Carolina Press.

Macculloch, J. A. 1905. *The Childhood of Fiction: A Study of Folk Tales and Primitive Thought*. New York: E. P. Dutton.

MacQueen-Pope, Walter. 1947. *Carriages at Eleven: The Story of Edwardian Theatre*. London: Hutchinson.

Magnanini, Suzanne. 2007. "Postulated Routes from Naples to Paris: The Printer Antonio Bulifon and Giambattista Basile's Fairy Tales in Seventeenth-Century France." *Marvels & Tales: Journal of Fairy-Tale Studies* 21, no. 1: 78–92.

———. 2008. *Fairy-Tale Science: Monstrous Generation in the Tales of Straparola and Basile*. Toronto: University of Toronto Press.

Mainil, Jean. 2001. *Madame d'Aulnoy et le rire des fées: Essai su la subversion férique et le merveilleux comique sous l'Ancien Régime*. Paris: Kimé.

Marchant, Alicia. 2015. "A Landscape of Ruins: Decay and Emotions in Late Medieval and Early Modern Antiquarian Narratives." In *Gender and Emotions in Medieval and Early Modern Europe: Destroying Order, Stucturing Disorder*, edited by Susan Broomhall, 109–25. London: Routledge.

Marsden, Jean I. 1995. *The Reimagined Text: Shakespeare, Adaptation, and Eighteenth-Century Literary Theory*. Louisville: University Press of Kentucky.

Marsh, Carol G., and Rebecca Harris-Warrick. 1988. "A New Source for Seventeenth-Century Ballet: *Le mariage de la grosse Cathos*." *Dance Chronicle* 11, no. 3: 398–428.

Martin, Ann. 2006. *Red Riding Hood and the Wolf in Bed: Modernism's Fairy Tales*. Toronto: University of Toronto Press.

Masquerade and Carnival: Their Customs and Costumes. 1892. Rev. and enlarged. London: Butterick Publishing.

Mathews, Mrs. 1839. *A Continuation of the Memoirs of Charles Mathews, the Comedian.*2 vols. Philadelphia: Lea and Blanchard.

Mayer, David. 1969. *Harlequin in His Element: The English Pantomime, 1806–1836*. Cambridge, Mass.: Harvard University Press.

———. 1974. "The Sexuality of Pantomime." *Theatre Quarterly* 4, no. 13: 55–64.

———. 2002. "The Victorian Performer, the Photographer, and the Photograph." *Theatre Survey* 43, no. 2: 223–51.

McClelland, Harry. 1903. *Little Red Riding Hood* (souvenir script). Crown Theatre, Peckham, December. Pettingell Collection, University of Kent, Canterbury.

McCormick, John, with Clodagh McCormick and John Philips. 2004. *The Victorian Marionette Theatre*. Iowa City: University of Iowa Press.

McDermott, Gerald. 1986. *Daniel O'Rourke: An Irish Tale*. New York: Viking Juvenile.

McKeon, Michael. 1984. "The Origins of the English Novel." *Modern Philology* 82, no. 1: 76–86.

McNeil, Kenneth. 2012. "Ballads and Borders." In *The Edinburgh Companion to Sir Walter Scott*, edited by Fiona Robinson, 22–34. Edinburgh: Edinburgh University Press.

Menninghaus, Winfried. 1999. *In Praise of Nonsense: Kant and Bluebeard*. Translated by Henry Pickford. Stanford: Stanford University Press.

Myers, Victoria, David O'Shaughnessy, and Mark Philp, eds. 2010. *The Diary of William Godwin*. Oxford: Oxford Digital Library. godwindiary.bodleian.ox.ac.uk.

Miller, Daniel. 1993. "A Theory of Christmas." In *Unwrapping Christmas*, edited by D. Miller, 3–37. Oxford: Clarendon.

Mitchell, Rebecca. 2017. "The Victorian Fancy Dress Ball, 1870–1900." *Fashion Theory* 21, no. 3: 291–315.

Moody, Jane. 2000. *Illegitimate Theatre in London, 1770–1840*. Cambridge: Cambridge University Press.

Moon, Marjorie. 1990. *Benjamin Tabart's Juvenile Library: A Bibliography of Books for Children Published, Written, Edited and Sold by Mr. Tabart, 1801–1820*. Winchester, UK: St. Paul's Bibliographies.

Mother Goose's Melody: Or, Sonnets for the Cradle. 1791. London: Francis Power.

Muratore, Mary Jo. 1991. "The Discourses of Imprisonment in Perrault's Contes." *Papers on French Seventeenth Century Literature* 17:159–66.

Newey, Katherine, and Jeffrey Richards. 2010. *John Ruskin and the Victorian Theatre*. London: Palgrave Macmillan.

Nicholson, David. 1979. "Gozzi's Turandot: A Tragicomic Fairy Tale." *Theatre Journal* 31, no. 4: 467–78.

O'Brien, John. 1998. "Harlequin Britain: Eighteenth-Century British Pantomime and the Cultural Location of Entertainment(s)." *Theatre Journal* 50, no. 4 (1998): 489–510.

———. 2004. *Harlequin Britain: Pantomime and Entertainment, 1690–1760*. Baltimore: Johns Hopkins University Press.

"Old Drury's Newest Pantomime." 1899. *The Sketch*, December 27, 1899, 382. Opie, Peter, and Iona Opie, eds. 1980. *The Classic Fairy Tales*. New York: Oxford University Press.

Orr, Bridget. 2008. "Galland, Georgian Theatre, and the Creation of Popular Orientalism." *The Arabian Nights in Historical Context: Between East and West*, edited by Saree Makdisi and Felicity Nussbaum, 108–30. Oxford: Oxford University Press.

Ostry, Elaine. 2002. *Social Dreaming: Dickens and the Fairy Tale*. New York: Routledge.

Palgrave, Francis. 1819. Review of "Fairy Tales, or the Lilliputian Cabinet, Containing Twenty-Four Choice Pieces of Fancy and Fiction, Collected by Benjamin Tabart. Tabart & Co. London. 1818." *Quarterly Review* 21, no. 41: 91–112.

Palmer, Melvin D. 1975. "Madame d'Aulnoy in England." *Comparative Literature* 27, no. 3: 237–53.

Palmer, Nancy, and Melvin Palmer. 1974. "English Editions of French *Contes des Fées* Attributed to Mme d'Aulnoy." *Studies in Bibliography* 27:227–32.

"The Pantomime." 1822. *London Magazine* 5, February 1822, 183–84.

"Pantomime Special Props." Pantomime Store. www.thepantomimestore.com/props.html. Accessed November 25, 2011.

"Parisian Shows." 1886. *Saturday Review*, July 17, 1886. 84–85.

Pask, Kevin. 2013. *The Fairy Way of Writing: Shakespeare to Tolkien.* Baltimore: Johns Hopkins University Press.

Pasquil's Jests mixed with Mothere Bunch's Merriments. 1604. London: Francis Grove.

Paul, Lissa. 2011. *The Children's Book Business: Lessons from the Long Eighteenth Century.* New York: Routledge.

Pemberton, T. Edgar. 1896. "The 'Book' of the Pantomime." *The Theatre*, January 1, 1896, 25–29.

Perrault, Charles. 2002. *The Complete Fairy Tales in Verse and Prose / L'intégrale des contes en vers et en prose: A Dual-Language Book.* Translated by Stanley Appelbaum. New York: Dover.

Pickering, David, ed. 1993. *Encyclopedia of Pantomime.* Andover, UK: Gale Research.

"Play for Children at Little Theatre: With Marguerite Clark a Charming Snow White in the Well-Loved Fairy Tale." *New York Times*, November 8, 1912, 13.

"Poets." 1828. *La Belle Assemblée, or Court and Fashionable Magazine; Containing Interesting and Original Literature, and Records of the Beau-Monde* 7:299–300.

Popple, Simon, and Joe Kember. 2004. *Early Cinema: From Factory Gate to Dream Factory.* London: Wallflower Press.

Prest, Julia. 2006. *Theatre under Louis XIV: Cross-Casting and the Performance of Gender in Drama, Ballet, and Opera.* London: Palgrave Macmillan.

Radcliffe, Caroline. 2010. "Dan Leno: Dame of Drury Lane." *Victorian Pantomime: A Collection of Critical Essays*, edited by Jim Davis, 118–34. London: Palgrave Macmillan.

Ragussis, Michael. 2010. *Theatrical Nation: Jews and Other Outlandish Englishmen in Georgian Britain.* Philadelphia: University of Pennsylvania Press.

Ravenhill, Mark. 2006. "That's Entertainment?" *Contemporary Theatre Review* 16, no. 3, 327–28.

Reid-Walsh, Jacqueline. 2006. "Pantomime, Harlequinades and Children in Late Eighteenth-Century Britain: Playing in the Text." *British Journal for Eighteenth-Century Studies* 29:413–25.

Rice, Charles. 1873. *Red-Riding Hood and Her Sister Little Bo-Peep (souvenir script).* Theatre Royal, Covent Garden. Pettingell Collection, University of Kent, Canterbury.

———. 1874. *The Babes in the Wood and the Great Bed of Ware* (souvenir script). Theatre Royal, Covent Garden. Pettingell Collection, University of Kent, Canterbury.

Richards, Jeffrey. 2015. *The Golden Age of Pantomime: Slapstick, Spectacle and Subversion in Victorian England.* London: I. B. Tauris.

Richardson, Alan. 1994. *Literature, Education, and Romanticism: Reading as Social Practice, 1780–1832.* Cambridge: Cambridge University Press.

Ritchie, Susan. 1993. "Ventriloquist Folklore: Who Speaks for Representation?" *Western Folklore* 52, no. 2/4: 365–78.

Ritson, Joseph. 1831. *Fairy Tales, Legends, and Romances, Illustrating Shakespeare and Other Early English Writers.* London: Frank & William Kerslake.

Rizzo, Laura Katz. 2015. *Dancing the Fairy Tale: Producing and Performing the Sleeping Beauty*. Philadelphia: Temple University Press.

"Romantic Tales, by M.G. Lewis" (review). 1808. *Critical Review, or Annals of Literature*, 3rd series, 15:355–66.

"Royal Amphitheatre, Westminster Bridge." 1807. *The Times* (London), April 15, 1807, 1.

Ruskin, John. 1867. "Correspondence: At the Play." *Pall Mall Gazette*, March 1, 1867, 3–4.

———. 1868. *Introduction to German Popular Stories*. Rev. ed. Translated by Edgar Taylor. London: Hotten.

Sala, George Augustus. 1865. *My Diary in America in the Midst of War*. 2nd ed., vol. 2. London: Tinsely Brothers.

———. 1875. "The Nemesis of Pantomime." *Belgravia* 5 (January): 340–49.

Sauter, Willmar. 2000. *The Theatrical Event: Dynamics of Performance and Perception*. Iowa City: University of Iowa Press.

Schacker, Jennifer. 2003. *National Dreams: The Remaking of Fairy Tales in Nineteenth-Century England*. Philadelphia: University of Pennsylvania Press.

———. 2007. "Unruly Tales: Ideology, Anxiety, and the Regulation of Genre." *Journal of American Folklore* 120:381–400.

———. 2011. "Fluid Identities: Madame d'Aulnoy, Mother Bunch, and Fairy-Tale History." In *The Individual and Tradition: Folkloristic Perspectives*, edited by Ray Cashman, Tom Mould, and Pravina Shukla, 249-62. Bloomington: Indiana University Press.

———. 2012. "Fairy Gold: The Economics and Erotics of Fairy-Tale Pantomime." *Marvels & Tales: Journal of Fairy-Tale Studies* 26, no. 2: 153–77.

———. 2013. "Slaying Blunderboer: Cross-Dressed Heroes, National Identities, and Wartime Pantomime." *Marvels & Tales: Journal of Fairy-Tale Studies* 27, no. 1: 52–64.

———. 2018. "Theater." In *Routledge Companion to Media and Fairy-Tale Cultures*, edited by Pauline Greenhill, Jill Terry Rudy, Naomi Hamer, and Lauren Bosc, 337–47. London: Routledge.

Schechner, Richard. 1992. "Drama Performance." In *Folklore, Cultural Performances, and Popular Entertainments: A Communications-Centered Handbook*, edited by Richard Bauman, 272–81. New York: Oxford University Press.

Scott, Clement, and Cecil Howard. 1891. *The Life and Reminiscences of E. L. Blanchard, with Notes from the Diary of Wm. Blanchard*. 2 vols. London: Hutchinson.

Scott, Virginia P. 1972. "The Infancy of English Pantomime: 1716–1723." *Educational Theatre Journal* 24, no. 2: 125–34.

Scott-Warren, Jason. 2016. "Meet the Chillesters: The Printed Counterfeit in Early Modern London." *English Literary Renaissance* 46, no. 2: 225–52.

Seifert, Lewis. 1991. "Tales of Difference: Infantilization and the Recuperation of Class and Gender in 17th-Century Contes de Fées." *Papers on French Seventeenth Century Literature* 17:179–94.

———. 1996. *Fairy Tales, Sexuality, and Gender in France, 1690–1715*. Cambridge: Cambridge University Press, 1996.

Senelick, Laurence. 2000. *The Changing Room: Sex, Drag, and Theatre*. London: Routledge.

———. 2005. "Boys and Girls Together: Subcultural origins of glamour drag and male impersonation on the nineteenth-century stage." In *Crossing the Stage: Controversies on Cross-Dressing*, edited by Leslie Ferris, 82–96. New York: Routledge.

Short, Sue. 2014. *Fairy Tale and Film: Old Tales with a New Spin*. London: Palgrave Macmillan.

Shukla, Pravina. 2015. *Costume: Performing Identities through Dress*. Bloomington: Indiana University Press.

Shuman, Amy, and Charles L. Briggs. 1993. "Introduction: Theorizing Folklore: Towards New Perspectives on the Politics of Culture." *Western Folklore* 52, no. 2/4: 109–34.

Sims, George Robert. 1881. *The Dagonet Ballads*. London: John P. Fuller.

———. 1895. *Dagonet Abroad*. London: Chatto and Windus.

"Sir Walter Scott and Mr. Crofton Croker." 1854. *Gentleman's Magazine*, n.s., 42 (July–December): 452–55.

"The Sixth and Last General Subscription Night." 1795. *Johnson's British Gazette and Sunday Monitor* no. 832, October 11.

Smiles, Samuel. 1891. *A Publisher and His Friends, Memoir and Coresspondece of the Late John Murray, with an Account of the Origin and Progress of the House, 1768–1843*. 2 vols. London: John Murray.

Soriano, Marc. 1968. *Les contes de Perrault: Culture savante et traditions populaires*. Paris: Gallimard.

Speaight, George. 1946. *Juvenile Drama: The History of English Toy Theatre*. London: MacDonald.

Spufford, Margaret. 1982. *Small Books and Pleasant Histories: Popular Fiction and Its Readership in Seventeenth-Century England*. Athens: University of Georgia Press.

Stedman, Allison. 2005. "D'Aulnoy's *Histoire d'Hypolite, Comte de Duglas* (1690): A Fairy-Tale Manifesto." *Marvels & Tales: Journal of Fairy-Tale Studies* 19, no. 1: 32–53.

Stern, Rebecca F. 1998. "Moving Parts and Speaking Parts: Situating Victorian Antitheatricality." *ELH* 65, no. 2: 423–49.

Stevens, Victor. 1900. *Little Red Riding Hood, or The Saucy Squire of Sunnydale* (souvenir script). Fulham Grand Theatre, London, December. Pettingell Collection, University of Kent, Canterbury.

Stewart, Susan. 1991. *Crimes of Writing: Problems in the Containment of Representation*. New York: Oxford University Press.

Stone, Kay. 1998. *Burning Brightly: New Light on Old Tales Told Today*. Peterborough, ON: Broadview Press.

Stott, Andrew McConnell. 2009. *The Pantomime Life of Joseph Grimadi: Laughter, Madness and the Story of Britain's Greatest Comedian*. Edinburgh: Canongate.

St. Pierre, Paul Matthew. 2009. *Music Hall Mimesis in British Film, 1895–1960*: On *the Halls on the Screen*. Madison, NJ: Farleigh Dickinson University Press.

Sturgess, Arthur, and Arthur Collins. 1899–1900. *Jack and the Beanstalk, Theatre Royal Drury Lane, Grand Christmas Pantomime*. London: Nassau Press.

Sullivan, Jill Alexandra. 2011. *The Politics of the Pantomime: Regional Identity in the Theatre, 1860–1900*. Hatfield, UK: University of Hertfordshire Press.

Summers, Walter. 1897. *Little Red Riding Hood* (souvenir script). Theatre Royal, Newcastle-Upon-Tyne, December. Pettingell Collection, University of Kent, Canterbury.

Sumpter, Caroline. 2008. *The Victorian Press and the Fairy Tale*. London: Palgrave Macmillan.

Szumsky, Brian E. 1999. "The House That Jack Built: Empire and Ideology in Nineteenth-Century British Versions of 'Jack and the Beanstalk.'" *Marvels & Tales: Journal of Fairy-Tale Studies* 13, no. 1: 11–30.

Tabart, Benjamin. 1818. *Popular Fairy Tales: Or, A Liliputian Library; Containing Twenty-Six Choice Pieces of Fancy and Fiction, by Those Renowned Personages King Oberon, Queen Mab, Mother Goose, Mother Bunch, Master Puck, and Other Distinguished Personages at the Court of the Fairies*. London: Sir Richard Phillips.

Taruskin, Richard. 1996. *Stravinsky and the Russian Traditions: A Biography of the Works through Mavra*. 2 vols. Berkeley: University of California Press.

Tatar, Maria. 1987. *The Hard Facts of the Grimms' Fairy Tales*. Princeton, NJ: Princeton University Press.

Taylor, Diana. 2003. *The Archive and the Repertoire: Performing Cultural Memory in the Americas*. Durham, NC: Duke University Press.

Taylor, Diana, and Marcos Steuernagel. 2015. Introduction. In *What Is Performance Studies?* edited by Diana Taylor and Marcos Steurnagel. Durham, NC: Duke University Press. scalar.usc.edu/nehvectors/wips/what-is-performance-studies-introduction.

Taylor, Edgar. 1823. *German Popular Stories, Translated from the Kinder- und Hausmärchen of MM Grimm, from Oral Tradition*. Vol. 1. London: Baldwyn.

———. 1826. *German Popular Stories, Translated from the Kinder- und Hausmärchen of MM Grimm, from Oral Tradition*. Vol. 2. London: James Robins.

Taylor, Millie. 2007. *British Pantomime Performance*. Bristol, UK: Intellect Books.

"Theatre." 1806. *Morning Post* (London), December 30, 1806.

"Theatre, Drury-Lane." 1804. *The Times* (London), January 4, 1870, 3.

"Theatres." 1826. *The Times* (London), December 27, 1826, 3.

"The Theatres: Christmas Pantomimes and Burlesques." 1870. *Illustrated London News* 56 (January 1): 27.

Thompson, Melissa C. 2000. "If the Shoe Fits: Virtue and Absolute Beauty in Fairy Tale Drama." *Youth Theatre Journal* 14, no. 1, 114–22.

Thoms, William J. [Ambrose Merton, pseud.]. 1846a. "Folk-Lore." *The Athenaeum*, August 22, 1846, 862–63.

———. 1846b. "Folk-Lore." *The Athenaeum*, August 29, 1846, 886–87.

The True Story of Jack and the Beanstalk, a Gift from the Drury Lane Theatre, Christmas 1899. 1899. London: Harrison.

Tsurumi, Ryoji. 1990. "The Development of Mother Goose in Britain in the Nineteenth Century." *Folklore* 101, no. 1: 28–35.

Tucker, Holly. 2003. *Pregnant Fictions: Childbirth and the Fairy Tale in Early Modern France.* Detroit: Wayne State University Press.

Tucker, Nicholas. 1997. "Fairy Tales and Their Early Opponents: In Defense of Mrs. Trimmer." In *Opening the Nursery Door: Reading, Writing, and Childhood 1600–1900,* edited by Mary Hilton, Morag Styles, and Victor Wilson, 104–16. London: Routledge.

Tuite, Patrick. 1998. "Assimilating Immigrants through Drama: The Social Politics of Alice Minnie Herts and Lillian Ward." *Youth Theatre Journal* 12:10–18.

Turner, Kay, and Pauline Greenhill, eds. 2012. *Transgressive Tales: Queering the Grimms.* Detroit: Wayne State University Press.

"Two Pantomimes." 1885. *Saturday Review,* January 10, 1885, 50–51.

Van de Water, Manon. 2012. *Theatre, Youth, and Culture: A Critical and Historical Exploration.* New York: Palgrave Macmillan.

Varty, Anne. 2008. *Children and Theatre in Victorian Britain: "All Work, No Play."* London: Palgrave Macmillan.

Verdier, Gabrielle. 1996. "Comment l'auteur des 'Fées à la mode' devint 'Mother Bunch': Métamorphoses de la Comtesse d'Aulnoy en Angleterre." *Marvels & Tales: Journal of Fairy-Tale Studies* 10, no. 2: 285–309.

Villiers, Abbé Pierre de. 1699. *Entretiens sur les contes des fées et sur quelques autres ouvrages du temps pour servir comme préservatif contre le mauvais goût.* Paris: Jacques Collombat.

Vlock, Deborah. 1998. *Dickens, Novel Reading, and the Victorian Theatre.* Cambridge: Cambridge University Press.

Walton, William. 1897. *The Sleeping Beauty and the Mystic Yellow Dwarf* (souvenir script). Theatre Royal, Edinburgh. Pettingell Collection, University of Kent, Canterbury.

Warner, Marina. 1990. "Mother Goose Tales: Female Fiction, Female Fact?" *Folklore* 10, no. 1: 3–25.

———. 1994a. *From the Beast to the Blonde: On Fairy Tales and Their Tellers.* New York: Farrar, Straus, and Giroux.

———, ed. 1994b. *Wonder Tales.* New York: Farrar, Straus, and Giroux.

———. 2014. *Once upon A Time: A Short History of Fairy Tale.* New York: Oxford University Press.

Wearing, 2014. *The London Stage, 1930–1939: A Calendar of Productions, Performers, and Personnel,* 2nd ed. Lanham, MD: Rowman and Littlefield.

Weltman, Sharon Aronofsky. 2002. "Pantomime Truth and Gender Performance: John Ruskin on Theatre." In *Ruskin and Gender,* edited by Dinah Birch and Francis O'Gorman, 159–76. London: Palgrave Macmillan.

———. 2007. *Performing the Victorian: John Ruskin and Identity in Theater, Science, and Education.* Columbus: Ohio State University Press.

Wiencke, Jeremiah. 1881. "Puerile Pantomime." *The Theatre*, October 1, 1881, 203–6.

Wood, Christopher. 2008. *Fairies in Victorian Art.* Suffolk, UK: Antiques Collectors Club.

Yates, Edmund, ed. 1860. *The Life and Correspondence of Charles Mathews, the Elder, Comedian. By Mrs. Mathews. A New Edition, Abridged and Condensed.* London: Routledge, Warne, and Routledge.

Yonge, Charlotte. 1869. "Children's Literature of the Last Century." *MacMillan's Magazine* 20:229–37, 302–10, 448–56.

Zipes, Jack. 1993. *The Trials and Tribulations of Little Red Riding Hood.* New York: Routledge.

———. 1997. "Introduction: The Rise of the French Fairy Tale and the Decline of France." In *Beauty and the Beast, and Other Classic French Fairy Tales*, edited by Jack Zipes, ix–xxiv. New York: Signet.

———. ed. 2000a. *The Great Fairy Tales Tradition: From Straparola and Basile to the Brothers Grimm.* New York: W. W. Norton.

———. ed. 2000b. *The Oxford Companion to Fairy Tales.* New York: Oxford University Press.

———. 2011. *The Enchanted Screen: The Unknown History of Fairy-Tale Films.* New York: Routledge.

———. 2012. "*German Popular Stories* as Revolutionary Book." In *Brothers Grimm, German Popular Stories: Adapted by Edgar Taylor*, edited by Jack Zipes, 15–40. Kent, UK: Crescent Moon.

———, Pauline Greenhill, and Kendra Magnus-Johnston, eds. 2015. *Fairy Tale Films beyond Disney: International Perspectives.* New York: Routledge.

Ziter, Edward. 2003. *The Orient on the Victorian Stage.* Cambridge: Cambridge University Press.

INDEX

Adams, Davenport, 205

Adams, D. J., 149–50n4, 149–50, 164n13

adaptation, 18, 37–38, 59, 70, 72, 81–82, 245–46

Adelphi Theatre (London), 29, 92, 94, 98, 101; Daniel Terry as owner of, 95

affordances, 22; of fairy tales, 28–29, 30–31, 56, 246; of costume, 31

"Aladdin," 4, 12, 15, 167. See also *Arabian Nights' Entertainments*

Alf layla wa-layla. See *Arabian Nights' Entertainments*

"Ali Baba," 15, 225; *Ali Baba and the Forty Thieves* pantomime (1867), 119–20; *The Forty Thieves* pantomime (1886), 134. See also *Arabian Nights' Entertainments*

Ames, Winthrop, 240

Andersen, Hans Christian, 105–6

antiquarianism, 57, 102–3; parodied by Thomas Crofton Croker, 96, 97; parodied by Walter Scott, 97n18

anti-theatricality, 5, 112; and francophobia, 185. *See also* theatricality

Arabian Nights' Entertainments: and children's repertoires, 4, 58; and British theater, 37–38, 39–40; *The Genii . . . an Arabian Nights' Entertainment* pantomime (1752–53), 38; and Italian theater, 37, 38; pantomime plots and characters derived from, 15, 192. *See also* "Aladdin"; "Ali Baba"; Galland, Antoine; Manley, Delarivier; "Sindbad"

artifice: and children, 117; and *contes de fées*, 15, 142–43, 148, 182–85; and fairy tales, 9, 56, 118, 149; folklore discourse about, 114–15; in pantomime, 4–5n2, 179, 182, 184–85, 186, 210–11; and theatrical cross-dressing, 211, 214; Victorian anxieties about, 112, 182. *See also* authenticity; spectacle

Askey, Arthur, 210–11

Astley's Royal Ampitheatre (London), 63n5, 63–64, 124–25

Athaneum (periodical), 107

Attridge, Steve, 217

d'Auban, Emma, 11

Augarde, Amy, 199